International Peacebuilding

CW00556575

International Peacebuilding offers a concise, practical and accessible introduction to the growing field of peacebuilding for students and practitioners.

This new textbook comprises three parts, each dealing with a key aspect of peacebuilding:

- Part I defines the core concepts and theoretical discussions that provide the philosophical grounds for contemporary peacebuilding activities.
- Part II divides the procedures of peacebuilding into three phases and examines some of the important features of each phase.
- Part III examines the key areas of the practice of peacebuilding.

The volume approaches peacebuilding from the viewpoints of individual actors or institutions, introducing a range of theoretical discussions with which students can critically examine contemporary peacebuilding practice, as well as presenting detailed case studies for key issues highlighted in the text. In doing so, the book aims to provide more concrete ideas on how peacebuilding programmes are planned and implemented in the field and which major issues should be addressed by peacebuilding practitioners.

This book will be essential reading for all students of peacebuilding, conflict transformation and post-conflict reconstruction, and is recommended reading for students of international organisations, international security and international relations in general.

Alpaslan Özerdem is professor of peacebuilding and co-director of the Centre for Trust, Peace and Social Relations, Coventry University, UK. He is the author/editor of numerous titles, including most recently *Youth in Conflict and Peacebuilding: Mobilization, Reintegration and Reconciliation* (Palgrave, 2015).

SungYong Lee is lecturer at the National Centre for Peace and Conflict Studies, University of Otago, New Zealand. He is co-editor of *Local Ownership in International Peacebuilding: Key Theoretical and Practical Issues* (Routledge, 2015).

International Peacebuilding

An introduction

Alpaslan Özerdem and SungYong Lee

LONDON AND NEW YORK

First published 2016
by Routledge
2 Park Square, Milton Park, Abingdon, Oxon OX14 4RN

and by Routledge
711 Third Avenue, New York, NY 10017

*Routledge is an imprint of the Taylor & Francis Group,
an informa business*

British Library Cataloguing in Publication Data
A catalogue record for this book is available from the British Library

Library of Congress Cataloging-in-Publication Data
Names: Özerdem, Alpaslan, author. | Lee, SungYong, author.
Title: International peacebuilding : an introduction / Alpaslan Özerdem and
    SungYong Lee.
Description: New York, NY : Routledge, 2016. | Includes bibliographical references
    and index.
Identifiers: LCCN 2015031451 | ISBN 9781138929081 (hardback) |
    ISBN 9781138929098 (pbk.) | ISBN 9781315681429 (ebook)
Subjects: LCSH: Peace-building. | Postwar reconstruction.
Classification: LCC JZ5538 .O98 2016 | DDC 327.1/72—dc23
LC record available at http://lccn.loc.gov/2015031451

ISBN: 978-1-138-92908-1 (hbk)
ISBN: 978-1-138-92909-8 (pbk)
ISBN: 978-1-315-68142-9 (ebk)

Typeset Times New Roman
by Apex CoVantage, LLC

Contents

Illustrations

Figures

Tables

Boxes

About the authors

Alpaslan Özerdem is Professor of Peacebuilding and Co-Director of the Centre for Trust, Peace and Social Relations, Coventry University, UK. With over twenty years of field research experience in Afghanistan, Bosnia-Herzegovina, El Salvador, Kosovo, Lebanon, Liberia, the Philippines, Sierra Leone, Sri Lanka and Turkey, he specializes in the politics of humanitarian interventions, disaster response, security sector reform, reintegration of former combatants and post-conflict state building. Professor Özerdem is also president of CESRAN International, a UK-based think tank working in international relations. He has published extensively in peer-reviewed international journals and has authored and edited ten books, including *Youth in Conflict and Peacebuilding: Mobilization, Reintegration and Reconciliation* (Palgrave, 2015) and he was co-editor of *Turkey and Human Security: Challenges of the 21st Century* (Routledge, 2013).

SungYong Lee is Lecturer at the National Centre for Peace and Conflict Studies, University of Otago, New Zealand. He has examined the conflict resolution and post-conflict peacebuilding processes in Cambodia, Angola, Guatemala, El Salvador, South Sudan and Thailand. Some of the key concepts that he is particularly interested in are postliberal peacebuilding, local ownership in postwar reconstruction, international mediation and regional organisations. With Professor Özerdem, Dr Lee recently co-edited *Local Ownership in International Peacebuilding: Key Theoretical and Practical Issues* (Routledge, 2015) and he has been serving as a co-managing editor of the *Journal of Conflict Transformation and Security (JCTS)*.

Acknowledgements

The authors express special thanks to Alan Hunter and WookBeom Park who provided many constructive comments on the contents of this book. Soren Aspinal and Jessica Aitken edited the first draft of the manuscript. We would also like to thank Andrew Humphrys and Hannah Ferguson of Routledge for the constant support that they have provided for this project.

Alpaslan Özerdem would like to thank his sister, Associate Professor Dr Füsun Özerdem, for her never-ending support and inspiration in his life.

SungYong Lee is extremely grateful for tremendous love from his family, Gyunyeol Lee, Sunki Park, Eunyoung Judy Cho and Suhyun Jason Lee, as well as Dr Daisaku Ikeda who has provided much philosophical inspiration for SungYong's journey of peace research.

List of abbreviations

ACVC	The Peasant Farmers' Association of the Cimitarra River Valley (Colombia)
ANC	African National Congress (South Africa)
ASEAN	Association of South East Asian Nations
AU	African Union (the successor of OAU)
AusAID	Australian Agency for International Development
BIRIs	Rapid Deployment Infantry Battalions (El Salvador)
CBOs	Community-based organisations
CGDK	Coalition Government of Democratic Kampuchea (Cambodia)
CONADEP	National Commission for the Disappeared (Argentina)
CWDA	Cambodian Women's Development Agency
DDR	Disarmament, demobilisation and reintegration of ex-combatants
DFID	Department for International Development (UK)
DNI	National Directorate of Intelligence (El Salvador)
ECOMOG	Economic Community of West African States Monitoring Group
ECOWAS	Economic Community of West African States
ESAF	Armed Forces of El Salvador (El Salvador)
FDC	Foundation for Community Development (Mozambique)
FMLN	Farabundo Martí National Liberation Front (El Salvador)
FUNCINPEC	National United Front for an Independent, Neutral, Peaceful, and Cooperative Cambodia (Cambodia)
ICC	International Criminal Court
ICGLR	International Conference on the Great Lakes Region
ICISS	International Commission on Intervention and State Sovereignty
ICRC	International Committee of the Red Cross
ICTR	International Criminal Tribunal for Rwanda
ICTY	International Criminal Tribunal for former Yugoslavia
IDPs	Internally displaced persons
IFRC	International Federation of the Red Cross
ILO	International Labour Organization
IMAT	International Military Advisory Team
IMF	International Monetary Fund
ISAF	International Security Assistance Force (Afghanistan)
KPNLF	Khmer People's National Liberation Front (Cambodia)
LACE	Liberia Community Empowerment Project
MSF	Médecins Sans Frontières (Doctors Without Borders)
NATO	North Atlantic Treaty Organization

NGO	Nongovernmental organisation
NUREP	Northern Uganda Rehabilitation Programme
OAS	Organization of American States
OAU	Organization for African Unity
ONUSAL	UN Observer Mission in El Salvador (El Salvador)
OSCE	Organization for Security and Cooperation in Europe
OSIEA	Open Society Initiative for Eastern Africa
PBI	Peace Brigades International
PNC	National Civilian Police (El Salvador)
PRK	People's Republic of Kampuchea (Cambodia)
PRZ	Peasant Reserve Zone (Colombia)
QIP	Quick impact project
RENAMO	Mozambique National Resistance (Mozambique)
RUF	Revolutionary United Front in Sierra Leone (Sierra Leone)
SSR	Security sector reform
TJS	Traditional justice systems
TRC	Truth and reconciliation commissions
UCP	Unarmed civilian peacekeeping
UNDP	United Nations Development Programme
UNESCO	United Nations Educational, Scientific and Cultural Organization
UNHCR	United Nations High Commissioner for Refugees
UNICEF	United Nations Children's Fund
UNITA	National Union for the Total Independence of Angola (Angola)
UNSC	United Nations Security Council
UNSG	United Nations Secretary General
USAID	US Agency for International Development
USIP	United States Institute of Peace
WIPNET	Women in Peacebuilding Network

Introduction

Peacebuilding is defined in *An Agenda for Peace* (UNSG 1992: 21) as "action to identify and support structures which will tend to solidify peace in order to avoid a relapse into conflict." However, what the definition does not tell us is what that peacebuilding action would look like, who does it, for what purposes and, equally importantly, whose peace is it that really matters for peacebuilding actors. With its initial conceptualisation in relation to peacemaking (bringing the armed conflict to a halt either through a negotiated settlement or military endorsement imposed externally) and peacekeeping (through the deployment of international military forces, often as United Nations (UN) blue berets, to separate warring sides), peacebuilding was heralded as a progressive way of thinking of peace. Consequently, it now directs many contemporary peace-supporting activities into more comprehensive, nuanced and context-oriented approaches.

The concept of peacebuilding reflects a complex and turbulent path of earlier international peace-supporting activities during the previous decades. Peacebuilding at its initial conceptualisation was a response to the challenge of frozen conflicts created by prolonged peacekeeping operations such as the UN peacekeeping presence in Cyprus and Lebanon. It was also a response to complex reconstruction challenges emerged as a result of the peace agreements of the early 1990s in such places as El Salvador, Guatemala, Cambodia and Namibia after their protracted armed conflicts. The international community found itself dealing with the challenges of restructuring and in some cases constructing state institutions from scratch. Peacebuilding started to become an umbrella term for everything that would need to be done from the peace agreement onwards. It was primarily a job for civilian actors such as the UN and international nongovernmental organisations (NGOs) with the involvement of international peacekeeping forces for security-related tasks, but still very much under civilian control and supervision.

In the mid-1990s, the disintegration of the former Yugoslavia and Soviet Union as well as protracted civil wars in a wide range of other contexts such as Afghanistan, Liberia, Sierra Leone, Sri Lanka and Sudan kept emphasising the importance of being able to build bridges between divided communities along their ethno-religious fault lines. For those contexts emerging from the socialist regime framework as well as civil war such as in Bosnia, Tajikistan and Kosovo, the peacebuilding process was not only about the restructuring of governance but also the transition of their economic systems towards a market economy. In other words, the liberal peace doctrine with its two main elements of 'democracy' and 'market economy' has defined the main contours of peacebuilding work by the international community regardless of how much such 'post-conflict' environments that the international community has involved as 'peacebuilder' around the world differed from each other.

With the liberal peace doctrine in mind, the scope of peacebuilding has been widened to include political, economic, social and psychological aspects. Kofi Annan remarks that creating conditions most conducive to peace involves priority on activities such as

> encouraging reconciliation and demonstrating respect for human rights; fostering political inclusiveness and promoting national unity; ensuring the safe, smooth and early repatriation and resettlement of refugees and displaced persons; reintegrating ex-combatants and others into productive society; curtailing the availability of small arms; mobilising the domestic and international resources for reconstruction and economic recovery, providing for reintegration and rehabilitation programmes, and creating conditions for resumed development.
>
> (UNSG 2001: 66)

NATO's military intervention in Kosovo and subsequent reconstruction process was another significant departure point for peacebuilding operations at this time; there was an important dilemma over its legality. To start with the intervention itself was undertaken without the approval of the UN Security Council, and the argument of legitimacy for the protection of human rights was how it was justified by NATO. Consequently, the peacebuilding efforts in the aftermath of the military intervention were effectively to do with the statebuilding of Kosovo as an independent state against the wishes of Serbia, which still includes Kosovo in its territory, though Kosovo has since declared its independence, which has so far been recognised by a considerable number of countries. Peacebuilding as a tool of statebuilding became a different type of project with Kosovo, disregarding the post–World War II security architecture in the shape of the UN to a large extent, and emphasising the reality of a much more unilateral and Western-centric security perspective in international relations.

While the legitimacy argument was used to counterbalance the shortcomings with the legality of the international community's presence in Kosovo, for the post-9/11 context peacebuilding operations like Afghanistan and Iraq, the entire legitimacy of the international community and its peacebuilding efforts has faced serious questions. The liberal peace project started to face its most significant crisis and its assumptions over what peace is and how it should look in terms of post-conflict governance and economic structures, and how it would and should be achieved through which approaches and modalities has started to face serious scrutiny and criticism. The liberal peace was clearly failing to achieve what it promised to do in terms of security, human development and post-conflict reconstruction in its new areas of operation. Peacebuilding has been carried out by those who have some dubious credentials in terms of their identity in the eyes of local populations – one day they were occupiers, next day peacekeepers and the following the providers of humanitarian aid and reconstruction. In such contexts, security sector reform was no longer part of overall peacebuilding efforts as was the case in the early 1990s, but in fact, security sector reform has become the peacebuilding process itself in contexts like Afghanistan.

The so-called Arab Spring has exerted another major blow to the liberal peace doctrine and the way it translates the challenge of peacebuilding into different programmes. With the new post-conflict contexts of Libya and what might be the case in Syria, there are now serious question marks about what the international community claims to know about the know-how of peacebuilding. The experience that has been accumulated over the last two decades in a wide range of contexts seems to become rather helpless to advise how societies emerging from dictatorial regimes like Libya could rebuild themselves from the ruins of their civil wars. The hybridity of peacebuilding, especially for the requirement of working with nonstate armed groups, especially with those who are anti-Western in their ideology, in the reconstruction of these societies has been demanding new approaches and methodologies.

Therefore, peacebuilding both as a concept and practice is now facing another critical departure point and, although the experience of the last two decades could guide the action to some extent, it is also important to recognise the fundamental problems with the way it has always envisaged what peace is and how it could actually be built.

Then, how have the theories and practice of peacebuilding been developed throughout the period? What does contemporary peacebuilding look like? This book aims to provide an understanding of peacebuilding to students with a general interest but without advanced knowledge. The structure, contents and presentation of this book are formulated to achieve this goal. In terms of the structure, this book consists of three parts that deal with three aspects of peacebuilding: concepts and theories, procedures and issue areas. In this sense, this book is by no means an encyclopaedic handbook of peacebuilding. Instead, it selects the topics that enable university students to begin the early stages of their research. It should be noted that this book pays more (but not exclusive) attention to civil war than interstate war because it is a more common type of conflict in the post-Cold War period and more relevant to practitioners working in the field.

As for its presentation style, this book adopts three strategies that the authors believe are useful in enabling readers to have a clearer sense of peacebuilding. First, it attempts to approach most issues from the viewpoints of individual actors or institutes. In other words, it analyses peacebuilding issues by asking how peacebuilding actors would perceive the issues and what major issues they would face during the planning and implementation processes. The topics and supporting examples discussed in this publication are selected under this criterion. Moreover, when discussing core concepts and related programmes, this book endeavours to provide descriptions and concrete examples rather than engaging in sophisticated conceptual or theoretical discussions. Although many new concepts have been suggested as ways of promoting (in the case of practitioners) or of indicating (in the case of academics) new trends in peacebuilding, it is often difficult or impractical to delineate clear distinctions between these concepts.

When explaining the practical dimensions of peacebuilding, such as socioeconomic reconstruction of social justice, we paid most attention to introducing three topics: the main objectives of the programmes, major projects frequently undertaken in contemporary peacebuilding and major challenges hampering the effectiveness of the peacebuilding efforts. Moreover, in addition to a large number of examples, this volume introduces the peacebuilding programmes implemented in Afghanistan, Cambodia, Colombia, El Salvador, Kenya, Mozambique and South Africa as case studies. These examples are selected mainly from the peacebuilding programmes facilitated by international peace-supporting actors such as nation states, major humanitarian agencies and international organisations. The reason for this is that this book mainly targets students who approach peacebuilding from external actors' viewpoints. However, since there are a variety of 'new' types of peace initiatives promoted by indigenous people within conflict-affected societies, Part III of this volume presents some of the contributions that these indigenous peace movements have made.

It is important to recognise that peacebuilding should ultimately be considered as a process, rather than a goal, and not from the perspective of achieving only a negative peace, which would simply indicate the ending of armed conflict, but rather a positive and sustainable peace, which can ensure security as well as socioeconomic, structural, political and cultural stability, thereby reducing the likelihood of relapse into or the continuation of violence. In order to achieve this, it is important to bear in mind that peacebuilding is a multifaceted and multiagency process accompanied by a wide range of challenges from the creation of a security environment and functional governance structures to responding to the basic needs of war-affected communities. In other words, peacebuilding encompasses processes ranging from micro-level changes in the opinions and behaviour of conflicting communities to macro-level institutional changes that address the structural causes of conflict.

Another important issue to remember in peacebuilding is that the process is highly politicised and deals with the complex and sensitive power dynamics of post-conflict societies. From setting the overall vision for peacebuilding to priorities different groups often contest its key principles and directions, as in most contemporary conflicts a peace deal does not often bring a complete halt to the conflict. Peacebuilding in the environments of armed conflict of some degree and coverage is a stark reality to consider by the international community. Peacebuilding, whether for conflict prevention or post-conflict reconstruction, is an evolving concept and practice. It has already gone through a number of generations and reincarnations. For it to have a purpose in the post-Arab Spring context, for example, it would need to reinvent itself. Therefore, the objective of this book is to take stock of peacebuilding as a concept and practice in terms of what we think we know about peace and how it could be built.

Structure of the book

This book consists of three parts that examine various dimensions of peacebuilding from three perspectives. Part I defines a number of the core concepts and theoretical discussions that provide the philosophical grounds for contemporary peacebuilding activities. The aim here is to familiarise readers with these essential analytical foundations so that they can understand and evaluate practical or academic outputs relevant to peacebuilding.

Chapter 1 reviews the theoretical perspectives relevant to peace and armed conflict. The chapter introduces various approaches towards peace, such as negative peace and positive peace, different levels of peace and non-European perspectives on peace. It then examines some of the issues related to armed conflict, such as the various sources of violence (e.g. cultural, structural and social causes) and forms of violence (e.g. physical vs. psychological violence; intended vs. unintended violence; manifest vs. latent violence; and direct, structural and cultural violence).

Chapter 2 provides an overview of the peace process. The chapter first reviews the historical development of international peace intervention over the past century, with a particular focus on the distinction between the peacebuilding activities conducted in the Cold War period and contemporary peacebuilding in the post–Cold War period. It then introduces a number of key terms that are most frequently used in contemporary peacebuilding: conflict resolution, conflict management, conflict transformation, peacekeeping, peacemaking and peacebuilding. Finally, the chapter considers the scope of the peace process as well as the roles played by various peacebuilding actors.

Chapter 3 introduces contemporary academic and practical discussions on liberal peacebuilding and standardised models of peacebuilding that reflect Western approaches towards peace. In addition to its philosophical origins, this chapter explains key features of liberal peacebuilding by focusing on six policy areas: promotion of democracy, market economy, the rule of law, emphasis on human rights, security sector reform and governance reform. It then suggests some key lines of critique on the liberal peacebuilding model; in particular, those highlighting the cultural insensitivity that gives priority to external rather than internal development agendas. Such critical views will provide readers with an analytical framework through which to examine the strengths and limitations of contemporary peacebuilding operations.

Part II divides the procedures of peacebuilding into three phases and examines some of the important features of the peacebuilding programmes implemented in each phase. Although a clear-cut division of the phases of peacebuilding cannot be made, this part is intended to provide readers with more a comprehensive understanding of how the priorities of peacebuilding projects shift in accordance with the transforming environment in conflict-affected societies.

Chapter 4 discusses conflict resolution, which pursues the cessation of violent conflict through peaceful means. The targets of analysis in this chapter are the peacebuilding projects that are typically implemented in the period between the start of peace negotiation and the implementation of a peace agreement. After providing an overview of the conflict resolution procedures (pre-talks, peace negotiation, peace agreement, endorsement and implementation), the chapter examines two practical issues: peace negotiation and actors in peacebuilding. Finally, three theoretical discussions relevant to the effectiveness of conflict resolutions are discussed: the timing of the peace process, the spoiler problem and the neutrality and strength of interveners.

Chapters 5 and 6 pay attention to the peacebuilding procedures used in the post-conflict periods. Chapter 5 explores the short- and mid-term reconstruction programmes that aim to bring about the stabilisation of war-affected societies. In addition to presenting the conceptual development of post-conflict reconstruction, this chapter describes the four phases of the postwar reconstruction process: emergency relief, rehabilitation, reform and modernisation and peace consolidation. The chapter ends by noting the formidable challenges facing contemporary international peacebuilding and the efforts to overcome such challenges.

Chapter 6 discusses conflict transformation measures that aim to promote consolidated peace and sustainable development in war-torn countries by focusing on four dimensions of transformation: actor-related transformation, relational transformation, structural transformation and cultural transformation. Moreover, it examines the significant contributions of conflict transformation as a new paradigm of international peacebuilding and discusses human security as the theoretical foundation for conflict transformation programmes. This chapter closes with a discussion on gender issues in peacebuilding.

From a more practical viewpoint, Part III examines the issue areas of peacebuilding. Through this, the book aims to provide readers with more concrete ideas on how peacebuilding programmes are planned and implemented in the field and which major issues should be addressed by peacebuilding practitioners. Each chapter explains the significance of the issue areas in the overall peacebuilding process and introduces some of the representative programmes in these areas, focusing on their core purposes, scope of issues and forms of methods.

Chapter 7 looks at security and political sector peacebuilding programmes, which have been considered the most urgent issues in many contemporary postwar peacebuilding operations. The types of project reviewed in this chapter are disarmament, demobilisation and reintegration of ex-combatants (DDR), the restructuring of security forces, electoral assistance and public administration reform. Moreover, after reviewing the limitations of institution-focused peacebuilding programmes, this chapter introduces new types of peacebuilding programmes that aim to address such limitations by adopting more inclusive and flexible processes.

Chapter 8 discusses the characteristics of social and economic reconstruction and how it provides a foundation for sustainable peace and development. In this chapter, the references made to representative examples of practical programmes in this area are rehabilitation of industrial infrastructure and refugee repatriation, employment generation and development of sustainable communities. Based on the introduction, this chapter develops a discussion on the negative impact of economically driven peacebuilding programmes.

Finally, Chapter 9 considers the issues of transitional justice and social reconciliation, which deal with the human rights crimes that occur during conflicts. After discussing the rationales behind the justice and reconciliation programmes and the conceptual issues relevant to them, the three main methods of promoting justice and reconciliation are presented: truth-telling, punishment of perpetrators and reparation for victims, reform of legal and judicial institution.

Part I

Concepts and theories of peacebuilding

1   Peace and armed conflict

Peacebuilding is concerned with the promotion and consolidation of peace through deterring and resolving violent conflicts. This goal raises a number of conceptual questions, such as: What sorts of peace are the projects pursuing? On the wider scale of (absolute) war to (absolute) peace, where should we place the type of peace being pursued? What types of conflicts are we trying to address? In the specific cultural and social context in which the conflict is taking place, which methods of achieving peace are likely to be most useful? Moreover, given that each conflict has its own specific context, intervening in a conflict for peacebuilding purposes without understanding the nature of the conflict concerned would be a mistake. Regardless of its good intentions, an intervention has the potential to further damage relationships between disputants and lead to an escalation of tensions. In developing effective peacebuilding programmes, therefore, it is essential to have a thorough understanding of the concepts of peace and armed conflict.

This chapter aims to introduce a number of conceptualisations that have widely been utilised in Peace and Conflict Studies. Since the 1960s, the complexity in the concepts of peace and conflict has been analysed in various ways, and the consequent conceptual developments have determined the key features of mainstream peace-supporting activities over the previous decades. For instance, the evolution of international peace intervention over the past fifty years reflects the philosophical foundational shift that has taken place over the same period: the way in which the once-dominant concept of negative peace has gradually given way to contemporary conceptualisations of positive peace.

Out of a variety of the current approaches towards peace and peacebuilding, this chapter will primarily discuss:

- Approaches towards peace: theoretical debate on negative peace, positive peace, non-Western approaches to peace and levels of peace;
- Sources of violent conflict (cultural factors, social/economic factors and contemporary issues);
- Academic discussions on the forms of violence (intended/unintended violence; manifest/latent violence; physical/psychological violence; and direct/structural/cultural violence).

Peace: approaches and types

Although peace is primarily defined as a "state existing during the absence of war" (Collins English Dictionary 2003), it is a broad and elusive concept, and understandings of its meaning may vary. For instance, while some may assume that 'truth,' 'beauty' and 'love' are synonymous with peace, others believe that 'harmony,' 'repose,' 'truce' and 'friendship' lie at the heart of the concept. More frequently, 'human rights,' 'justice' and 'freedom' are regarded as its central values (Sandy and Perkins 2008). Hence, in attempting to understand peace-related discussions or projects, it is useful to identify exactly to which types of peace these debates or programmes subscribe.

Negative peace, positive peace and non-Western approaches towards peace

In peace studies, the distinction between positive peace and negative peace is one of the most widely accepted criteria. This distinction was first suggested by Johan Galtung (1967), one of the founders of peace studies as an academic discipline. Galtung criticised traditional Western approaches towards peace, categorising them as forms of 'negative peace' and called for a more comprehensive and functional conception of peace. This idea has been explored and developed further in many academic works.

Negative peace

Negative peace denotes "the absence of organized collective forms of violence" (Galtung 1967: 4). From this viewpoint, a wide range of states, from the temporary cessation of combat and separation of two enemies to the establishment of stable peace, are considered forms of peace. Moreover, this definition acknowledges spontaneous or individual violence as accept-able conditions of a peaceful society.

Many academic debates and publications in peace studies are based on the above assump-tion, especially those that ascribe to the realist perspective. For instance, Raymond Aron, a well-known French philosopher, argues that peace is a state of "more or less lasting suspen-sion of rivalry between political units" (1966: 151). Consequently, peace research based on negative peace ideas focuses on eliminating or minimising active violence. Examples of strategies that employ this line of reasoning include peace mediation for the resolution of civil conflicts, military intervention to provide buffer zones between two warring enemies and the demilitarisation of ex-combatants in the post-conflict period (Barash and Webel 2009). Moreover, since the concept of negative peace defines peace as the 'absence of vio-lence,' the characteristics of the violence under consideration need to be identified in order to clarify the meaning of peace. Hence, in defining what constitutes peace, the following questions are frequently asked: "What type of violence? Violence by whom? And Peace with whom?" (Galtung 1996: 226).

In the West, the concept of negative peace has a long tradition. The meaning of peace as the 'absence of war' is found in the New Testament and is in evidence in the classical depic-tion of the Greek goddess Irene, whose name is also the Greek word for peace. Since the Roman era, peace has been commonly understood in terms of *absentia belli* (the absence of war), with the 'state' being the fundamental unit of analysis. Hence, external peace has com-monly referred to a condition in which the state is not engaged in external wars (e.g. a regional war, an interstate war or a world war), while internal peace has indicated that the state has no internal war (e.g. no insurgency or civil war).

Moreover, it has been commonly believed that peace can be maintained through a 'social contract,' and, indeed, one of the origins of the word 'peace' is the Latin word *pax*, which is also the root of the word 'pact.' The idea here is that the state of peace (defined as an absence of war) is founded on "contractual, conscious, and mutually agreed upon" relationships (Young 2010: 354). Nevertheless, although violence has traditionally been considered the opposite of peace, it has also been understood as a useful tool to achieve or protect peace. The Roman phrase *'sivispacem, para bellum'* ('if you want peace, prepare for war') reflects the notion that peace can be established and maintained by deterring potential aggressors through the building up of defensive strength (or sometimes, offensive defence).

It was during the Cold War period, when realist views of peace became a dominant perspective in academic debates, that the basis of contemporary international relations was formed. As mistrust and rivalry between the liberal (or capitalist) camp and the communist (or socialist) camp determined the interactions between states during this period, academics saw no good opportunities for pursuing more than the absence of war in the international community. Hence, most of the peacebuilding operations conducted by the United Nations (UN) and other international/regional organisations during this period drew upon this version of the concept of peace. Examples of this include most traditional forms of international peace-supporting activities such as third-party mediation, traditional UN peacekeeping operations, military intervention for providing buffer zones between warring enemies and demilitarisation of ex-combatants in post-conflict period.

Positive peace

A number of Western thinkers and scholars believe that the traditional concept of negative peace is not useful in the promotion of stable peace. According to them, approaches based on negative peace are likely to fail to reflect and address the fundamental issues that lie behind the violence. Moreover, these approaches inherently possess potential for appropriation "in the interest of the status-quo powers at the national or international levels, and . . . become a conservative force in politics" (Galtung 1967: 2).

Hence, the necessity of a wider and more comprehensive conceptualisation of peace had been raised for many years, which Galtung terms 'positive peace.' Since, in this context, 'positive' represents the most ideal condition of peace that a person can think of, positive peace has no agreed definition. Instead, people have proposed their own versions of positive peace according to their positions. For instance, although he did not use the term of positive peace, Albert Einstein defined peace as "not merely the absence of violence but the presence of just, of law, and of order" (cited in Sandy and Perkins 2008: 6), while Reardon (1988: 16) regards peace as "the absence of violence in all its forms," which includes physical-psychological, explicit-implicit, direct-indirect and individual-structural violence. Moreover, Barash and Webel (2009: 7) propose positive peace as "a social condition in which exploitation is minimised or eliminated and in which there is neither overt violence nor the more subtle phenomenon of underlying structural violence." Nevertheless, there are some key elements of positive peace that are commonly found in these definitions. These include peace zones (space safe from violence), peace bonds (positive relationship between social actors), social justice (fair and equal treatment of all social constituents), eco mind (harmonious coexistence between human and environment) and link mind (people's awareness of interdependency) (Boulding 2000; Galtung 1996; Standish and Kertyzia 2015; Synott 2005).

Theories based on positive peace generally pursue the creation of proactive and optimistic values in society and seek to transform negative social relations into positive ones, work towards the harmonious coexistence of different peoples, promote reconciliation between conflicting parties and reconstruct nonviolent patterns of behaviour through empathetic understanding. For instance, structural peace refers to conditions of

> (1) reciprocity, as opposed to mental conditioning of one by the other; (2) integration in the sense of all relating to all, as opposed to fragmentation; (3) holism, the use of many faculties, as opposed to segmentation; and (4) certainly inclusion as opposed to exclusion, marginalization, and/or second-class citizenship.
>
> (Young 2010: 352)

Nevertheless, there is no consensus on the definition of positive peace yet and its scope still continues to expand.

Non-Western approaches towards peace – There are various approaches towards peace and peacebuilding that reflect non-Western perspectives. Although they have not been pro-actively reflected in recent academic discussions for conceptualising peace, these views frequently offer highly important elements required for building solid and durable peace.

In Hinduism, for instance, the term *shanti*, while literally meaning 'peace,' specifically means much more than the external or material dimensions of peace. Instead, the concept adopts as a key element of peace the notion of a person's "inner peace, with oneself, with no part of the body-mind-spirit doing violence to other parts" (Galtung 1996: 226). Moreover, *ahimsa* refers to "no harm, including to self (inner peace) and to nature" (ibid.). In the *Bhaga-vad Gita*, one of the most important Hindu epics, the story of Arjuna emphasises that fighting should be based not on hatred or personal desire, but on selfless duty or compassion for others (Barash and Webel 2009).

The concept of peace in the Confucian cultural tradition, such as *hep'ing* in China, denotes "harmony between the international, social, and personal spheres as a necessary condition" for peace (Young 2010: 355) rather than mere nonviolent relations between different social actors. In addition, traditional Confucian teachings emphasise the value of obedience and order both within the person and society in the belief that true peace can be achieved only through social harmony and balance. Hence, conflict resolution in many societies in East Asia is more about correcting misarranged relations than compromising contradictory inter-ests or perspectives.

The concepts of peace in many Muslim countries are strongly influenced by religious tradi-tion and they frequently emphasise justice as a key element. The utmost peace can be achieved only through one's submission to Allah and only within Dar ul-Islam (the House of Submission). In Khalifah (the Islamic community), all people are equally blessed by God regardless of their background, race, language or history. In addition, justice, "the placement of everything in their proper order" is an essential part of the concept of peace in the Islamic world (Ali IbnAbiTalib cited in Mirbagheri 2012: 85).

While these perspectives present dissimilar points of emphasis, they enable recent aca-demic discussions to develop the concept of positive peace in more diverse and nuanced ways. In addition, the illumination of such non-Western perspectives of peace creates wider opportunities for peacebuilding practice to reflect the needs and opinions of local actors in conflict-affected societies that, in most cases, do not share Western cultural backgrounds.

Levels of peace

Another useful framework for understanding the conditions of peace is 'level,' which views peace as a 'ladder' of stages. Although categorisation of the levels of peace varies among scholars and analysts, many studies commonly refer to the following four levels: frozen peace, cold peace, normal peace and warm peace (see Table 1.1).

Frozen peace

This level refers to a situation in which coercion is the primary means of dealing with conflict. While on the surface things appear to carry on as normal, the causes of conflict (both underly-ing and immediate) have not been resolved and the probability for violence to erupt remains high. An authoritarian regime's imposition of a 'state of emergency,' which curbs basic human rights and behaviours, best describes the level of frozen peace. This level of relation-ship is characterised by a one-way flow of communication (orders are transmitted from the

Table 1.1 Levels of peace

	Frozen peace	Cold peace	Normal peace	Warm peace
Main issues in conflict	Unresolved	Mitigated but not fully resolved	Resolved	Resolved or transcended
Channels of communication	Unilateral communication by authoritarian actors	Only official level	Mostly official level with early-stage transcommunity or national ties	Highly developed transcommunity or national ties
Collaboration	None or exploitation	Exploratory	Possible	Active
Possibility of return to war	High	Present	Possible	Unthinkable

Source: This table is adapted from Miller (2005: 232).

dominant group to the dominated group) and there is no cooperation or participation to achieve social goals. As a result, it is frequently debated whether frozen peace can be considered a type of peace at all. Palestine under the control of Israel is frequently discussed as an example of this level of peace.

Cold peace

At the level of cold peace, parties in disagreement recognise each other's rights to existence, access resources and so on. Although there is a level of interaction and cooperation between disputants, the underlying and immediate issues surrounding the conflict generally remain unresolved. While the probability of returning to violence is reduced at this level, it has not disappeared completely and might easily be triggered. Cold peace is often regarded as a step towards the resolution of a conflict and offers an opportunity for achieving a sustainable and higher level of peace. The relation between North Korea and South Korea is frequently cited as an example of this level of peace.

Normal peace

At this level, the major issues that had caused serious tensions or violent conflicts between disputants have been largely resolved or mitigated, and the relations between them are more or less normalised (or indifferent). The possibility of cooperation is higher than in conditions of cold peace, and in international relations cases, transnational collaboration between civil societies emerges. Examples of this level of peace are the improvement in the relationship between China and the US in the early 1990s and the social settlement in post–civil war El Salvador.

Warm peace

Warm peace describes a situation in which the issues pertaining to rivalries and incompatibilities between states or within society have been addressed. This level of peace is characterised by cooperation between the various actors, effective organisation of civil society and the existence of active conflict resolution processes. Although differences between the various groups of such societies may persist, these differences are no longer seen as threats to societal security.

By suggesting the levels of peace, many studies aim to move beyond the binary categorisation of peace and conflict. For instance, the discourse on third-party peace intervention and the UN's peacekeeping operations, which had previously simply focused on whether peace could be maintained by using certain intervention methods, began to ask what types of peace can be achieved via the traditional methods. Sometimes, these levels are utilised for developing a new research project. Bayer (2010) adopts the categorisation of different levels of peace and argues that democracy can help states that maintain mid-level peace achieve a higher level of peace, but that it does not have a positive impact in terms of improving the relations within lower-level peace. Through this, he challenged a widely accepted assumption that democracy is universally more likely to improve relationships between former belligerents.

Thus, the contents of peacebuilding became diversified and professionalised by adopting the concept of different levels of peace. Through this process, since the early 2000s, international peacebuilding became more comprehensive in its scope and projects were equipped by more specified procedures of implementation that should be achieved through gradual transformation of social conditions.

Armed conflicts: sources and forms

As peace has been understood as the absence of certain types of violence in many previous studies, conflict has been a core topic of theoretical discourse in Peace and Conflict Studies. In this section, two elements of conflict analysis that are particularly relevant to peacebuilding are introduced: sources and forms of conflicts.

Sources of violent conflicts

Responses to armed conflicts need to be different according to the diagnosis of their causes. Examination of thirty-four comprehensive peace accords signed in the post–Cold War period demonstrates that, although most peace processes commonly considered security assurance as a key condition for peacebuilding, there were significant variations in the contents of peace accords; and the primary determinants of these contents are the perceived causes of conflicts (Joshi, Lee and Mac Ginty 2014). For instance, economic development, redistribution of national wealth and respect for cultural/ethnic diversity were important issues in the peace process in Guatemala, where extreme economic polarisation and the suppression of social minorities offered important sources of armed conflicts. In contrast, the Angolan peace process took political power sharing as a key point of negotiation because the competing economic and political interests between power elites were primary catalysts of the conflicts. In this sense, determining the sources of a military conflict is a crucial step in any effort to prevent or resolve it.

This section presents a number of representative sources of contemporary armed conflicts. Although violent human actions are highly probable under certain circumstances, violence is still by no means inevitable. Thus, although some of the major factors deeply related to contemporary military conflicts are presented shortly, these factors should be regarded not as *causes* but as *sources* of violence.

Nevertheless, identifying and defining the sources of a conflict is a complex process because there may be a large number of factors involved in its emergence (and continuation): while some may be fundamental to the outbreak of the conflict, others may function as catalysts.

Cultural factors

Cultural heritage that defines people's identity, such as language, religion, ethnicity and nationality, can be an important source of the conflict between individuals and groups. Some scholars have posited that cultural factors are more likely to cause violent conflict than other factors since actors are less likely to compromise on such issues (Huntington 1993). Many previous examples of violent conflict demonstrate that people fight to maintain their own cultural identity or to remove others, and various discussions in peace studies point to the significant roles played by the following three factors in the emergence and development of a violent conflict. In particular, ethnicity and religion have been argued to be two most out-standing causes of contemporary civil conflicts (Elbadawi and Sambanis 2000; MacFarlane 1999 cited in Haynes 2011).

ETHNICITY

Ethnic diversity itself does not necessarily bring about military conflict. Indeed, some research shows that ethnic diversity sometimes contributes to a reduction in the severity of a military conflict, as ethnic groups may learn the skills relevant to mitigating con-flict and aiding negotiation of their interests while interacting with other ethnic groups. Nevertheless, when a society fails to develop effective institutions for managing the incompatible interests of different ethnic groups, the groups' interests in obtaining or protecting their prosperity and power can lead to intense competition, and diversity may then become a significant source of conflict. As ethnicity is one of the strongest sources of people's identity, this competition is likely to lead to exclusive ethnic nationalism within ethnic groups. Moreover, as the rise of ethnic nationalism in one group can be viewed as a threat by others, similar forms of nationalism will develop among other ethnic groups (Collier 1999; Gurr 1970). While the conflicts in the former Yugoslavia, Chechnya, Rwanda, Sudan (Darfur) and Sri Lanka are total civil wars mainly caused by ethnic tensions, the violence in Moldova, Azerbaijan and Georgia was slightly less significant.

RELIGION

Although many religious philosophies emphasise the virtue of embracing different ideas, some theological themes are interpreted in such a way so as to encourage (or at least permit) aggression against heathens and pagans. Violent actions such as suicide bombings have been hailed and encouraged by some religious groups as emblematic of self-sacrifice, heroism and loyalty to the faith. A most striking event that had huge impact on contemporary international security was the 9/11 terrorist attack in New York. Since then, Islamic fundamentalism has been cited as a major cause in the violent con-flicts in Bosnia, Chechnya, Afghanistan and other parts of the world. The situation has been made worse by the stereotyping of Middle Eastern countries as 'terrorist nations' and the indiscriminate use of the term 'Islamic fundamentalism' (Rupesinghe 1998: 9). Some followers of other religions have also exhibited religious extremism. For exam-ple, Orthodox Judaism has gained strength in the political arena in Israel, and right-wing Christian movements (advocating anti-abortion policies) have gained popularity in the United States.

LEGACIES OF COLONIALISM

Although many cultural identities are inherited, they are sometimes created, modified or reconstructed. A representative example of this is the influence of colonialism on the development of cultural identities in Africa, Latin America, Asia and elsewhere. Many of the aspects of ethnic identities were strongly affected by the legacy of colonial policies, and this has contributed to the emergence of ethnic conflicts in these regions/areas. For instance, the arbitrary boundaries drawn by Europeans in their quest to establish states in Africa and Asia divided once cohesive communities and in some cases brought together groups who had long been in competition or conflict. Moreover, colonial administrations in many countries utilised the policy of 'divide and rule,' which led to fierce intertribal rivalries. As the colonial masters withdrew after independence, the struggle for power that ensued transformed these intertribal rivalries into bitter and protracted armed conflicts in some regions. This was particularly the case in Africa, where a number of groups are still engaged in armed conflicts over political and economic resources (Rupesinghe 1998).

Social/economic factors

There has been extensive research on the causality or correlation between a number of social and economic issues and military conflicts. If cultural factors draw clear distinctions between social groups, socioeconomic factors serve to promote the tensions and competition between them. More specifically, such research focuses on the political and economic interests of the actors who engage in conflict. If armed conflict brings huge economic returns or geopolitical benefits to individuals or even the state, there is always a strong motivation for prolonging it. Consequently, individuals and organisations need to be aware of such significant information to enable them to propose attractive alternatives when planning to intervene.

POVERTY

The academic community is largely in agreement on the role that poor economic conditions play as a long-term source of violent conflicts. If a society does not offer adequate opportunities for the fulfilment of people's needs, the possibility of violence increases. Moreover, the competition between social groups becomes more intense in cases where resources are limited, and violent conflict is therefore more likely to erupt (Collier and Sambanis 2005). Nevertheless, some analysts insist that poverty itself does not create sufficient conditions for the outbreak of war, but in the wider context, it can be instrumental in building tensions that provoke outbreaks of violence (Rupesinghe 1998). This link between poverty and military conflict can be described as a 'vicious cycle': one the one hand, poverty can lead to tensions that may trigger an armed conflict, while on the other, prolonged and destructive conflicts can erode income-generating opportunities and thereby reinforce economic hardship in conflict zones. Here, one important key word emphasised by many researchers is 'opportunities.' A conflict does not occur simply when the level of poverty is serious; rather, people conduct military conflicts only when they see sufficient prospects of achieving their goals in this way, or at least to gain better trade-offs.

INEQUALITY

Socioeconomic inequality sometimes plays a bigger role than poverty per se in initiating violent conflicts. Inequalities in economic wealth or political power usually produce an exclusive social hierarchy that heightens social tensions. Economic growth is normally uneven, increasing the interests of some groups while subjecting others to new forms of poverty. Discrimination in public spending and taxation, high asset inequality and governments' economic mismanagement frequently make the tensions based on inequality more visible. If the disadvantaged groups' attempts to redress the social disparity continually fail, their anger and resentment is likely to increase tensions and raise the likelihood of violence. The dominant groups are also tempted to use violence to maintain their privilege against "the challenges posed by endemic economic crises, foreign competition, and workers' demands" (Cheldelin, Druckman and Fast 2003: 60). Under such circumstances, people's strong anxiety can be organised rapidly if the discrimination is against certain social identity groups. The conflicts in most Central American countries, such as El Salvador, Nicaragua and Guatemala, are mainly caused by extremely unequal distribution of economic wealth and lack of other opportunities to address such problems.

POLITICAL SYSTEM

The type of political system in a country can strongly affect both the possibility of war breaking out and its progress. Societies in which people are free to express their grievances and seek their redress through peaceful means (e.g. via dialogue or political deliberation) are less likely to experience violent conflict than other types of societies. The academic discourse on the role of the political system in preventing violent conflicts increased with the emergence of Democratic Peace Theory, which argues that "democracies had rarely if ever gone to war with each other" (Russett 1993: 9). Although the empirical validity and theoretical soundness of this theory have been criticised by a significant number of academics, it has become a foundation of most peacebuilding projects operated by Western states and international organisations. Further research has followed on the relation between the various types of political systems and military conflicts. Some studies have found that 'nondemocratic but nonautocratic' states are most war prone, whereas some have stressed that the period of transition towards democracy is the phase in which the outbreak of violent conflict is most probable (Jaggers and Gurr 1995).

Contemporary issues

In addition to the cultural and socioeconomic sources of conflict, there are two contemporary issues that have attracted particular academic attention in recent times: the proliferation of small arms and light weapons and environmental degradation.

PROLIFERATION OF SMALL ARMS AND LIGHT WEAPONS

The growth in the global arms trade has made small arms and light weapons readily available to those factions able to afford them. It is estimated that there are half a billion small arms currently in circulation worldwide, causing the death of approximately half a million people annually. Unlike nuclear, chemical or biological weapons, nation states and the international community have encountered serious challenges in controlling and preventing the proliferation of small arms and light weapons. The widespread availability of small arms continues to pose a major threat to human security and has been implicated as a factor in starting and prolonging a large number of violent conflicts, since "war is possible as soon as weapons are available with which to fight it" (Smith 2004: 5).

ENVIRONMENTAL DEGRADATION

Environmental degradation in many cases causes a rapid reduction in three types of renewable resources (water, forests and fertile soil), and the scarcity of these resources initiates or propels military conflicts. For instance, the lack of water due to chronic drought frequently causes serious interclan conflicts in sub-Saharan Africa. When the problem of scarcity is combined with the issue of uneven distribution, the risk of violence becomes much higher. Thus, as global climate change has increased the frequency and intensity of such formidable natural disasters, the conflicts caused/catalysed by environmental degradation are becoming a central issue in Peace and Conflict Studies.

Forms of violence

What, then, are the major forms of violence that affect human beings? A narrow definition of violence might concentrate on physical and actual violence only, but there is a much wider range of forms of violence, each of which has a strong impact on human behaviour. This section presents a number of the distinctions suggested by Johan Galtung.

PHYSICAL AND PSYCHOLOGICAL VIOLENCE

Whether a form of violence affects the body or mind is a fundamental criterion for categorising the type of violence. Physical violence refers to violence that harms the human body or physical objects. Galtung (1969: 169) suggests that physical violence can be categorised into two groups: biological violence and physical violence that constrains human movements (e.g. imprisonment). The effects of physical violence on human behaviour are clearly evident and have been well explored in previous peace studies (in fact, most previous academic discussion on the impact of warfare focuses on this aspect). By contrast, psychological violence includes the types of action that might affect human psychology, including "lies, brainwashing, indoctrination of various kinds, threats, etc." (Galtung 1964: 24), and the impact of psychological violence is not always easily identifiable. However, an increasing number of studies apply systematic analysis on psychological violence (Krippner and McIntyre 2003; Martz 2010).

INTENDED VIOLENCE AND UNINTENDED VIOLENCE

In traditional models of moral judgement, including Judaeo-Christian ethics and Roman jurisprudence, the intention or purpose of a person's behaviour is considered more important than the consequences of their behaviour. As a result, many previous studies have tended to neglect the impact of unintended violence, even though unintended violence in human society may have devastating effects on human well-being. One example is structural violence, which has serious effects on people's lives but may not reflect the intention of a certain person or a group to harm the people. Another is environmental pollution, in which case, although the effects may be unintentional, careless disposal of rubbish may have serious consequences.

MANIFEST VIOLENCE AND LATENT VIOLENCE

While manifest violence refers to forms of violence that are observable, latent violence denotes potential violence that may not yet be apparent. For instance, regarding the British and French colonialism in sub-Saharan Africa, although manifest violence of the colonialist powers targeted a relatively small number of people, the fear of African populations of potential violence enabled the UK and France to control the countries. Many previous studies have failed to recognise the potential impact of latent violence. As Galtung (1969) argues, it is important to include this form of violence in an analytical framework because as the level of potential violence increases, so social tension and instability intensify. In fact, the inclusion of latent violence in the equation significantly expands the scope of peacebuilding operations to include efforts to address the 'invisible' dimensions of war-affected societies.

DIRECT VIOLENCE, STRUCTURAL VIOLENCE AND CULTURAL VIOLENCE

Galtung later devised a more comprehensive categorisation of the forms of violence by looking at three dimensions: direct, structural and cultural violence. *Direct violence* denotes armed hostile action that can be traced to a perpetrator. War, extortion, torture, rape, ethnic cleansing and genocide are some examples of direct violence. In most conflicts, direct violence is used extensively by an armed population to intimidate innocent civilians into submission and cooperation. *Structural violence* concerns the manipulation of the structures that exist in society by people/groups in order to suppress others. Although these structures generally support the functioning of society for the benefit of all, they can be exploited to engender structural violence. Suppression of human rights, gender/age discrimination, institutional violence (as within the police or military) and exclusion of some religious groups are examples of structural violence.[1] *Cultural violence* has strong links with the day-to-day activities and perceptions of a social group. Various aspects of culture (e.g. religion, ideology, language) can be used to justify violence against certain sectors of society, thus preventing people from meeting their basic needs and reaching their full potential. For instance, while the common language shared by a particular social group serves to promote effective communication and social cohesion within that group, it can become a focal point for cleavage between that group and others.

Conclusion

This chapter has considered a number of the perceptual and theoretical aspects of peace and armed conflict. First, the meaning of peace was discussed, primarily focusing on the two distinct perspectives of negative peace and positive peace as well as the levels of peace. As described briefly earlier, these definitions and concepts determine the nature of field practice in various peacebuilding sectors. In fact, the scope of peace operations has constantly widened according to transformations in the concepts and theories of peacebuilding. For instance, the categorisation of negative peace and positive peace is useful for understanding the unique characteristics of previous international peacekeeping and peacebuilding practices. Although the majority of mainstream practitioners and decision makers have advocated the realisation and maintenance of negative peace (that is, an absence of war) in peacebuilding operations during the past several decades, in recent times projects based on the assumptions of positive peace have gradually gained in popularity.

This chapter then analysed the sources of violence by focusing on three areas: cultural factors, social/economic factors and contemporary issues. However, the sources of violent conflict discussed are not mutually exclusive. Since two or more sources in combination may lie behind the onset of a military conflict, ascertaining the most salient sources of the conflict and finding ways to respond to them is a difficult part of conflict transformation. Moreover, various factors intervene in determining the forms and dynamics of conflicts. As new causes and more subtle forms of violence have been identified in the post–Cold War period, the goals and methods of peacebuilding have increasingly diversified. Hence, correctly identifying the sources and forms of targeted violence is considered key to the success of a peace process, as these factors limit the methods that can be employed in peace-supporting programmes aimed at tackling/eradicating violence. Recognising this, various frameworks for systemic conflict analysis have been adopted by many peacebuilding organisations. Some of the elements commonly included in such analytic frameworks are historical context; interaction between political, economic, social and security sources; actors; social structures; and external influence.

Finally, this chapter introduced and discussed the forms of violence conceptualised by Johan Galtung, as well as a few tools for conflict analysis. Although such categorisations are highly useful from a theoretical perspective, the primary goal of Galtung's conceptualisation was to call people's attention to the dimensions of violence that have largely been neglected. In addition to physical, intended, manifest and direct types of violence, he proposed to consider the victims of violence in its less visible and tangible forms. However, it took a long while before the field practice of peacebuilding began to address these issues. Although these ideas were first released in the late 1960s, the issues of psychological violence or structural violence only began to be reflected in peacebuilding practice in the early 2000s.

Discussion questions

*   Can conflict and peace be mutually exclusive?
*   Is positive peace a realistic goal in the contemporary peace process?
*   Is war a socially constructed phenomenon? Why or why not?
*   Are there outstanding 'new' methods of warfare? What impact do they have on the strategies for conducting armed conflicts?
*   In what way does 'unintended violence' help us in understanding contemporary armed conflicts?

Note

1   In many academic discussions, institutional violence is considered a part of structural violence. It is true that institutional violence frequently represents a dimension of social violence. For instance, discrimination against women within a private company in terms of salary and opportunities for promotion may reflect the structural discrimination of a society. However, strictly speaking, institutional violence refers to the violence perpetrated by institutions and should be distinguished from general structural violence.

Recommended reading

Cortright, D. (2008) 'What Is Peace?', in *Peace: A History of Movements and Ideas*. Cambridge: Cambridge University Press: 3–17.

Galtung, J. (1969) 'Violence, Peace, and Peace Research'. *Journal of Peace Research* 6 (3): 167–91.

Levy, J. and Thomson, W. R. (2010) Chapters 2–4, in *Causes of War*. London: Wiley Blackwell: 28–54, 83–127.

Mueller, J. (2005) 'Six Rather Unusual Propositions about Terrorism'. *Terrorism and Political Violence* 17: 487–505.

Ramsbotham, O., Woodhouse, T. and Miall, H. (2011) Chapters 1 and 4, in *Contemporary Conflict Resolution* (3rd ed.). London: Polity: 3–34, 94–122.

Reiter, D. (2003) 'Exploring the Bargaining Model of War'. *Perspectives on Politics* 1 (1): 27–43.
Themnér, L. and Wallensteen, P. (2014) 'Armed Conflict, 1946–2013'. *Journal of Peace Research* 51(4): 541–54.

2   The peace process

Historical evidence shows that it is never easy to mitigate armed conflicts and promote consolidated peace. Since the first modern forms of international peace-supporting activities appeared in the mid-19th century, peace processes have evolved in various ways seeking more effective methods of achieving their goals. Hence, while there is general agreement upon the broad definition of a peace process – a wide range of international, national and local efforts to stop, minimise, eliminate and transform violent conflicts – the detailed characteristics of peace processes vary according to the contexts in which the programmes are implemented. Although they may present similar features at a glance, each of these programmes its own distinctive conceptual foundations and principles of operation. Nevertheless, some key terms that identify such different forms of the peace process are either being used interchangeably or without drawing clear distinctions between them. Such conceptual ambiguity occasionally causes misunderstanding among field practitioners as well as academics.

This chapter therefore introduces the various strands of international peace-supporting activities by focusing on:

* Historical developments of peacebuilding projects
* Key concepts relevant to peacebuilding
* Procedures and major methods of peacebuilding
* Roles of peacebuilding actors.

Historical development of peace operations

How have international peace-supporting activities and humanitarian interventions developed over the previous decades? The traits of international third-party intervention have changed in accordance with the distinctive characteristics of the era. Particularly since the establishment of the United Nations (UN) immediately after World War II, international peace-supporting operations have greatly diversified in terms of their methods, their scope of action and their participating actors.

Period of emergence

The modern concept of peace-supporting operations by the international community emerged in the 19th century, the era of the 'balance of power.' Besides mutual treaties, European states established common security codifications, institutions and trade regimes to discourage slavery and piracy at sea and measures to control their waterways and to promote postal and telecommunications services. As seen in the collapse of the Ottoman Empire and the division of Kosovo, some European countries participated in forms of external humanitarian intervention, although their chief aim was to secure the order and stability of the international system. In the late 19th century, nongovernmental organisations (NGOs) such as the International Committee of the Red Cross (ICRC) began to participate in humanitarian assistance to war victims and to promote international norms for humanitarian operations. In its aftermath, although no military action was conducted, the establishment of the League of Nations in 1919 extended the scope of cooperation in the international community.

The Cold War period

With the establishment of the UN on 24 October 1945, a new era began. The 1945 UN Charter states that the UN is entitled to use "a set of techniques which it can use in order to secure the peaceful settlement of disputes, including fact-finding, good offices, conciliation, mediation and negotiation" and to use coercion and armed force "if necessary to maintain or restore international peace and security" (Miall, Ramsbotham and Woodhouse 1999: 34). The Korean War (1950–53), in which armies from sixteen nations participated, was a striking example of the UN's role in collective security.

In a further development, the UN began to intervene in a number of areas lying within the scope of the nation state's domestic jurisdiction, which were traditionally regarded as areas of strict noninterference. In such military interventions, three major methods are used: peace-keeping-type activities (e.g. in the Balkans, the Middle East and the Indian subcontinent), peace enforcement action (e.g. Korea and Congo) and management of transition (e.g. Congo and Dutch West New Guinea) (Bellamy et al. 2004: 71). These interventions by the UN (and other international organisations) could take place only with the consent of the conflicting parties.

The first UN peacekeeping mission, involving the deployment of military observers to the Middle East to monitor the Armistice Agreement between Israel and its Arab neighbours, was authorised in 1948. Since then, the UN Security Council has authorised peacekeeping missions in more than a hundred countries, with varying degrees of success. The form of the UN's early interventions is frequently categorised as 'first-generation peacekeeping.' The UN's early operations were conducted by unarmed or lightly armed military forces, and their main purposes were monitoring the implementation of a truce or creating a buffer zone between warring parties while peace negotiations took place. The UN peacekeeping missions in this period strictly followed three guiding principles: involvement only with the consent of all parties at war, strict impartiality and the use of force only for self-defence.

Nevertheless, the UN's military interventions rarely achieved UN Security Council consensus due to the strong rivalry between the bipolar bloc coalitions. Moreover, many countries regarded the UN as an agency of the United States and did not consider it a neutral mediator. While the rivalry between the two global camps served to limit the number and the scope of collective actions conducted under the name of the UN, individual states such as the US and the UK played diverse roles in various international tensions in this period. As a result, UN officials, including former secretary-generals such as Dag Hammarskjöld and U Thant, opted for the use of 'quiet diplomacy' to encourage conflicting parties to join the negotiating table. For instance, the UN played a significant role as a mediator in cases such as the Cyprus conflicts (1967 and 1974), the war between Iraq and Iran and in the withdrawal of the Soviet Union from Afghanistan.

Regional organisations also began to get involved in attempts to resolve regional conflicts. For example, the Organisation for African Unity (OAU), which was established in 1963, played a significant role in African conflicts in both positive and negative ways. Sometimes the OAU provided military aid to rebels (e.g. independence movements against colonialism or anti-apartheid groups in South Africa) and actively promoted a number of projects helping the refugees of conflicts and natural disasters. Nevertheless, the OAU's failure to gain uni-lateral consent from member states to intervene in conflicting states hampered its ability to mediate in the internal conflicts of the region.

In a number of cases, high-profile individuals contributed to the peaceful resolution of conflicts. Some of these figures include Tanzanian President Nyerere in Burundi, US President Jimmy Carter in the conflicts in the Middle East and Ethiopia's Emperor Haile Selassie in the Sudanese civil war. Another good example is the Commonwealth Eminent Persons Group's political pressure on the South African government regarding its policy of apartheid.

The post–Cold War period

The collapse of the Cold War system brought considerable changes to the international security arena: the disappearance of bipolar constraints (a new system), the emergence of NGOs (new actors), renewed interest in mediation (a new motive) and international norms recognising the need for international intervention (new norms) (Crocker, Hampson and Aall 1999). These changes led to the significant expansion of international peace operations – quantitatively, qualitatively and normatively – and to a new conception of peacebuilding in the early 1990s.

In terms of quantity, peace interventions have increased in number in the post–Cold War period, with the UN having conducted more peacekeeping operations in the five years from 1989 to 1994 than in the previous forty years. In addition, the number of civil war cases being terminated through negotiation has increased. According to Wallensteen (2007), 39 per cent of armed conflicts have been ended through peace negotiation in the post–Cold War period, while the Uppsala Conflict Data Program (2009) reports that that 61 per cent of the conflicts terminated between 1989 and 2006 (74 out of 122) were resolved by the signing of peace agreements.

With regard to actors, the UN began to play a more active role from the early 1990s. *An Agenda for Peace* (UNSG 1992), which was announced by the UN Secretary-General Boutros Boutros-Ghali in 1992, insisted that third-party intervention by the UN should change direc-tion and shift its focus towards peacebuilding. After acknowledging "the increasing ethnic, religious, social and cultural tensions within state boundaries, the problems of population growth, trade barriers, debt burdens and the disparity between the rich and the poor as potential sources of regional instability," the report suggested that the UN needed to extend the breadth of its concern and to expand the methods it uses (Rupesinghe 1998: 17). The establishment of the Peacebuilding Commission at the UN in 2005 is in this sense a significant development. The Commission, which aims to coordinate post-conflict peace-supporting activities, clearly demonstrates the UN's stronger commitment to peacebuilding.

In the post–Cold War period, the scope of peacekeeping has expanded to include second-generation operations which are engaged in "various police and civilian tasks, the goal of which is a long-term settlement of the underlying conflict" (for example, the peacekeeping operations in the Balkans and Africa in the 1990s) (Doyle 1996: 484). Furthermore, third-generation peace-keeping operations which are also called 'peace-enforcing' operations with their scope extending "from low-level military operations to protect the delivery of humanitarian assistance to the enforcement of cease-fires and, when necessary, assistance in the rebuilding of so-called failed states" (Doyle 1996: 484). Third-generation operations are conducted under the mandate of Chapter 7 of the UN Charter (collective security) and, sometimes, without the consent of the UN.

UN peace intervention methods also diversified during the 1990s. In addition to the recruitment of military forces for peacekeeping operations, human resources were drawn from members of civilian police forces, diplomatic actors and nongovernmental professionals (Ramsbotham, Miall and Woodhouse 2005). Military interventions were supplemented by a range of projects such as emergency relief, institution (re)building programmes, economic rehabilitation and community building. In normative terms, the concept of liberal-democratic peace had been widely accepted as the postwar system standard (Carment and Rowlands 1998), but as the cultural issues involved in intervention attracted greater attention and came under greater scrutiny, new types of intervention began to be considered. For instance, many external interveners began to adopt interactive conflict resolution methods, which employ "small group, problem-solving discussions between unofficial representatives of identity groups or states engaged in destructive conflict that are facilitated by an impartial third party of social scientist-practitioners" (Fisher 1997: 239). The peacebuilding ideas that provided strong conceptual grounds for these changes were actively adopted in the UN's major documents of this period: *An Agenda for Peace* (1992), *Supplement to an Agenda for Peace* (1995), *Agenda for Democratization* (1996), *Report of the Panel on United Nations Peacekeeping* (*the Brahimi Report*, 2000), *A More Secured World: Our Shared Responsibility* (2004), *In Larger Freedom: Towards Development, Security and Human Rights for All* (2005) and *Report of the Secretary-General on Peacebuilding in the Immediate Aftermath of Conflict* (2009).

The collapse of the Cold War system widened the scope for cooperation between major powers. The Gulf War in 1991, in which the UN's collective security force was deployed, was a notable example of this increased cooperation. In the process of consent building, the Soviet Union supported the US resolution authorising the use of force against Iraq. Moreover, in addition to the involvement of relatively neutral developed countries in Europe and North America in peace-supporting operations (including the Republic of Ireland and the Scandinavian nations), many Asian countries (Bangladesh, Pakistan, South Korea, India) and African nations (Nigeria, Ethiopia, Ghana) have actively participated in international peacebuilding since the mid-1990s.

The roles of regional organisations such as the African Union (AU, the successor of OAU), the Organization of American States (OAS) and the North Atlantic Treaty Organization (NATO) became much more prominent in conflict intervention. In Africa, for instance, the AU has made great efforts to mediate conflicting parties by sending envoys to countries such as the Central African Republic (2003) and Zimbabwe (2005) in addition to peacekeeping operations in Burundi and Sudan. In Europe, while NATO has played significant roles in various military operations, from peacekeeping (e.g. operations in the former Yugoslavia in 1994) to direct military action (e.g. the war in Bosnia-Herzegovina in 1995), the EU's activities have focused on preventive diplomacy and postwar assistance.

Concepts of the peace process

This section articulates some concepts that are widely used in contemporary academic discussions related to international peacebuilding. First, three terms that describe the approaches towards conflicts and de-escalation of conflicts – conflict management, conflict resolution and conflict transformation – will be explained. Each of these terms represents fundamental assumptions that determine peace-supporting activities in different phases discussed earlier.

Conflict management, conflict resolution and conflict transformation

Conflict management

Conflict management is a conservative approach to peace operations and refers to a set of strategies undertaken by third-party interveners to end a conflict and minimise its negative impact on people or the environment. As a response strategy, conflict management is often based on the assumption that human beings are by nature aggressive, and conflict will be an inevitable feature of society as a long as people interact (Miall 2004). This realist view assumes that disagreements and violent conflicts are very difficult to resolve, if not impossible. Hence, the core aim of conflict management is often limited to suppressing the outbreak and/or escalation of violence rather than addressing the underlying factors responsible for the conflict.

Several strategies are available for managing international and intrastate armed conflicts. Each strategy is guided by one core principle: containing violence and disruptive behaviour of the hostile parties in the conflict to a minimum. Since containment is an important factor in conflict management, it is safe to conclude that such strategies should aim at separating fighting parties to reduce hostilities, providing safe corridors for delivery of humanitarian aid and initiating peace talks to end the conflict. Key methods of peace-supporting activities until the late 1980s, such as mediation and traditional peacekeeping, are based on the ideas of conflict management.

Conflict resolution

Conflict resolution is a higher level of response than conflict management and is concerned with addressing the causes of conflict and building stronger, lasting relationships between competing groups. This approach is based on the assumption that a conflict normally comes out of contradictory views and/or interests of different actors and such sources of conflict can be addressed. Hence, conflict resolution operations endeavour either to mediate the competing interests of warring parties by facilitating peace negotiation or to de-escalate the risk of conflicts by alleviating extreme poverty or antagonism (Ramsbotham et al. 2005).

A variety of coercive and noncoercive methods are employed for conflict resolution. Frequently used noncoercive methods include the provision of good offices for negotiation, rule building for interparty interaction, suggesting feasible common targets for competing parties and transmission of information and diplomatic persuasion. When noncoercive methods do not bring about the expected outcomes, external interveners sometimes apply coercive economic and military incentives/pressure, which are more coercive.

Conflict transformation

The conflict transformation model adopts a more nuanced approach to the emergence and transformation of conflicts. Although both conflict resolution and conflict transformation assume that the sources of conflict can be addressed, conflict transformation pays attention to various social issues related to structural violence. The proponents of conflict transformation argue that conflicts originate from a series of social changes that lead suppressed or marginalised individuals/groups to challenge norms and structures. Accordingly, this approach tries to identify and resolve the wider social and political causes of conflict. The focus of conflict transformation, therefore, differs significantly from conflict management and conflict resolution and emphasises the following: relationship-centred strategies (not content-centred); long-term (rather than short-term) processes addressing cultural, contextual or structural issues (including grievances and the root and immediate causes of conflict); building or reconstructing relationships (interactions and networks); and creating or reforming structures (institutions or policies that govern people).

It should be noted that these terms are nevertheless interpreted in different ways, and no universally accepted definition of each term exists in the contemporary peacebuilding arena. Conflict resolution in particular is subject to definitional problems, as it one of the most commonly used terms to describe the process of bringing armed conflicts to an end. While it is sometimes used to distinguish between activities that aim to address the causes of conflicts and conflict management programmes, it is also understood as a general term that refers to the efforts of third parties to de-escalate military violence. Recently, as the concept of post-conflict peacebuilding has become more prominent, conflict resolution has come to refer to the processes of de-escalating ongoing military conflicts, as distinct from conflict transformation, which emphasises longer-term efforts.

Peacekeeping, peacemaking and peacebuilding

While conflict resolution, management and transformation emphasise the procedural aspect of peace activities, peacekeeping, peacemaking and peacebuilding denote external interveners' approaches to peace intervention. The distinctions between the notions of peacekeeping, peacebuilding and peacemaking are largely determined by the types of approaches that interveners choose to employ and the fundamental assumptions upon which these approaches are based.

Peacekeeping

In many cases, peacekeeping is used to denote a wide range of activities that often include peacebuilding and peacemaking operations. However, traditional definitions of peacekeeping specifically refer to the deployment of armed forces that aim "to end immediate violence and hostilities" (Chetail 2009: 1). Peacekeeping missions are normally mandated to maintain law and order, monitor ceasefire agreements, protect relief aid convoys and propose programmes for disarming and demobilising combatants. The missions, therefore, often focus on reducing the fighting on the ground by separating combatants while plans are made for diplomatic efforts to end the conflict by promoting peace negotiations, brokering ceasefires and maintaining transitional peace. In short, the main emphasis of peacekeeping is on halting military conflict. In principle, such intervention takes place only when the military factions consented to the operation.

Peacekeeping missions have been undertaken mainly by national/international agencies such as state military forces, the UN and regional organisations. As most projects are politically sensitive, traditional peacekeeping operations require consent from the immediate parties to the conflict and usually rely on noncoercive and impartial means. Representative examples of peacekeeping are the operations undertaken by UN peacekeeping forces during the Cold War period (such as those in Cyprus and Lebanon), whose fundamental task was to provide a buffer zone between two or more disputing military factions in order to reduce the chances of encounter/engagement.

More recently, unarmed civilian peacekeeping has been attempted by some civil society organisations as an alternative to military peacekeeping. These organisations usually take on the nonmilitary parts of traditional peacekeeping operations, such as monitoring ceasefire agreements and playing advocacy roles for minority groups (e.g. protective accompaniment, media coverage to ensure the implementation of ceasefire provisions) (Berghof Foundation 2012).

Peacemaking

As the limitations of traditional peacekeeping that mainly concerns neutral intervention to sustain peace-supporting activities and reduce violence became clear, more proactive operations to nurture more peaceful conflict resolution were initiated. While peacebuilding mainly concerns a wider range of field practices, peacemaking is more about state-oriented activities focusing on diplomatic or policy-oriented programmes.

Thus, from a narrow perspective, peacemaking is normally defined as diplomatic efforts to encourage disputing parties to choose negotiation rather than violent conflict. Ratner's definition is a good example, which identifies peacemaking as "the diplomatic process of bringing the sides to a conflict together toward a settlement (both before and after the signature of any peace agreement)" (1997: 21). Like peacekeeping, this method can only be implemented following consent of the disputants and they are frequently applied together with peacekeeping operations. From a broader perspective, the concept of peacemaking occasionally includes 'peace enforcement.' In the circumstances where combatants target civilians and commit human rights abuses, peacemaking mandates may be changed to include peace enforcement, which allows the use of threats or force to compel conflicting parties to negotiate. In such cases, further enforcement measures, such as economic sanctions and military interventions, are applied together with traditional diplomatic methods like mediation, arbitration and judicial settlement.

Moreover, contemporary peacemaking projects tend to aim to achieve Western ideals of peace. In particular, many peace agreements signed in the 1990s and 2000s are criticised as primarily representing the views and interests of international actors. Many of these agreements are facilitated by Western third parties and include key ideas that are popularly supported by the mediators, either implicitly or expressed explicitly: "a monopoly over the use of force," "the rule of law," "the control of interdependence . . . limiting the inclination to use violence and force," "democratic participation," "social justice (welfare and rights)" and "a political culture of constructive and peaceful management of conflicts" (Young 2010: 407–8).

Peacebuilding

Peacebuilding was first conceptualised by Johan Galtung as peace-supporting activities that aim to facilitate durable peace by addressing root causes of armed conflicts. In 1992, the UN produced a similar definition of peacebuilding, as "action to identify and support structures which will tend to strengthen and solidify peace in order to avoid a relapse into conflict" (UN 1992: para 21) and describing its purpose as "support for the transformation of deficient national structures and capabilities, and for the strengthening of new democratic institutions" (UNSG 1992). Later critical reflection on previous peacekeeping operations, which had tended to sustain the status

Figure 2.1 Development of concepts on peacebuilding

quo in the society in which they had operated, gradually led to calls for projects that focused on longer-term social transformation, addressed the fundamental causes of conflict and aimed towards developing a more sustainable peace.

This new conception of peacebuilding challenged previous approaches towards security and peace "by taking people, rather than states, as the referent of security and by moving beyond a narrow focus on military security" (Tschirgi 2013: 197). Peacebuilding programmes therefore aim to effect changes not only in social and institutional structures but also in people's behaviour and perception (Jeong 2005). In this sense, peacebuilding expanded the scope of peacemaking significantly by bringing a wider range of issues to international peace-supporting activities. Schmelzle and Fischer (2009) categorised such expanded missions into three areas: altering structural contradictions, improving relations of conflict parties and changing individual attitudes and behaviour.

Two types of peacebuilding are commonly employed. The first type deals with the issues that emerge immediately after a ceasefire. In the aftermath of large-scale violence, a range of problems such as the demobilisation of military forces, the establishment of state authority, the restoration of public services and refugee resettlement require urgent attention. Peace-building programmes in this period therefore attempt to provide provisional methods of managing transitional periods. Once the war-torn society has achieved a relatively stable level of peace, the focus of peacebuilding programmes can shift to addressing the fundamental sources of the violent conflict and the second type of peacebuilding, which pursues longer-term transformation of social structures, can take place.

Although they approach peace-supporting efforts from different perspectives, the key ideas of peacekeeping and conflict management are very similar. Similarly, the core concepts of peacebuilding are highly consistent with the themes of conflict transformation. In fact, these terms and concepts were developed in similar periods of time. While peacekeeping was a dominant form of international peace-supporting activities when the concept of conflict management was utilised as a prominent theoretical foundation. After having rapid expansion of its scope, the international peace operation is being developed into long-term peacebuilding based on the conceptual ground of conflict transformation.

Scope of the peace process

What, then, are the core components of the peace process? What are the main issues addressed through the peace process? This section answers these questions focusing on the phases of conflict prevention, peace negotiation, post-conflict recovery and conflict transformation (see Figure 2.2). Although a variety of methods with different goals are generally employed in parallel, competition, force and accommodation are more frequently used during the peace negotiation period, while accommodation and cooperation are more commonly observed in the post-conflict phase.

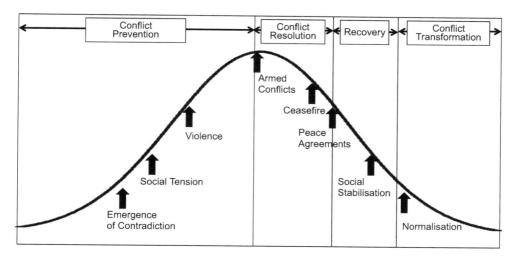

Figure 2.2 The scope of the peace process

Conflict prevention

Although the importance of conflict prevention measures had been emphasised since the 1950s, it was only in the 1990s that preventive actions were adopted as an essential element of peacebuilding. As identifying and addressing the signs of potential violent conflicts as early as possible are central to these actions, three main types of activity have been promoted by major international organisations: early warning, preventive diplomacy and peacekeeping operations.

Early warning refers to any initiatives that aim "to detect potential peace breaking issues or situations" (Ramcharan 2009: 235) so that external actors can implement relevant measures to reduce the risk. Specifically, it identifies "a) wars and armed conflict; b) state failure; c) genocide and politicide; d) other gross human rights violations; and e) humanitarian emergencies caused by natural disasters" (Wulf and Debiel 2009: 5). Although the UN and other regional organisations (e.g. the Organization for Security and Cooperation in Europe [OSCE] and the AU) developed their own early warning systems and established networks for collaboration between 2000 and 2005, evaluating the likelihood of the occurrence of violent conflicts remains a challenge. In particular, precisely determining the moment when the threshold for the eruption of violent conflict has been reached – that is, "when parties to a conflict decide, or feel compelled to use or escalate violence to achieve their aims" – is a complicated task (UNSG 2011).

Preventive diplomacy is one of the most common measures employed by the UN and other external actors to "prevent disputes from arising between parties, to prevent existing disputes from escalating into conflict and to limit the spread of the latter when they occur" (UNSG 1992). Some of the UN's traditional preventive diplomacy methods include (1) facilitating good offices of the secretary-general, (2) dispatching envoys and (3) organising unofficial groups of international leaders called 'Friends of UN Secretary-General' (UNSG 2011). Recently, the organisation has also established permanent regional offices in West Africa, Central Asia and Central Africa and uses the offices for conducting proactive preventive diplomatic actions. Although such diplomatic measures have mediated a large number of potentially risky conflicts over the past decade, these quiet successes are not widely reported by the media.

As discussed above, traditional (first-generation) peacekeeping has been employed as another key preventive action measure. By dispatching nonaggressive military forces to act as a buffer between the conflicting parties, this measure is intended to reduce the frequency and intensity of the interaction between them.

Peace negotiation (conflict resolution)

Peace negotiation is a process that brings disputants together to negotiate their demands with the aim of ending an ongoing military conflict. Although a large number of definitions highlight different aspects of negotiation, there is a general agreement that negotiation is a process by which compromise is reached. In addition, these definitions assume that negotiations have four core elements: board (set up), players (important actors), stakes (issues and their salience for players) and moves (strategies and tactics) (Starkey, Boyer and Wilkenfeld 1999). In short, no matter what specific forms they have, the actions that actors communicate to build a voluntary agreement can be defined as negotiations.

Negotiation in conflicts can be understood as one of the most competitive types of negotiation in the international arena for several reasons. When a war begins, actors believe that their contradicting interests cannot be harmonised through nonviolent means. Moreover, once a war begins and casualties occur on both sides, the level of a faction's trust toward its counterpart decreases dramatically. Even when leaders wish to negotiate, the rank and file are so filled with anger that they tend not to allow it. Under these circumstances, the actors in peace negotiations seek resolutions that can convince the warring factions to agree to end the war through peaceful means (strategies employed by actors will be discussed later).

Hence, various ways to improve the effectiveness of peace negotiation have been suggested. First, some researchers seek ways of 'changing the bargain to a nonzero-sum game' based on the assumption of actors' rationality. Some propose methods for finding common interest among actors and for manipulating the game so that it becomes 'interest-based bargaining.' For instance, Fisher and Ury suggest a number of effective methods to enable this to occur: "separate the people from the problem; focus on interests, not positions; invent options for mutual gain; and insist upon using objective criteria to judge the merits of possible solutions" (Fisher and Ury 1991 cited in Starkey et al. 1999: 115). Axelrod (1990) argues that there are three interrelated features of cooperative negotiation: negotiations need to be sequential games, the gains that actors expect in the forthcoming games should be sufficiently large and reciprocity should be guaranteed.

In contrast, nonpositivist theorists point to the critical role that cultural issues play in civil conflicts as causes, reflectors, amplifiers or inhibiters. First, cultural issues can be the direct cause of conflicts. In ethnic war, for example, ethnic identity provides the fundamental motivation for violent resistance to the (perceived) discrimination of rival parties. Second, cultural symbols and narratives are sometimes the mirror for tensions among groups. For instance, the religious parades in Northern Ireland serve to galvanise the anger of opposing sides. Third, according to how the cultural expressions are used, they can be either amplifiers or inhibiters of conflicts. For example, although the parades in Northern Ireland are reflections of existing tensions, they may also cause subsequent tensions or violent reactions (Ross 2007). Nonpositivist theorists therefore maintain that understanding the cultural traits of actors is the first step towards a successful peace negotiation.

Post-conflict recovery and reconstruction

Once a peace negotiation process succeeds in convincing belligerents to sign peace accords and to agree to a ceasefire, the promotion and maintenance of sustainable peace in the post-conflict period becomes the central part of the peace process. The focus of peacebuilding in this phase is the programmes that are implemented to improve public security, promote economic recovery, facilitate social healing and develop democratic institutions. Most contemporary post-conflict reconstruction programmes focus on the establishment of democratic political institutions and a market-oriented economic system (Jeong 2005). This section briefly discusses major peacebuilding programmes from both short-term and long-term perspectives.

There are programmes that aim to provide immediate support to enable the reestablishment of social security and the building of social and economic systems in war-torn societies. The short-term management and recovery plans discussed during the political negotiation between disputing military factions are mainly concerned with restructuring the security, political and public service sectors. In addition, international and local actors also make efforts to restore the social and economic dimensions of societies that have been devastated by war. Examples of such initiatives are as follows:

The *disarmament, demobilisation and reintegration of ex-combatants* (DDR) is a typical strategy undertaken in an effort to reform the security sector. Since overcoming mistrust is an indispensable factor for successful DDR, various strategies are employed to build trust both between the former rival combatants and between the factions and interveners, including the exchange of reliable information, transparent inspection and verification of the disarmament process and acceptance of mutual security. In addition, sufficient support for the rehabilitation and reintegration of ex-combatants into their societies (e.g. emergency food aid, transitional allowances, skills training, health support and cash grants) should be provided (Özerdem 2009).

Providing *interim security* during the transitional period is another important issue. Since the majority of the security forces formerly under the control of warring factions will have disarmed or demobilised by this point, the transitional period is prone to experiencing a security vacuum, especially given that few national leaderships or international interveners actually possess the capabilities to provide transitional arrangements for control of the security dimension. As a result, disarmed former combatants, returning refugees and other people have been victimised by remaining security forces or other militias in many cases (Call and Stanley 2003).

Attempts to *protect and enhance human rights* are also made in most peacebuilding programmes. For those who have been subject to severe violence and indignity, having confidence in exercising their political, economic and civil rights is an important but difficult issue. Together with judicial, security and political support (e.g. enhancing law enforcement on human rights violations, promotion of disciplined criminal proceedings, effective control of security officials and political campaigns on human rights), social and psychological support (e.g. rebuilding social capital, creating work opportunities and providing psychological treatment) are essential elements of human rights protection.

Transitional authorities control the administration during the interim period between ceasefire and the first general election and play particularly important roles in preventing the occurrence of violent conflicts. Power sharing (consociationalism) and autonomy acknowledgment (federalism) are two key ideas that have been applied in most of the political transition projects in post-conflict societies during the 1990s and 2000s. While power-sharing aims to provide mechanisms through which the parties can work as equal partners during the interim period and pursue coexistence in the postelection phases, the objective of autonomy acknowledgement is to grant certain levels of power to regional or ethnic groups (Jeong 2005).

Since chronic wars greatly damage the conditions for economic activities, *economic rehabilitation and development* are high-priority goals. Recovery of basic infrastructures such as buildings, roads, ports and electricity can be done in a relatively short period. However, it takes much longer to address both the destruction of human capital due to massive displacement and deaths and the weak and inefficient national institutions managed by untrained public servants. In addition, the existence of a patron-client system nurtured by a war economy is often another significant barrier to the development of a post-conflict political economy.

As regards the social dimensions of peacebuilding, *refugee resettlement and land transfer* are two of the most prominent issues. As the sudden influx of a large number of returning refugees and internally displaced persons (IDPs) will have a huge impact on post-conflict societies, a cautiously designed repatriation plan is necessary. Nevertheless, the relatively short-term resettlement plans of previous peacebuilding projects and the interim authorities' lack of capacity have led to insufficient support being given to both refugees and impoverished local communities. Land transfer is a core means by which to assimilate refugees and other war affected people into a productive life. However, as the issue of land rights is often a major factor in many belligerents' initial decision to engage in long-term military struggle, redistribution of land has frequently been a barrier to the implementation of peace accords.

The provision of *health services* (e.g. disease control and children's immunisation) is a particular challenge in post-conflict societies because the demand for medical treatment usually far exceeds available supplies. Nevertheless, since health care is a common issue for all former military factions and has no direct relation to the political power structure, it may provide an opportunity for the opposing parties to begin to associate and collaborate more closely. For instance, while sharing the same health infrastructure and undertaking the same health training, they can rebuild intercommunal communication.

Conflict transformation and stable peace

Many peace operations in the early 1990s ended upon the completion of the reconstruction projects set out in peace accords. As the concept of peacebuilding has grown in prominence, however, programmes for long-term social transformation and reconciliation have been included in most peace operations in the 2000s. A representative example of the various types of programme being undertaken in pursuit of stable peace is *reconciliation*, which is "a process of mutual accommodation comprised of acknowledgment of past wrong doing and contrition for the perpetrators in exchange for forgiveness offered by the victims" (Jeong 2005: 156). By acknowledging the past and reconciling former enemies, it enables both victims and perpetrators of misdeeds to move on to future-oriented activities and thus reduce the possibility of violence resuming. In many peacebuilding processes, truth recovery schemes have been adopted as a core step in the reconciliation process. In many cases, however, various issues related to "amnesties, partial involvement of former combatants, and compensation" have diminished the effectiveness of the processes (Darby and Mac Ginty 2003: 195).

Attempts are also generally made to *transform political, security and judicial institutions*. These reforms are usually intended both to reduce the social cleavages or ethnic tensions caused by violent conflicts and to develop democratic systems for social representation and protection of human rights. Security sector reforms, for instance, tend to pursue the 'military merger' of all the opposing parties' military forces into a single army and the development of a new sense of identity (Arnson and Azpuru 2003). In cases where government armies have committed serious human rights violations during the war period, the size of armies tends to be significantly reduced in order to reduce military power (Call and Stanley 2003).

In terms of political transformation, efforts to replace the old patron-client relationships (which had sustained the former factional leaders) by democratic representation systems at the national and local levels are made.

At the local level, *community development* has been a major goal of many programmes run by international organisations, local governments and NGOs. Local populations are encouraged to reconsider their own strengths and to devise development strategies that rely on their own skills and resources (Jeong 2005). Moreover, social capital such as the informal networks of peasant groups, local self-help loan systems and micro-entrepreneurship are promoted by external peace facilitators.

As the first phase of DDR programmes that focused on disarmament and demobilisation came to an end, the longer-term reintegration of ex-combatants into society became a principal goal of DDR. In fact, due to insufficient reintegration support, many demobilised ex-combatants have caused serious social problems or have been re-recruited as soldiers. Recognising this, a wide range of vocational skill training, effective insulation from military groups from other countries, credit programmes and self-help systems within ex-combatants' communities have/are being attempted in many countries. These programmes generally aim to deal with "the motivation and determination of former combatants themselves," "the acceptance and support of the community" and "the facilitation of measures provided for employment and income generation" (ILO 1995 cited in Özerdem 2009: 21).

Main actors in peacebuilding

When, up until the end of the Cold War, the traditional concept of conflict management and peacekeeping dominated international peace-supporting activities, the actors involved in the processes were also fairly limited. Although a number of prominent NGOs such as Oxfam, Médecins Sans Frontières (MSF) and ICRC were active, most peacekeeping operations were decided and operated by the UN and a few nation states (mainly the members of the UN Security Council). Nevertheless, while the scope of international peacebuilding rapidly expanded during the 1990s, the types of peacebuilding actors significantly diversified by including regional and intrastate actors with different areas of expertise. Gradually, the NGOs and local communities have become considered core actors who are able to effect real societal transformation. As summarised in Figure 2.3, this section will categorise the actors into four groups and provide a more comprehensive elaboration of the significance of each group in conflict transformation processes.

Intergovernmental organisations

At the stage of conflict resolution towards ceasefire or de-escalation of conflicts, the UN has been the most vigorous actor in peace negotiation processes. As a mediator, it has provided the main momentum and opportunities for talks in peace processes in El Salvador, Angola, Mozambique, Liberia, the Central African Republic, Tajikistan and the Western Sahara (Wallensteen 2007). The UN's legitimacy as an impartial external actor helped the organisation to play relatively effective roles in these operations. However, the UN's impartiality and autonomy have not always played positive roles in peace processes. Doyle confirms that many smaller non-Western states have doubted the impartiality and neutrality of the organisation (and of the Security Council, in particular) (Doyle 1996: 485–86). Moreover, critics have also noted that the UN frequently lacks operational efficiency and that it relies heavily on the financial, military and human resources of member states (Crocker et al. 1999).

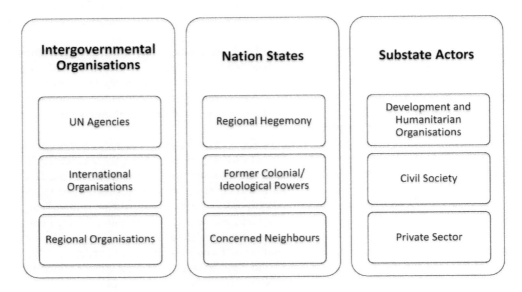

Figure 2.3 Main actors in peacebuilding

Whilst the UN has long been a key actor in peace mediation processes, the roles of regional organisations are now becoming more prominent in post-conflict peacebuilding processes. A number of regional organisations, including NATO in Europe and the Economic Community of West African States (ECOWAS), sometimes play critical roles in peace negotiations. Increasing numbers of cases are dealt with by regional security organisations. Examples include NATO's intervention in the war in Kosovo, the Economic Community of West African States Monitoring Group (ECOMOG) intervention in Liberia (consisting mainly of Nigerian military forces) and the intervention by the International Military Advisory Team (IMAT), led by the British army, in Sudan (Ramsbotham et al. 2005: 149). While some organisations, including the OSCE in Europe, were intentionally established 'to bridge the divide in an existing conflict and provide a venue for discussion and dialogue,' others like the Association of South East Asian Nations (ASEAN), the OAS and ECOMOG were founded on broader shared interests.

The roles of the European Union (EU) and the AU are particularly prominent in the post–Cold War period. As the UN has increased its reliance on regional organisations in conflict resolution, both the EU and AU have been key actors in many regional conflicts. In recent years, the AU has played a more significant role and has moved towards conflict prevention and early response strategies, and the EU has expanded its concerns outside Europe to other parts of the world.

Both international and regional organisations employ a wide range of strategies to de-escalate military conflicts, including military measures (to deter opposing forces), constitutional measures (to promote democratic politics), governance measures (to enhance the capability of local government and society) and financial measures (to construct infrastructure). By adopting the concept of conflict transformation, these actors may achieve considerable successes in conflict de-escalation and prevention. For instance, the OSCE high commissioner's intervention in Estonia significantly reduced the risk of armed conflict by transforming the economic policies in favour of the Russian-speaking communities and by introducing an electoral system that allowed cross-ethnic voting.

Nation states

Many of the interveners are national states with a centralised power structure. Among the various actors, this section focuses particularly on regional hegemons, former colonial or ideological powers and concerned neighbours.

Regional hegemons

Actors in this category intervene in civil wars in neighbouring states "in order to press their own claims to territory, economic benefits or access to natural resources, or support the socio-political ambitions of allies" (Bellamy, Williams and Griffin 2010: 44). Examples include Russia in Georgia and Nigeria in West Africa. Although they exhibit strong enthusiasm and have effective power, these actors are highly likely to be partial to certain factions and may be motivated to pursue narrow national interests. Since the collapse of the global bipolar system in the late 1980s, the role of regional hegemons has been increasing. South Africa's mediating role in recent internal conflicts in neighbouring countries such as Zimbabwe demonstrates the enhanced and complicated roles of regional hegemons in conflict resolutions. In addition, many regional hegemons such as China, India and the US are also global powers.

Former colonial/ideological powers

Many Western countries that had previously colonised the states in civil war also intervene. In the Cold War period, a few hegemonic states also participated in civil war peace processes. Since former colonial powers 'have close economic, political and social ties with their former colonies' (Bellamy, Williams and Griffin 2010: 44) and Cold War hegemons strongly supported developing states, they had relatively strong leverage. Most peace processes in the Cold War era and some in the post–Cold War period (including the UK in the case of Sierra Leone and France in the case of Rwanda) provide examples of these close ties and leverage. More recently, these countries have created a number of value-based groups such as the Community of Democracies and have restructured the role of institutions like the Council of Europe, in which members closely cooperate in peacekeeping activities.[1]

Concerned neighbours

If the countries neighbouring the states in civil war are vulnerable to the impact of the war, they often try to intervene. As Ramsbotham, Woodhouse and Miall (2005: 113) put it, civil wars "have external effects on the region through the spread of weaponry, economic dislocation, links with terrorism, disruptive floods of refugees, and spill-over into regional politics when neighbouring states are dragged or the same people straddle several states." As a result, states tend to be deeply concerned about the security issues of their neighbours and try to minimise the external effects of their neighbours' violent conflicts. However, despite their strong desire to resolve the conflicts, in many cases they lack the ability to intervene effectively and are therefore unable to contribute significantly to the resolution of the conflicts.

Development and humanitarian organisations

Although their material resources are much smaller than those of state actors, development and humanitarian agencies are actively involved in most contemporary peacebuilding processes (in particular, the activities conducted in the post-conflict phases). Of the various external peace supporters, it is the NGO practitioners who have initiated and sustained the programmes in a manner most suited to the concept of conflict transformation. A large number of NGOs have operated development programmes in sectors ranging from landmine disposal to consultancy on national police reform.

Owing to the sheer number of organisations working in a wide variety of fields, it is impossible to generalise their roles; however, support for refugees in politically unstable areas, reintegration of ex-combatants, rehabilitation of industry and the capacity building of local communities are some examples of their activities. For instance, Oxfam facilitated talks in Northern Kenya between local elders and set the codes of honour and conduct in order to promote communication and reconciliation between the nomadic pastoral communities and agricultural communities, which have experienced intense conflicts.

In many cases, NGOs are able to develop a more comprehensive understanding of the root causes of the conflict and to work more closely with local people due to their relatively smaller sizes and local-based networks and working environment. While it is clear that they also experience various problems/challenges, NGOs have proven their capabilities in developing bottom-up conflict transformation programmes (e.g. facilitating workshops between different tribal groups, mediation of local conflicts and initiatives for cross-cultural understanding).

Civil society and private sector

In conflict management and conflict resolution perspectives, the contributions of civil society and the private sector to peacebuilding have been underappreciated in academic discourse until recently. International interveners facilitate peace processes, and national leaders or military factions participate in the processes by using their material and nonmaterial resources, with civil society playing a passive role. Some of the case studies employing these perspectives even go so far as to doubt the existence of meaningful civil society. In conflict transformation theories, however, it is the local actors themselves who "have the greatest responsibility, and the greatest opportunity, for transforming their own conflicts" (Miall 2004: 14). Hence, projects based on the notion conflict transformation have tried to place local people at the centre of their implementation and to reflect local needs. Nevertheless, an exaggerated expectation of local communities and their ability to play the leading role may cause serious problems. Previous experience shows that underdeveloped communities are vulnerable to local patrons or demagogues and that this increases the risk of the resumption of conflict (Fischer 2006).

Nevertheless, past peacebuilding processes demonstrate that the role of the private sector is particularly significant in economic regeneration. In addition to creating jobs, private companies sometimes address the causes of conflict by providing alternatives to conflict-related employment (e.g. the narcotics industry or the weapons trade). Moreover, as the idea of corporate social responsibility became more prevalent, more private companies began to take actions that are intended to have a positive impact on their societies through exercising their economic influence, relatively large financial resources, skilled workforce and connections at all levels of society. Occasionally, private companies contribute to facilitating peace negotiations (Carbonnier 2009). Nevertheless, the private sector remains a minor contributor to peacebuilding, and its contribution is made in indirect ways.

Conclusion

This chapter reviewed the history and development of international intervention for conflict resolution from the earliest forms of international intervention in Europe and humanitarian assistance by the ICRC in the 19th century to recent peacebuilding programmes in Timor-Leste and South Sudan. In particular, it notes the significant increase in the frequency of peacebuilding projects in the post–Cold War period and the expansion in the scope of activities. Then, this chapter articulated some of the key terms used in peace studies, including conflict resolution, conflict management, conflict transformation, peacekeeping, peacemaking and peacebuilding. Finally, the main procedures, major actors of peacebuilding and methods employed by peace facilitators in each stage of a peace process are presented. During the peace negotiation process, state- or interstate-level actors (e.g. the US and the UN) play prominent roles, and most methods used involve pursuing successful negotiation between warring factions. In the post-conflict period, however, a wider range of actors, including nongovernmental actors, participate in peacebuilding projects that aim at the promotion of sustainable peace in the war-torn society. Moreover, the exploration reveals that the characteristics of peacebuilding projects have changed significantly in terms of their frequency, actors, scope of activities and purposes and especially so in the post–Cold War period.

In understanding contemporary peacebuilding trends, it is worth mentioning that the emergence of two new themes – peacebuilding and conflict transformation – has determined the new features of contemporary international peace activities implemented since the late 1990s. Moving beyond the cessation of conflicts, people began to think about how to transform the post-conflict 'no war, no peace' situation into a state of consolidated peace. Moreover, by shifting the focus of activities to community and individual levels, international peacebuilding actors identified a large number of conflict-related issues that had been frequently neglected, including psychological trauma, local culture, roles of leaders, human needs and impact of external intervention. Such transformation of the theoretical ground accordingly made significant shifts in the focus of field practice from deterring the occurrence of violence to addressing the causes of conflicts. New types of actors (e.g. NGOs, civil associations and local community leaders) also began to play important roles.

The new theoretical ground, however, does not have a universal influence on the peacebuilding projects implemented across the globe. The transition to a new generation of peacebuilding is being made at different rates depending on the type of peacebuilding, location of the implementation, key actors who operate the programmes and the social and structural contexts. For instance, while a large number of international NGOs supporting the community development in Bosnia-Herzegovina advanced the theme of conflict transformation, the security sector reforms currently being implemented in Afghanistan still very much reflect the concept of conflict management. Hence, the programmes explained in Parts II and III are proposed and developed in different generations of peacebuilding.

Discussion questions

- Are there any problems caused by the increased roles of the international organisations such as the UN in conflict resolution and post-conflict reconstruction?
- Can a humanitarian intervention of external states be completely humanitarian?

- What impact do new trends in contemporary peacebuilding (i.e. conflict transformation) have on international politics?
- Does the increased roles of intrastate actors such as NGOs and the private sector affect the Weberian concepts of the state?
- Are there effective and realistic alternatives to coercive intervention in situations of dictatorship, genocide and war crimes?

Note

1 Since these communities are based on democratic values, Wallensteen (2007) refers to them and their underlying ideology as a *Pax Democratica*.

Recommended reading

Bellamy, A. J. Williams, P. and Griffin, S. (2010) 'Peace Operations in Global Politics', in *Understanding Peacekeeping*, edited by Bellamy, A. and Williams, P. Cambridge: Polity: 13–41.

Kathman, J. and Wood, R. (2011) 'Managing the Threat, Cost and Incentive to Kill: The Short and Long-Term Effects of Intervention in Mass Killings'. *Journal of Conflict Resolution* 55 (5): 735–60.

Kuperman, A. (2008) 'The Moral Hazard of Humanitarian Intervention: Lessons from the Balkans'. *International Studies Quarterly* 52 (1): 49–80.

Lowe, V. (ed.) (2008) Chapters 7 and 9, in *The United Nations Security Council and War*, Oxford: Oxford University Press.

Weiss, T. (ed.) (2012) 'The Feudal System, or Dysfunctional Family', in *What's Wrong with the UN and How to Fix It* (2nd ed.). London: Polity: 73–111.

Woodhouse, T. (2001) 'Conflict Resolution and Peacekeeping: Critiques and Responses'. *International Peacekeeping* 7 (1): 8–26.

3　The liberal peacebuilding model

Since the collapse of the Cold War system, the liberal peacebuilding model has shaped the key features of contemporary international peacebuilding and has delineated the scope of peace in many conflict-affected countries. The end of the Cold War brought fundamental changes to the international security arena, and peacebuilding operations were expanded quantitatively, qualitatively and normatively. Since the most prominent actors in international aid programmes during the 1990s were European and North American states and organisations, the themes contained within the liberal peacebuilding model naturally became the standards that informed the efforts to (re)construct peace in war-affected countries. Moreover, as the theory of 'democratic peace,' which argues that (liberally constituted) democratic countries are more likely to be peaceful than others, gained currency among both academics and politicians, the tendency to rely on the liberal peace agenda increased.

Nevertheless, it became clear over time that these new types of international peace-supporting activities faced various obstacles and had limitations that prevented them from facilitating durable peace in conflict-affected societies. While some countries returned to armed conflict within a few years, other countries came to be ruled by more authoritarian and repressive types of governance than had been the case in the pre-conflict period. These failures have led to extensive discussion within the international academic community, much of which has focused on criticism of the liberal peacebuilding model and the formulation of proposals for alternatives. For instance, more inclusive and reflective procedures for the planning and implementation of peacebuilding programmes have been emphasised at the policy-making level, while promotion of partnerships with local actors and efforts to move beyond the traditional models of practice have been encouraged at the field practice level.

Given these recent developments, this chapter closely examines the liberal peacebuilding model by focusing on four learning objectives:

- The conceptual and philosophical grounds of the liberal peace tradition
- The key features of liberal peacebuilding
- The criticism of liberal peacebuilding
- Efforts to overcome the limitations of liberal peacebuilding.

The liberal peace tradition and liberal peacebuilding

At the heart of the liberal peace framework is a liberal epistemology of peace that has determined the nature of major peacebuilding operations in the post-Cold War period. It is generally agreed that the fundamental tenets of the liberal peace have their origins in the constitutional peace plans of the Enlightenment period. These central values were then refined by developments in the idea of institutional peace and the enhanced roles of civil society during the imperial and postcolonial period. However, given that there are differing theoretical strands within the liberal peace tradition, it is difficult to define a set of what might be considered the universal features of the liberal peace. Despite this theoretical and definitional problem, it is clear that all liberal peace theories share a number of commonalities.

For instance, a fundamental assumption of the majority of liberal peace theories is that an individual is a sovereign actor and the government is an agent that reflects the will of citizens. This tendency to conceptualise individuals and collectives as rational actors means that liberal peace theories therefore tend to emphasise tolerance, diversity, equal opportunity and protection of individual property. Furthermore, it is widely accepted by liberal peace theorists that the government's main roles should be providing security to citizens, enforcing the rules and regulations of the society, mediating conflicts and supporting citizens' pursuit of happiness. Regarding some of the specific elements that constitute peace, the liberal peace highlights the state's right to exercise a monopoly over the use of force, "the rule of law," "democratic participation," "social justice (welfare and rights)," and "a political culture of constructive and peaceful management of conflicts" (Young 2010: 407–8).

During the Cold War period, the majority of academic output concluded that the central concepts of liberal peace would bring about more durable peace. Drawing particularly on the democratic peace ideals espoused in Immanuel Kant's *Toward Perpetual Peace* (1795), the studies produced in this period argued that democracy, economic interdependence and international organisations are the three pillars of sustainable peace. First, the argument that democratic institutions are instrumental in attaining a sustainable peace is based on the proposition that because the democratic system "create[s] an accountable relationship between the state and the voters" (Doyle 2005: 464), and because the overwhelming majority of citizens have no wish to suffer the sacrifices of war, "democracies rarely, if ever, make war on each other" (Russet and O'Neal 2001: 49) unless there are significant "cultural, structural and ethical reasons" (Newbrander 2012: 40). Second, it is argued that international peace can be enhanced through trade and mutual economic collaboration. Mutual economic interdependence and the material incentives afforded by trade (termed the 'power of money' by Kant) reduce the risk of armed conflict as all actors involved have so much to lose if war erupts (Doyle 2005; Keohane and Nye 1977). Third, international organisations can contribute to international peace by regulating and sustaining the interaction between states. In other words, by supporting these states to engage in continued interactions, international organisations can make states more reluctant to breach international norms and rules. Thus, rather than seeking short-term benefits through aggressive actions, states are more likely to choose to secure more sustainable gains within the international system.

With the collapse of the Soviet Union and the end of the Cold War, civil war became the most common form of armed conflict, and liberal notions of peace were actively adopted in major international peace-supporting activities in the 1990s. Although international peacebuilding activities rapidly increased in terms of their number, size and forms, these activities were primarily initiated and led by international organisations and nation states from the global North (mainly from Europe and North America) and were therefore strongly underpinned by the liberal notions of peace. As a result, the liberal prescriptions for peace were firmly embedded in the peacebuilding programmes in this period. The prevalence of liberal peace themes in the post–Cold War period is attested to by the fact that these themes were explicitly presented in the following major UN documents on the direction of peace-supporting activities throughout the 1990s and 2000s: *An Agenda for Peace* (1992), *Supplement to an Agenda for Peace* (1995), *Agenda for Democratization* (1996), *Report of the Panel on United Nations Peacekeeping (the Brahimi Report,* 2000), *A More Secure World: Our Shared*

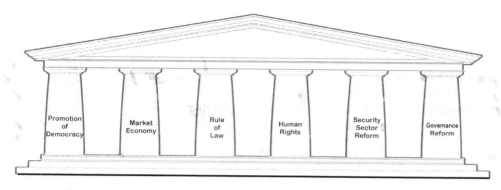

Figure 3.1 The key features of liberal peacebuilding

Responsibility (2004), *In Larger Freedom: Towards Development, Security and Human Rights for All* (2005), and *Report of the Secretary-General on Peacebuilding in the Immediate Aftermath of Conflict* (2009).

Accordingly, many of the peacebuilding programmes implemented in conflict-affected societies shared common themes (or agenda priorities) that reflected the liberal peace world view. While the specific features of these programmes varied, six broad principles that underpinned their conception and operation can be identified (see Figure 3.1).

Promotion of democracy

The promotion of democracy is one of the prime concerns in contemporary peacebuilding. In assuming that the rational empowered individual can make prudent decisions for themselves and their community, liberal peace theories argue that constitutional democracy is a model that can facilitate and sustain peace in conflict-affected countries. Reflecting this idea, many of the seminal documents issued by international organisations and major donor agencies have emphasised the importance of offering "credible and inclusive processes of political dialogue" as a key goal of postwar reconstruction (UNSG 2011: 3).

In particular, Western forms of 'free and fair' election are usually pursued as a primary goal of political peacebuilding, and transforming the country's political landscape from a one-party state to a competitive but peaceful multiparty system is regarded as a long-term objective (Roberts 2011). In the field, the measures employed for implementing elections include detecting and deterring fraudulent behaviour, providing training support for election personnel, ensuring security during the election period and ballot verification (Lee and Mac Ginty 2012). Beyond the election process itself, longer-term programmes for nurturing civil society and democratic governance are implemented, primarily targeting traditional associations, village leaderships, community-based organisations (CBOs), local nongovernmental organisations (NGOs), trade unions and youth organisations.

Security sector reform

Security sector reform (SSR) is generally regarded as one of the most urgent issues to be tackled in the post-conflict reconstruction process. As security affects various social dimensions such as the economy, governance and culture, SSR has a potentially wide-ranging and intersectional impact on the post-conflict society. In practice, therefore, SSR takes various forms that require fundamentally different approaches. For instance, while demilitarisation of militia groups is a military-oriented process that often involves rigorous external verification, efforts to establish local community-based patrol groups require the adoption of a more flexible and culturally sensitive approach. In the field, common SSR projects include landmine clearance, the staged withdrawal of foreign military forces, the containment and/or dissolution of former armed factions, the building of new judicial systems and the introduction of new measures for the oversight of security forces (Newman, Paris and Richmond 2009). In particular, disarmament, demobilisation and the reintegration of ex-combatants (collectively termed DDR) and reform of the police force have been traditionally considered the "most important factor determining the success of peace operations" (UN 2004: 72).

Irrespective of the varied efforts to reform of the security sector that are actually employed in the field, one obvious feature of traditional SSR is that it usually revolves around the statebuilding agenda and is ultimately state-centric (Richmond 2005). In this, it reflects the Weberian conception of the state, and contemporary peacebuilding tends to assume that the transition to stable peace in post-conflict societies requires successful institutionalisation of liberal values at the state level.

Market economy

Another key element of liberal peacebuilding is developing a free-market economy based on constituencies' rights of private property. Since poverty or extreme economic disparity were, at least in part, the cause or the catalyst of a large number of contemporary conflicts, many international actors have assumed that democratisation and marketisation are mutually reinforcing mechanisms for peace. Most international financial organisations, such as the World Bank, the International Monetary Fund (IMF) and the Asian Development Bank, have therefore sought to promote sustainable development of the conflict-affected country's national economy through the support of private industry and the pursuit of fairer distribution of wealth.

Three prominent goals of such programmes have been to "facilitate equitable movement of goods and services," create "a rewards-based meritocracy" and build "efficiency and ultimately connections to global markets" (USIP n.d.a.). In peacebuilding practice in the field, a range of programmes has been implemented to achieve these goals, including reforming legal regulations (e.g. clarifying individual property titles), building infrastructure (e.g. public finance institutions, transportation systems for logistics) and developing and supporting the private sector (e.g. providing incentives for local investment and establishing financial services for micro enterprises).

Rule of law

Liberal peace approaches favour the regulation of society by equitable and established rules rather than by the arbitrary rule of persons. These approaches argue that transparent and equally applicable regulations and institutions are necessary in order to sustain a peaceful and democratic society. Given that this conception of society (that is, one governed by impartial laws) is central to another key element of the liberal peace – protecting private property rights and markets – it is unsurprising that establishing the rule of law as a peacebuilding strategy features prominently in a large number of UN documents. For example, *A More Secure World: Our Shared Responsibility* (2004: 72) contends that a peaceful society "require[s] dedicated support on the broader aspects of peacebuilding strategy, especially in the area of rule of law."

In practice, major peacebuilding programmes widely implement measures for (re)forming national constitutions as well as (re)building judicial and legal systems. Two key elements of such projects involve efforts to make judicial decisions independent from political or military influence and to ensure that judicial systems are made more available to the less empowered and poorer members of the society. In some cases, transitional justice programmes are implemented in an attempt to address human rights violations committed during the armed conflicts (Locula 2011). Where this occurs, various forms of truth and reconciliation committees and/or criminal courts are often established to investigate human rights abuses and to bring war criminals to justice.

Emphasis on human rights

Since the First Geneva Convention for the Amelioration of the Condition of the Wounded and Sick in Armed Forces in the Field (1864), human rights have been repeatedly confirmed as an international norm. Subsequent conventions such as the later Geneva Conventions, the Genocide Convention, the Rome Statute of the International Criminal Court and the many refugee conventions have consolidated the international community's commitment to guaranteeing fundamental human rights in conflict situations. Hence, as the peacebuilding role of the UN and other international organisations became increasingly prominent in the early 1990s, human rights came to be regarded as an indispensable requirement for political settlement and sustainable development (UNSG 2005). A significant number of postwar reconstruction programmes have also emphasised human rights protection in various ways. In particular, gender equality and the rights of youth have received prominent attention.

The types of programmes typically undertaken in this area include distributing immediate aid to ensure food security, building effective mechanisms for refugee repatriation, resuming primary education for children and building public health systems. Nevertheless, despite the repeated emphasis on human rights in the peacebuilding discourse, a recent study shows that the issue of human rights has been treated as a second-tier priority in many peacebuilding processes (Joshi, Lee and Mac Ginty 2014).

Governance reform

A notion of 'peace-as-governance' has been another key theme underlying many peacebuilding activities (Richmond 2005). Governance reform programmes highlight the importance of effective and efficient institutions of governance, with concepts such as accountability, transparency, equity, democracy and integrity considered prerequisites for good governance in conflict-affected societies. For instance, the UN's *A More Secure World: Our Shared Responsibility* (2004: 23) states that strong 'commitments to sound policies and good governance at all levels' should be regarded as core elements of the postwar peacebuilding process.

Since governance is a broad term, the programmes for promoting good governance cover a wide range of issues. For instance, the reform of state administration tends to include downsizing the bureaucratic system, decentralising governmental delivery mechanisms, enhancing interdepartmental collaboration and taking steps to promote government accountability. Policies for economic governance aim to facilitate an environment in which a market economy can flourish; common policies include establishing public finance institutions, restoring and developing infrastructure and supporting private entrepreneurs. In terms of social rehabilitation, many peacebuilding programmes emphasise capacity building, the rule of law and social transparency.

A statement of the president of the UN Security Council on the objectives of peacebuilding summarises these key elements well:

> These actions should focus on fostering sustainable development, the eradication of poverty and inequalities, transparent and accountable governance, the promotion of democracy, respect of human rights and rule of law and the promotion of a culture of peace and non-violence.
>
> (cited in Call 2008)

Moreover, while the specific measures employed in individual peacebuilding programmes may vary, the aforementioned elements of liberal peacebuilding have been adopted in most contemporary peace processes. For example, the promotion of democracy and security sector reform were highlighted in more than 75 per cent of all comprehensive peace accords signed in the post–Cold War period (Joshi et al. 2014), and the development of a market economy was promoted by international financial institutions such as the World Bank and the IMF in most postwar reconstruction programmes implemented in the same period (World Bank 2015).

Criticisms of liberal peacebuilding

Although international peace-supporting activities based on the liberal peace have made solid contributions to statebuilding and to reducing the level of violence in conflict-affected societies, it has become clear over time that liberal-democratic peacebuilding presents various problems and has limitations in terms of bringing about sustainable peace (Futamura, Newman and Tadjbakhsh 2010; Mac Ginty 2011). In particular, since third-party interveners are necessarily external actors, they are unable to comprehend fully the characteristics of local societies and are thus unlikely to promote the peacebuilding mechanisms most appropriate for the recipient societies. Due to these perceptual limitations of major donor communities, a range of local resources that could have made significant contributions to promoting sustainable peace, such as indigenous forms of conflict resolution, informal community-driven security systems and religious dimensions of peacebuilding, have been neglected.

For instance, the arrangements for promoting democracy in many post-conflict reconstruction processes have often involved efforts to pursue the simple transplanting of Western forms of 'free and fair' elections on to the post-conflict society in the belief that it was the only way for promoting a consolidated peace in the society (Lyons 2004). Although elections can prove highly useful in helping to bring a war to an end, in establishing and legitimising new leadership, and in wider conflict management in postwar societies (Lyons 2004), a significant number of previous efforts to address armed conflicts through the promotion of democracy have failed to achieve their goals. While some of the issues faced have been the result of practical problems before/during/after the election, such as a failure to set an adequate time frame for the election/democratic transition, insufficient voter support and a lack of voter education (Lee and Mac Ginty 2012; Obi 2007), others represent more fundamental limitations of the Eurocentric view of democracy (Harris 2012; Sisk and Reynolds 1998).

Furthermore, against the expectations of many peacebuilders, the arrangements imposed for the transition to democratic governance have actually resulted in the resumption of violence in some war-torn societies. For example, the 1992 elections in postwar Angola, which were supervised and verified by the UN, triggered further armed conflict between former belligerent groups. In Liberia, although the 1997 postwar election succeeded insofar as a new leadership came to power, the new government led by Charles Taylor immediately began the suppression of other political parties, and opposition to his rule ultimately culminated in the start of the Second Liberian Civil War in 1999. In the case of Rwanda, a poorly designed and structured power-sharing arrangement contributed to the onset of the 1994 massacre of Tutsis.

In many cases, the liberal peace agenda has achieved only limited success in meeting the immediate goals of external actors. For example, the attempted restructuring of the primary unit of political activity in Sierra Leone, an effort supervised by the Department for International Development (DFID) and other international organisations, has failed to achieve its aims. Recognising the role that chieftaincy has played as a key driver of violent conflicts in the country, the interveners made efforts to reduce the significance of the role of chiefdoms in people's daily activities by establishing twelve district and five urban councils. These councils have led regional administration since 2003. In addition, new local Ward Development Committees were promoted as an alternative to traditional chiefdom. Despite these efforts, chieftaincy remains the key political and social unit in Sierra Leone.

The conflict resolution process in Cambodia presents a similar example of the failure of the liberal peace agenda to secure the immediate goals of external actors. The international interveners, which included the UN, the US and Australia, set a comprehensive postwar political reconstruction plan based on liberal peace ideas. However, most of the major elements of the plan, including prescriptions on the composition of the interim authority, the electoral process and the postelection power structure, were either postponed, abandoned or altered to favour the national actors' interests (Lee 2011).

The evidence of such failures has led to the emergence of academic debate since the late 1990s on the problems of liberal peacebuilding as a barrier to durable peace. Within this debate, criticism of the dominant influence of the Western community's approach to peacebuilding has primarily come from two distinct viewpoints. First, one group of studies argues that these interventions are, by nature, illegitimate and ineffective. From a normative perspective, it is argued that the transplanting of the liberal peace agenda onto conflict-affected countries is a new type of imperialism that aims to deter the self-determination of local communities (Shinoda 2015). For the commentators who embrace this perspective, liberal peacebuilding is part of a "larger hegemonic project whose ideological purpose is to spread the values and norms of dominant power brokers" (Pugh 2008 cited in Paris 2010). By examining the peace processes in Bosnia and Timor-Leste, for example, Chandler (1999) showed that liberal peacebuilding programmes can erect barriers to self-government by the people in conflict-affected societies, and Chopra (2000) described the early phase of postwar reconstruction as a process of establishing the "UN's Kingdom."

By focusing on the trends in contemporary peacebuilding practice, other studies have paid more attention to the power disparity between external interveners and local actors. Many of these studies assume that programmes based on 'alien rules' are likely to be much less effective and/or efficient than projects based on local knowledge. Nevertheless, even in cases where international peacebuilders aim to move beyond their liberal peace themes and adopt local perspectives, peacebuilding programmes have little choice but to promote the liberal peace agenda. In the aftermath of armed conflicts, when the social and economic situations for local people may be extremely difficult, the ability of local actors to plan and promote reconstruction and peace is inferior to that of external supporters. Moreover, irrespective of the wishes of local actors and the approach to peacebuilding that they might want to pursue, the very structure of international aid reinforces the donors' agenda.

Other studies take a more moderate view, arguing that such fundamental criticisms of liberal peacebuilding fail to provide any concrete alternatives to address the existing problems. Although they accept that peacebuilding often results in counterproductive outcomes due to the influence of the donors' viewpoints and agendas, this does not mean that the current forms of peacebuilding should be abandoned completely but should instead be supplemented by other measures. Within this academic tradition, particular structural and practical limitations of international peacebuilding activities have been recognised, including the poor coordination of aid agencies, insufficient understanding of local contexts (social power structures, tensions between power groups, cultural violence), a lack of appreciation of the institutional limitations of the local governance system and the promotion of Eurocentric criteria for planning and evaluating projects. Since the late 1990s, a wide range of academic research and practical reports detailing ways to address these limitations has been produced.

Reflecting these concerns and proposals, peacebuilding operations in the early 2000s began to expand the scope of their operations, extend the duration of their presence in the post-conflict society and limit their intrusion into the domestic governance process.

Local ownership, hybridity and beyond

In response to the problems of liberal peacebuilding, practitioners and analysts began to seek an alternative way of pursuing peace. Notable among these efforts is the promotion of 'local ownership.' The idea behind this concept is that, since local populations know their own social contexts intimately and therefore understand the best strategies for promoting peace in their society, they should plan, initiate and conduct the peacebuilding programmes. Accordingly, many academics have stressed the importance of supporting local communities in developing a strong commitment to their own governance projects and to drawing on their "inner resources of wisdom, courage and compassionate non-violence" (Curle 1994: 96; similar views can be found in Edgren 2003; Lopes and Theisohn 2003; and Shinoda 2008).

Similarly, in the field of practice, national ownership had been recognised by the early 2000s as "the single most important determinant of the effectiveness of capacity-building programmes" (UNSG 2002 cited in Wilén 2009: 341). Then secretary-general of the UN, Kofi Annan, recognised that no international initiative "imposed from the outside can hope to be successful or sustainable" (UNSC 2004: 7). In 2006, he reemphasised his position by stating that "peacebuilding requires national ownership, and must be home-grown. Outsiders, however well-intentioned, cannot substitute for the knowledge and will of the people of the country concerned" (UNSG 2006, n.p.).

In response to this new approach, various UN agencies and NGOs adopted a range of strategies to enable local actors to participate in their own peacebuilding programmes. For instance, the UNDP, the EU and other international/regional organisations promoted local capacity-building programmes in countries such as Cambodia, Uganda and Mozambique through focusing their efforts on governmental civil servants and local elites (Lee and Özerdem 2015b; UNDP 2008). Other donor groups, especially NGOs such as Oxfam and World Vision, implemented more community-oriented peacebuilding programmes. By the early 2000s, the promotion of local ownership had become "a key principle of civil conflict management" (Ropers 2000 cited in Reich 2006: 27).

At the same time, academic debates also began to focus on the most appropriate ways in which to foster effective, accountable and inclusive local participation and ownership. As regards the short-term prospects for local ownership and participation, a large number of studies conclude that an early transfer of peacebuilding ownership to local communities tends not to serve to achieve the goals of peacebuilding. For instance, Futamura and Notaras (2011) argue that an international presence or leadership should be maintained during the post-conflict transitional period. Reich (2006) contends that while local ownership is a desirable goal as a policy ideal, it should not be incorporated into concrete implementation plans as a project objective. For these analysts, local ownership during the transitional period means that local people should be limited to determining the delivery mode of the peacebuilding programme rather than setting its goals, long-term strategies or resource mobilisation in the immediate post-conflict period.

As regards the issue of local ownership from a long-term viewpoint, contemporary studies propose a number of new models of collaboration between external actors and local communities. Underpinning all such studies is the rejection of the simplistic dichotomised imposer-acceptor relationship. Liden, for example, proposes a cosmopolitan model that "exemplifies a model of global governance where a cosmopolitan human rights agenda is consistent with the communitarian defence of political autonomy and cultural diversity" (Liden 2009: 616; Heathershaw 2008 presents a similar view). Another group of studies employs the concept of hybridity to underline that varied forms and standards of peace may coexist within a peacebuilding programme. Thus, in order to promote durable peace in a given context, it is necessary to pursue the most appropriate balance between the various forms and standards of peace existing in that context (Mac Ginty 2011; Richmond and Mitchell 2011).

In regard to the practical methods that may be employed in pursuit of this model, studies have highlighted the following two factors: integrating the issue of local needs into Western conflict analysis and decision-making frameworks, and establishing and developing long-term projects for local empowerment. Some of the specific methods that have been put forward to address these factors and pursue the goal of local participation and ownership follow. A group of studies stresses the importance of the process of local ownership promotion rather than the outcomes. Ropers suggests a continuous process of generating multiple options and spaces for peacebuilding and utilising feedback loops to review progress as an effective method of bringing local players more fully into the peacebuilding process (Ropers 2008). Both Sommers and Harris propose the provision of peace education that teaches the core values of conflict resolution and nonviolence to local communities as a useful approach (Harris 2004; Sommers 2002). The UNDP (2008: 73) presents the usefulness of a 'dialogue forum' that "allow[s] all parties to discuss and contribute to shaping programme design." By drawing on the experiences of the DDR programmes conducted in Sierra Leone, Afghanistan and the Somaliland region, it argues that such a forum can contribute not only to reflecting local needs but also to strengthening the capabilities of local actors such as the government, the army, civil society organisations and traditional leaders to plan and conduct demilitarisation projects. Other studies highlight that provisional multiactor national governing bodies may play a significant role in providing ideas to national actors on post-conflict reconstruction issues as well as fostering local capacity (Gerstl 2015; Mackenzie-Smith 2015).

However, more recent studies warn of the 'romanticisation' of local resources, arguing that indigenous culture does not necessarily make a positive contribution to constructive peace-building. Although local actors may possess detailed knowledge that can be utilised to develop a peaceful society, it is also true that local people in the aftermath of conflict (which has often been preceded by periods of colonisation and a consequent lack of proper opportunity to develop and inherit cultural traditions) may not be ready to develop their capacity

(Mac Ginty 2011). For instance, many local cultures and communities are sites of "power asymmetry, patriarchy and privilege," where local patrons and organisations can simply pursue their selfish interests rather than the sustainable development of their societies (Ramsbotham, Woodhouse and Miall 2011: 236). These patrons and organisations tend to refuse all external attempts to counter or intervene in their interest-seeking activities by accusing interveners of external imperialism. In such cases, transferring ownership to a local population at an early stage of post-conflict reconstruction is likely to have a negative impact on the society. In addition, post-conflict societies often witness the emergence of 'mushroom NGOs.' These NGOs are locally run organisations that spring up in the wake of a peacebuilding (or aid) project and exist primarily to secure income from foreign-funded projects. Although these NGOs utilise local human resources, they make efforts to "fulfil the needs of outsiders more adequately than supporting inside development needs" (Reich 2006: 13–14).

More fundamentally, some studies claim that because ownership is a complex process that involves various issues such as information sharing, consultation, and monitoring and assessing success, the capabilities of local communities to take on ownership cannot be strengthened simply by providing external support. In the early period of external interveners' adoption of the ideals of local ownership and participation, it was reported that international donors' superficial application of 'local participation' ideas and programmes frequently caused problems. For instance, although local people participated in the development programmes, they were not involved in meaningful and sustainable ways. In some extreme cases, local communities were forced to join in the planning process without any knowledge or understanding of the process, and the decisions made therefore tended to reflect the goals of donors. As a result, some commentators denounced this as a 'tyranny of participation' (Cooke and Kothari 2001).

Developing local capacity necessarily involves a long and complex process of social engagement that includes information sharing, skill transfer, personal consultation and monitoring and evaluation (M&E). Moreover, due to donors' own commitment and exit plans, externally led postwar development programmes have to achieve two different and sometimes contradictory objectives: facilitating a suitable environment for proactive local participation, and maintaining the progress and quality of the programmes to meet the standards of donor agencies. Thus, creating an effective, accountable and inclusive model for developing local capacity has become an important goal of the contemporary academic peacebuilding discourse (Boyce, Koros and Hodgson 2002; Culbertson and Pouligny 2007; Peake, Gormley-Heenan and Fitzduff 2004).

In light of the criticisms outlined previously, the recent discussions on 'hybrid' forms of governance are noteworthy. The concept of hybridity was first developed in anthropological and sociological studies of postcolonial contexts. In the late 1990s, these conceptual discussions were introduced into Peace and Conflict Studies in an effort to reappraise the peacebuilding dominant discourse of the time. The concept of hybrid peace is particularly significant in that it enables contemporary discourse to move beyond a binary conceptualisation of peacebuilding as a process characterised by an external/indigenous dichotomy, and instead move the discussion towards a comprehension of peacebuilding as a more flexible and dynamic process. In other words, the emergence of the concept of hybridity in research on peacebuilding means that the traditional presuppositions of liberal/external/peace-oriented intervention versus nonliberal/indigenous/conflict-oriented movements are being replaced by a more nuanced approach towards governance in conflict-affected societies. Although the detailed discussion of hybridity varies widely within the literature, the studies in the critical tradition of Peace Studies generally highlight that peacebuilding involves the hybridisation of various factors such as actors, social structures, cultural contexts and external influence.

The varied use of the concept of hybridity within the field of Peace and Conflict Studies has led to academic debate developing in a number of directions.

The majority of studies attempt to examine the complex nature of hybrid peace in contemporary post-conflict societies. For example, Öjendal and Lilja (2009) consider the democratisation process in Cambodia to have in fact been the institutionalisation of the patron-client system tradition within a formally democratic governing structure. By focusing on everyday agencies (individuals or organisations) of peacebuilding, Richmond and Mitchell (2011) present the various 'states' of hybridity as the results of constant interaction between external actors' liberal actions and local agencies' resistance. Höglund and Orjuela (2012) note how the fundamental division that exists between external donor groups and national actors (and their competing interests) can make the interaction between the actors more complex.

From a more practical perspective, another group of studies seek to discover the forms of hybridisation (or the processes that contribute to hybridisation) that foster peace in conflict-affected countries. Boege, Brown, Clements and Nolan (2008), for example, present various practical suggestions for building sustainable peace in Vanuatu, the Solomon Islands, Timor-Leste, Tonga, Bougainville and Papua New Guinea, emphasising the importance of establishing constructive linkages between central state institutions and local customary authorities by enhancing 'grounded legitimacy.' By examining the *Infrastructures for Peace* projects of the United Nations Development Programme (UNDP), Kumar and Haye (2011) argue that successful hybridisation is more about the process of constant dialogue and mediation between external actors and domestic actors than about certain types of forms. Richmond and Mac Ginty (2015) similarly claim that positive peacebuilding requires more active participation from the local agencies rather than the simple juxtaposition of local elements and international themes.

Conclusion

This chapter has discussed how the liberal peacebuilding model has come to be the dominant form of contemporary peacebuilding, the criticisms it has faced and the ways in which it has been supplemented in recent years. In one sense, international peacebuilding can be regarded as being in a transitional phase: while the limitations of liberal peacebuilding have become clearer over the past decade and the model has faced increasing criticism, the exploration of alternative approaches to peacebuilding has as yet failed to provide clear evidence of the direction in which contemporary peacebuilding should develop.

Although the normative criticisms of liberal peacebuilding have provided insights that might help to inform a new approach to peacebuilding, many practitioners argue that these criticisms fail to present concrete proposals on what actually needs to be done in the field. Moreover, after a decade of solid progress, critical debates have reached the point of intellectual stalemate, with the same themes and ideas being repeated using different examples and little progress being made in further developing the scholarship in the area (Heathershaw 2013; Lee 2014). Perhaps of greater concern is the fact that some recent studies have exhibited a tendency to present exaggerated or oversimplified arguments by ignoring the distinction between forceful peacekeeping operations led by prominent nation states (i.e. the US or the UK) and other ground-level peacebuilding programmes, thereby misjudging the achievements and problems of contemporary peacebuilding, oversimplifying the moral complexity of international aid and defining the liberal peace too broadly (Paris 2010).

In addition, practical attempts to reflect such views in the field have thus far failed to show meaningful outputs. For instance, recent empirical studies confirm that the level of local ownership that has actually been achieved in many peacebuilding programmes has fallen far short of the idealised form of ownership advocated by many scholars and has generally amounted to little more than a relatively equal partnership between external supporters and internal actors. Moreover, in many cases, such local 'partners' of peacebuilding tend to be the local power elites, government officers or NGO practitioners, not the local population whose voice had long been ignored. In this sense, at the risk of overgeneralisation, it can be tentatively concluded that an advanced level of local ownership that would afford local residents the opportunity to participate fully in peacebuilding has not yet been developed in most postwar societies.

Given that many peacebuilding programmes require long-term commitment, it might be considered premature to judge the achievements of relatively recent programmes. It should be noted, however, that international peacebuilding actors in the field already often struggle to run their existing programmes, and any extension of the scope of their programmes can cause further problems. In fact, the recent shift in the peacebuilding paradigm has meant that many major peacebuilding operations have become more comprehensive, lengthier, reflective and collaborative. As a result, they require more human and material resources and a wider range of advisory/technical support for a longer time period, but the ongoing post-2008 economic downturn means that mobilising resources from the traditional donor countries has become more difficult. As a result, many aid agencies and donor organisations have reported that limited resources are causing a range of problems.

Although efforts to develop better models of international peacebuilding continue to attract the keen attention of both field practitioners and academic researchers, many of the examples of peacebuilding introduced in Part III of this book represent typical forms of liberal peacebuilding. This is because liberal peacebuilding, despite critiques from different perspectives, is still the dominant form of contemporary peace-supporting practice in conflict-affected countries. We encourage readers, therefore, to critically investigate and evaluate the utilities and limitations of the traditional forms of peacebuilding practice. This book intends to aid such investigation by raising questions for discussion and by introducing some of the newly developed forms of peacebuilding.

Discussion questions

- Can external interveners promote a fundamental transformation of conflict-affected societies?
- What are the short-term and long-term effects of 'aid conditionality'?
- Although local ownership is a useful concept when considering the aims of long-term peacebuilding programmes, the local culture frequently contains violent or conflict-oriented features. How can such features be transformed?

Recommended reading

Futamura, M. and Notaras, M. (2011) *Local Perspectives on International Peacebuilding*. Research Article Series. Tokyo: United Nations University. Available at: http://unu.edu/publications/articles/local-perspectives-on-international-peacebuilding.html#info

Joshi, M., Lee, S. Y. and Mac Ginty, R. (2014) 'Just How Liberal Is the Liberal Peace?' *International Peacekeeping* 21 (3): 364–89.

Mac Ginty, R. (2011) Chapters 1–2, in *International Peacebuilding and Local Resistance: Hybrid Forms of Peace*. Palgrave Macmillan: 19–67.

Part II

The three phases of peacebuilding

4   Conflict resolution

In January 1979, a group of former Khmer Rouge soldiers – with backing from Vietnam – toppled the Khmer Rouge regime and established the People's Republic of Kampuchea (PRK) regime. At that time, three resistance movements – one of which was the previous Khmer Rouge regime – immediately began military operations close to the border with Thailand, and another civil conflict began in Cambodia. As the conflict grew in intensity between the PRK government and the resistance groups – which had external support from the Soviet Union and China, respectively – the number of casualties increased dramatically until the mid-1980s.

In response to such severe armed conflicts, what can be done by the international community? The practice of 'conflict resolution' emerged to address this question, aiming to terminate armed conflict and, where possible, address the causes of conflict. This chapter explores a number of the practical dimensions of conflict resolution with particular attention to:

*   Analysis of conflict resolution procedures
*   Key methods of third-party intervention
*   Timing of peace intervention
*   Spoiler problems in conflict resolution
*   Neutrality and strength of interveners.

By definition, conflict resolution includes a wide variety of efforts ranging from activities associated with peace negotiation to those of post-conflict social redevelopment. As discussed in Chapter 2, however, contemporary academic discussions frequently regard it as a relatively short-term effort to resolve ongoing military conflicts as distinct from programmes aimed at longer-term post-conflict development. In line with these recent debates, this chapter limits the scope of conflict resolution to the time period from the initiation of the peace process to the implementation of peace agreements, with the main analytic focus being on peace negotiation and emergency relief during and immediately after the conflicts.

The five stages of conflict resolution

The conflict resolutions in the post–Cold War period have taken various paths towards the production of peace agreements. For instance, while the peace process in South Africa (1994–97) was mainly driven by bilateral talks between the government and the African National Congress (ANC), the peace negotiation in Angola (1994–2002) was accommodated and closely monitored by three external observing parties (Portugal, the Russian Federation and the United States). Furthermore, whereas the Cambodian peace process finished with a single comprehensive peace agreement in 1991, the conflict resolution in Guatemala produced multiple peace accords.

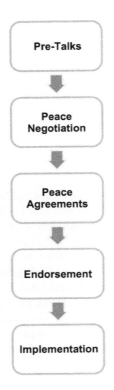

Figure 4.1 The stages of conflict resolution

Nevertheless, an examination of the basic structure of recent peace processes reveals that they have generally adopted the following steps: pre-talks, peace negotiation, peace agreements, endorsement and implementation (see Figure 4.1).

Pre-talks

Pre-talks denote the discussions that take place before the start of formal peace negotiations. Negotiating parties in the pre-talks phase have various concerns that include: Can the negotiation bring about a better alternative than the status quo? Can there be a fair agreement? Are we skilful or powerful enough to ensure that the likely outcome of the negotiation will favour our interests? Furthermore, since chronic armed conflicts increase the levels of distrust between disputants, negotiating parties are likely to be suspicious about the intentions of their 'enemies.' The main aim of pre-talks is therefore to assuage these fears and convince disputants to enter the negotiation process. Since the success of a negotiation and peace process ultimately depends on the level of cooperation that is achieved between the disputing groups, the focus of third-party interveners and disputing parties in the pre-talks phase should be on confidence building before a commitment to enter negotiations is made.

The negotiators may discuss procedural issues related to the negotiation, such as logistics, the location for the talks, security during the negotiation, participants, the time frame, mediators, the topics to be discussed, goals, the number of representatives from the other side, the structure of the negotiation and so on. Some frequently used forms of pre-talks are indirect diplomacy through mediating actors, shuttle diplomacy and secret face-to-face meetings.

Pre-talks are often characterised by distrust and half-hearted commitments. However, despite the challenges, a successful pre-talk will always lay a strong foundation for the rest of the peace process. Thus, external mediators or facilitators may intervene to support the talks. Their main roles during the pre-talk phase are minimising the technical barriers to negotiation by transmitting messages and information between the disputants, providing suitable locations/venues for talks, providing diplomatic incentives and pressures, and proposing the general rules for the negotiation.

Peace negotiation

If pre-talks successfully facilitate the conditions for negotiation, the official peace negotiation process then begins. As success in conflict resolution depends on getting conflicting parties to talk and reach agreement on the best way to resolve the conflict, negotiation plays a central role in the peace process. In this phase, the conflicting parties can increase the possibility of resolving incompatibilities and agreeing on strategies/ways to live in a more peaceful or cohesive manner.

Peace negotiations frequently fail to produce fruitful outcomes due to various obstacles. For instance, negotiations that take place during military conflicts are likely to be a competitive game,[1] which assumes that the relationships between negotiators are based on zero-sum interests. In addition, since the trust levels between groups are eroded once a war begins and casualties occur on both sides, negotiating actors tend to be very wary of their counterparts and their potential deceptions. Moreover, even when leaders wish to negotiate, their supporters and constituencies may refuse to engage due to negative sentiments against the opposing factions.

To overcome these challenges, the initial phase of negotiation frequently takes place in the form of 'secret talks,' in which the interveners hold separate and secret discussions with the leaderships of the conflicting parties. These talks may provide interveners with more information on obstacles to the peace process and can go a long way towards reducing the levels of suspicion held by disputants.

Successful completion of secret talks leads to official 'multilateral talks' where the representatives of conflicting parties come together for face-to-face discussions. In this phase, the negotiation may encounter difficulties as the key causal issues or those contributing to the conflict are openly discussed. In practice, many negotiations were complicated by the sheer number of conflicting parties participating in the talks (e.g. in Guatemala and Namibia), while others faced difficulties due to the involvement of external actors and their support for particular factions (e.g. in Cambodia and Angola).

Under these circumstances, many external interveners in contemporary peace processes become involved in order to contribute to increasing the likelihood of successful negotiations and may typically intervene by means of security guarantees, economic sanctions and military threats in addition to the measures outlined earlier.

Peace agreements

A successful process of peace negotiation results in a peace agreement (or a series of agreements) that defines the principles and terms of engagement and proposes the strategies for achieving lasting peace. A peace agreement often provides guidelines for ending hostilities and supporting marginalised groups in playing active roles in the political arena. It may also specify the arrangements for governance or power sharing in the future, the position of combatants and victims in the new administration and so on. As a result, peace treaties are considered important road maps for postwar societies in terms of nation building and reconstruction.

The formats of peace agreements vary depending on the characteristics of the precedent negotiations (e.g. ceasefire agreements, interim or preliminary agreements, comprehensive and framework peace accords, and follow-up agreements focusing on implementation). Recent agreements issued in the post–Cold War period tend to be more comprehensive and incorporate accords on issues ranging from security to cultural concerns.

Care should be taken during the process of drafting and documenting the terms of the agreement. Although vague wording may sometimes be employed to circumvent deadlocks in the negotiation, clear presentation of agreed provisions is generally considered important in order to reduce challenges in the implementation stage. In many cases, the terms of the peace will be tied to a timeframe that conflicting groups and interveners are expected to make efforts and take measures to achieve.

Although the production of a peace accord may be regarded as marking the end of an armed conflict, it is frequently the start of another phase of conflict resolution. In fact, many peace processes collapse in the stages of endorsement and implementation. Hence, external interveners frequently participate in the signing of the agreement in order to enhance its legitimacy and promote its enforcement among the disputing parties.

Endorsement

The agreed peace accords should gain the backing of all concerned actors within the national factions, which include the internal power groups of each military faction, combatants and agents, prominent social leaders and constituencies.

In countries with little or no history of democracy, intrafactional endorsement is critical to successful implementation of peace accords. In particular, in cases where the factional representatives sent to a peace negotiation are not core power group members (e.g. the Farabundo Marti National Liberation Front [FMLN] in El Salvador and the National Union for the Total Independence of Angola [UNITA]), it is imperative that the leadership's endorsement of the agreements reached during the negotiation is secured. Gaining intrafactional endorsement of a peace accord, however, is not always possible due to the existence of various internal groups within the factions, each of which may have different (sometimes contradictory) interests, norms and viewpoints.

In societies with relatively extensive experience of democratic political movements (e.g. the UK and Ireland in Northern Ireland), the governments or major military organisations may hold public sensitisation sessions to inform their citizens about the peace agreement (including its terms), the plans for implementation and the implications for the country. Although the process of endorsement normally takes place after the signing of peace agreements, opinion on the direction that the negotiation is taking may be sought during the negotiation process itself (e.g. the referendum in South Africa in 1992).

Implementation

The implementation of peace agreements covers various issues such as the disarmament, demobilisation and reintegration of ex-combatants (DDR), provision of interim security, protection of human rights, elections for selecting a new leadership, economic rehabilitation, refugee resettlement and land transfer. Some of these issues may seriously affect the fundamental interests of former militant groups (e.g. their chances of political survival). As a result, the implementation of a peace accord is frequently considered the most fragile part of the entire peace process.

There is a range of factors that may cause the failure of or delays in the implementation process, one of the most notable of which is the 'spoiler' who continuously refuses to participate in negotiations or who agrees/endorses peace accords without being seriously committed to them (such as the Revolutionary United Front in Sierra Leone [RUF]). However, even in cases where all actors are willing to undertake and commit to the agreements, implementation might not be easy. For instance, in cases of prolonged military conflict and embedded distrust between factions, any real or perceived signs of defection by any faction can cause the peace process to collapse.

External interveners may support the implementation process by supervising and verifying the consistency and continuity of peace accord implementation by national actors. Some states and international organisations provide financial, technical and legal support to the implementation projects and, when necessary, apply diplomatic and economic pressure to ensure that national actors abide by the provisions set out in the agreement. In addition, other organisations and nongovernmental organisations (NGOs) may monitor the progress of all related parties' implementation of the peace accord.

Third-party mediation

In most contemporary conflict resolution processes, third-party mediation is considered an essential element in facilitating peace negotiation between two or more warring parties. Mediation is performed by "an acceptable, impartial, and neutral third party who has no authoritative decision making power to assist contending parties in voluntarily reaching their own mutually acceptable settlement" (Moore 1986: 6). Mediatory roles can be divided into two categories: deal making and orchestrating. Deal making tries to produce substantive forms of compromise, while orchestrating places greater emphasis on the process of mediation itself. A typical method of orchestrating mediation is via establishing a forum in which the parties to the conflict can continue their negotiations in a neutral and free environment.

The main purpose of the efforts in the initial phase of a peace process is nurturing an environment appropriate for starting a negotiation. Such early mediation is undertaken either by a limited range of actors such as states and international or regional organisations or by internationally well-known individuals. In third-party mediation of peace negotiations, the following methods are widely used.

Providing good offices

Due to the distrust between rival factions, there is always a high risk of prenegotiation talks collapsing. Efforts therefore focus on providing an environment in which all the factions can get together and talk. As Stevens argues, the chance of successful negotiation becomes higher when negotiators and mediators "(1) create a contract zone;[2] (2) help the parties to save face and to recreate the contract zone, and (3) assist the parties to weigh and to rank existing alternatives and create a truly integrative strategy" in the stage-setting phase (Stevens 1963 cited in Lewicki, Weiss and Lewin 1992: 235). In order to do this, interveners need to make contact and establish connections with the warring factions.

Building the rules of negotiation

When opposing factions in a conflict express their intention to negotiate, they usually move on to exploring and signalling stages. The negotiating parties need to agree on basic issues such as the people who will participate in the negotiation, inviting mediators and the basic principles of the negotiation. Since all factions are highly suspicious about possible deception by their counterparts, and since many factions are not familiar with bilateral or multilateral negotiation, the early stage of a negotiation is extremely fragile. The mediators' neutral suggestions on the negotiation's principles and conditions may contribute to its sustainability.

Suggesting the contents and feasible targets of negotiation

When players agree to the basic rules of the negotiations, each player presents more detailed and concrete proposals. During this stage, the interveners use compromise strategies to entice factions to remain at the negotiating table. When factions approach each other, the interveners help them to produce explicit resolutions. First, interveners sometimes help the factions compile a list of issues of mutual interest to discuss. The biggest challenge for interveners is making the factions believe that they will not be victimised or have their positions undermined by the negotiations. Second, from time to time the mediators present their own suggestions or compromise proposals to the factions. After the issue list is agreed to by the factions, the negotiators begin specific bargaining. Since it is highly likely that factions will have completely different views on many issues and demand unacceptable things from each other, it is therefore important that the suggested proposals should be seen as beneficial, or at least not harmful, to all factions.

Transmission of information

Although the conveying of information is a prerequisite for successful negotiation in all phases, obtaining precise information is a major challenge in any negotiation. Peace facilitators contribute to the development of good communication channels between the adversarial actors. Most commonly, peace facilitators act as messengers, conveying the messages of one actor to another (e.g. Norway in the Israel-Palestine conflict). Another common role is that of a mediator who transmits each party's will as well as their own suggestions. Recognising this, Avruch (1998) affirms the critical role that clear and effective communication plays in the success of international negotiations and stresses the importance of intervention in conflicts.

Diplomatic incentives and pressure

A variety of skills that utilise the diplomatic power of interveners are utilised to strengthen the effectiveness of mediation. Among the many diplomatic resources that interveners employ, one frequently used method is diplomatic recognition. In the modern international political system, obtaining national sovereignty for a state is essential. Therefore, when a faction wins a war, obtaining recognition as the legitimate authority from the international community is of paramount importance to the victorious party. Diplomatic alignment is also widely used for managing a negotiation. When the negotiation has stalled on the most important issues, the consensus of interveners and supporters sometimes helps the factions to find a breakthrough.

Theoretical debates on conflict resolution

This section introduces a few theoretical discussions that have attracted academic attention during the past decade. First, it considers the debates on the timing for initiating a peace process. In this respect, William Zartman's proposal that a 'mutually hurting stalemate' signals the 'ripe' moment has been at the centre of extensive debate. In addition, the section presents the academic discourse related to Stephen Stedman's spoiler problems and two factors that determine the behaviour of warring factions during peace negotiation: fear (as a motivation) and the quantity of resources available to warring parties (as an intervening condition). Finally, the discussions on how to make third-party mediation more effective will be introduced by focusing on the strength and neutrality of third parties.

Timing (ripeness)

One of the most significant practical problems facing a conflict resolution programme is the timing of its initiation. Many academic approaches recommend early involvement in violent conflicts because a late intervention is likely to have a more complicated situation and have to deal with higher costs (e.g. a heavier toll on the human population, destruction of the social infrastructure and greater economic impacts). For peace-supporting practitioners, however, early intervention is always easier said than done. For example, as the early stages of a violent conflict do not attract strong attention from the international community, it is difficult to mobilise the material and nonmaterial resources to initiate a conflict resolution process. In addition, early conflict resolution efforts may be criticised as interference in a country's national sovereignty. Early intervention also sometimes extends the duration of conflicts by providing new sources of conflict to the warring parties (Vaux 2001). Hence, determining the appropriate time to initiate peacebuilding projects (including international peace negotiation and humanitarian support during violent conflict) has been a central topic in both academic and practical debates.

While there have been a number of useful proposals on appropriate timing, the model of ripeness suggested by William Zartman has attracted the most attention. The ripeness model argues that the presence of a mutually hurting stalemate is a good indicator of the ripeness for intervention to end the conflict. It assumes that three conditions determine the ripeness for resolution: the high costs of the war, a balance of power and certain domestic political institutions (Zartman 2003). As to the costs of war, research suggests that peaceful settlements are more likely to be achieved as the benefits of war decrease and the costs of war increase: when the limited resources of combatants run out, the expected outcomes of victory become less attractive, and domestic pressure increases. As regards the balance of power, scholars generally agree that when combatants clearly realise that a balance of power exists, they are more likely to come to the negotiating table. When such a situation applies, "no one side can achieve a great enough superiority to be sure that aggressive action would be crowned with success" (Organski 1968, cited in Walter 2002: 9). Finally, when domestic political constraints are combined with the previous conditions, the chances of compromise increase. This is particularly true in democratic societies. The American Civil War, in which Abraham Lincoln signed a peace agreement rather than pursue a complete victory, is considered a representative example, although the US in the 18th century was by no means an established democratic country.

However, some commentators point out that the mutually hurting stalemate should not be taken as a self-fulfilling condition since ripeness is an issue of perception. As Zartman (2003) himself admits, a fundamental condition is that the actors need to perceive the ripeness. Furthermore, Lederach (1999: 31, 33) contends that ripeness is "extremely weak in its predictive capacity from the standpoint of a practitioner" and requires analysts or practitioners to have the "capacity to envision a longer-term process and recognise opportunities for constructive change in the midst of crisis." In this sense, although ripeness theories are based on the concept of rationality, the validity of these theories is subject to the inevitable limitations of negotiators.

In addition, there may be multiple moments or degrees of ripeness, and interveners need to recognise or create chances to intervene rather than waiting for the mutual hurting stalemate to develop. Nor is the concept of ripeness universally applicable in all cases: studies show that the conditions are not relevant to cases such as the negotiations for the Oslo Accords between Israel and Palestine (1993) and the peace negotiation in South Africa in the mid-1980s (Rothstein 2007).

Spoiler problems

Spoilers are those actors who do not want an end to armed conflict through peace negotiation and make efforts to prevent the negotiation from progressing. As many of the peace negotiations conducted in the 1990s became deadlocked, prolonged and sometimes collapsed due to these spoilers, extensive debates on identifying the motivation and behaviour of spoilers and ways of responding effectively to their actions took place in the academic literature.

As regards their motivations, Stedman suggests that fear is the primary motivation behind disputing parties' decisions to become spoilers. Spoilers may perceive peace negotiation as a threat for a variety of reasons. Some actors refuse to negotiate due to the ideological or religious background of their movements. Some radical Islamic movements, for example, believe that they lose the normative grounds of their beliefs and causes if they compromise or negotiate with their enemies. Moreover, the warring factions that benefit from the war economy consider the peace negotiations and programmes a threat to their financial security. The RUF in Sierra Leone and UNITA in Angola were reluctant to join peace negotiation because of this. In addition, there are actors who believe that they will be marginalised in the postnegotiation national political/social arena. For instance, the Khmer Rouge in Cambodia and the Serbian authority in the Kosovo war refused to negotiate partly because they saw no chance to increase (or at least sustain) their power and influence.

Nevertheless, not all would-be spoilers are determined to boycott negotiation. After consideration of the utility of a peace negotiation, some national leaderships establish their positions and strategies based on the resources under their control. The resources under a faction's control include not only material (economic and military factors) but also non-material resources (psychological and cultural factors). The importance of a particular resource can vary according to the type of conflict. For instance, in comparing greed-based conflicts with grievance-based ones, the former is much more dependent on economic and military assets. Moreover, some types of wars, such as guerrilla wars, demand much fewer resources. In fact, there are various nonmaterial factors that can have a critical effect on the progress of a conflict and negotiations, such as the perceived and projected moral position of the factions, individual negotiation skills, network/connections with external states, domestic frictions, education and the like. Spoilers that possess abundant resources are more likely to be *outside spoilers* who systematically refuse peace negotiation, while actors with fewer resources tend to become *inside spoilers* who enter into agreements and then renege on promises.

How, then, do peace facilitators prevent warring factions from becoming spoilers or, if they are already spoilers, convince them to return to negotiation? In most peace processes undertaken in the 1990s, external peace facilitators applied three strategies: inducement, coercion and socialisation. Since inducement and coercion have already been discussed, we will look only at socialisation briefly here. Socialisation is about 'taming' warring factions and tying them to the negotiation through their adherence to a set of norms. In the early phase of negotiation, external interveners propose a set of norms that are hoped and believed to be acceptable to all disputing parties and demand that the parties abide by these norms. As the interaction between the national parties and external peace facilitators intensifies, the disputing parties gradually come to regard the norms as desirable and important principles. Nevertheless, the inducement, coercion and socialisation strategies frequently failed to elicit the expected behaviour from disputing groups, and the debate on the most effective response to spoilers is therefore ongoing.

Strength and neutrality

Another issue that had attracted extensive academic attention is the utility of two factors that are believed to improve the effectiveness of third-party intervention: strength and impartiality.

First, intervention is seen as a process involving the exercise of power. The intervener should possess the "power to reward, power to punish, and power to induce parties" to reach the agreement that the intervener wants them to reach (Smith 1994: 447). Especially when warring factions are reluctant to abide by the negotiation proposals, the strength of interveners can leave the negotiators little choice but to accept mediation. Hence, most studies highlight the role of military operations and economic sanctions as coercive methods of intervention. However, some people disagree with this idea. For instance, Fisher (2001: 19) argues that although coercive methods are useful for promoting an "initial settlement," they are counterproductive for developing "the values of autonomy and free choice" among the national actors. Other commentators claim that since most interveners have limits to their ability "to police the terms of settlement' and 'to observe and control the actions of the disputants," external intervention is also likely to prolong the conflicts (Watkins and Rosegrant 2002: 271). Moreover, in some cases, interveners who have relied too heavily on pressure are likely to bring about a situation that leads to a dangerous win-lose outcome, to rebellion, and to more conflict.

Second, for mediators, impartiality and neutrality are considered essential elements of successful intervention. This idea is based on the assumption that warring factions cannot trust mediators if the factions believe that they are involved in some way with the other side. Thus, it is believed that neutrality and impartiality make it easier for warring factions to accept the legitimacy of the intervention and give interveners more opportunities to promote creative suggestions (Bercovitch and DeRouen 2005). In particular, American mediation discourses tend to stress that an ideal mediator is "completely impartial and unbiased, ideally unconnected" to the negotiating parties (Avruch 1998: 83). However this assumption faces criticism from a variety of viewpoints. In a more practical sense, scholars claim that neutrality does not necessarily provide the basis for successful intervention. While some provide evidence of the ineffectiveness of impartial and nonforcible intervention in war zones, others demonstrate that mediators who are favourable towards one national party can play significantly productive roles. In some extreme cases, people argue that letting the conflicts "burn themselves out" or "intervening decisively on one side" might prove better options than simple impartial mediation (Ramsbotham, Woodhouse and Miall 2005: 142).

On a fundamental level, there is the question of whether a third party can be purely impartial and unbiased. As peacekeeping operations generate opportunities for state interests, most actors become involved in seeking economic and security interests. Moreover, even in the case where external actors have no particular economic or security interests, they should potentially have ideological and cultural biases.

Case study: multiparty mediation in the Cambodian peace negotiations

Going back to the introduction of this chapter, what did happen in the peace negotiations in Cambodia? Like many other peace processes where a large number of third parties are involved in pursuing different goals, the peace mediation in Cambodia was marked by a few formidable issues: coordination, limitations of noncoercive methods and dealing with spoilers.

The civil war in Cambodia started in 1979 between the PRK government backed by Vietnam and the SSR and the three resistance groups that had ruled the country. While the National United Front for an Independent, Neutral, Peaceful, and Cooperative Cambodia (FUNCINPEC) and the Khmer People's National Liberation Front (KPNLF) were led by the former king and a former prime minister who took more nationalistic and pro-Western postures, the third of these, the Khmer Rouge, aimed to continue its radical Maoist 'revolution' in the country. In 1981, these three groups created an alliance called the Coalition Government of Democratic Kampuchea (CGDK) to develop a more effective resistance movement. After seven years of total war, negotiations between the PRK and the CGDK began in 1987.

A large number of regional and international actors had participated in the development and escalation of the conflicts in the country (see Figure 4.2). Hence, the issue of coordination of these actors was a key challenge to the peace negotiations. At the international level, there were two significant countries that interacted closely with the national factions during the negotiations: the United States, which played a key role in the coordination of the external actors' policies; and China, a global power with strong regional interests. Both countries called for the withdrawal of the Vietnamese army from the Cambodian territory and provided diplomatic and material support to the resistance groups. On the other hand, the USSR indirectly supported the PRK government through its communication with Vietnam. Although the role of the United Nations (UN) was important, the organisation functioned more as a forum for debate rather than a unilateral organisation that had a specific position on the conflict. Japan and France facilitated a number of peace talks as neutral mediators.

At the regional level, the members of the ASEAN played significant roles, both collectively and individually. The tension between the Indochinese communist countries (Vietnam, Cambodia and Laos) and the ASEAN states (Indonesia, Malaysia, Singapore, Thailand and the Philippines) that had existed during the Cold War period was reflected in ASEAN's mediation activities. In particular, the Thai leaders, who had had a long-standing fear of Vietnamese imperial forces, considered the war to be a result of Vietnam's invasion, which constituted a direct threat to internal security in Thailand. In contrast, Indonesia and Malaysia behaved like more impartial third parties.

Thus, the third-party intervention was dominated by strong pro-CGDK/anti-Vietnam activities led by China, the US and Thailand. For instance, China provided economic and military aid to the Khmer Rouge through Thailand whilst the US indirectly provided material

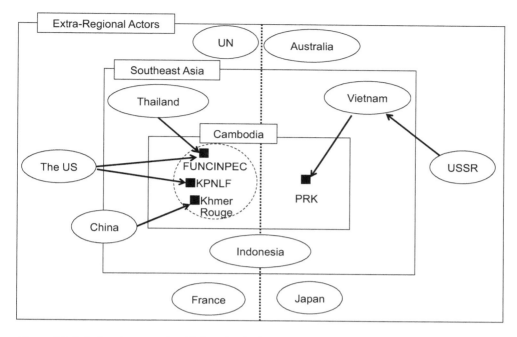

Figure 4.2 Relations between the third parties in the Cambodian peace negotiations

aid to the two noncommunist resistance parties. Diplomatically, in addition to open condemnation of the invasion, the US and China made efforts to convince the UN not to recognise the PRK regime and to deny it legitimacy. Vietnam continued its total involvement in the Cambodian civil conflicts by providing massive amounts of human, economic, military and diplomatic support.

Another challenge was the Khmer Rouge's constant refusal to negotiate with the PRK government. Rather, since it had lost its power through armed struggle with the PRK, the party's goal was to return to central government. Moreover, the Khmer Rouge considered the PRK to be the puppet regime of the Vietnamese 'imperialists' – the Khmer Rouge's longstanding enemy. Relying on communist revolutionary ideology, the party presented a highly rigid posture in its position throughout the negotiation process.

Under such circumstances, diplomatic efforts of other mediators such as Indonesia, France and Japan generally turned out to be less significant. Between 1985 and 1989, a large number of noncoercive methods were applied to bring the warring factions to proceed for further negotiation. While Indonesia, France, Japan and China contributed to the Cambodian peace negotiations by providing good offices and applying diplomatic pressure on the national factions, Australia and the United States produced comprehensive peace proposals. Nevertheless, the continued mediation failed to convince national belligerents sufficiently to reach to a ceasefire.

These challenges were gradually overcome in the late 1980s when the new waves of international politics emerged. The USSR under Mikhail Gorbachev identified the normalisation of ties with China as its diplomatic priority and took more reconciliatory approaches towards the US after the mid-1980s. In response, after 1987, China gradually revised its regional strategies and improved its relationships with the Soviet Union and Vietnam, which it had hitherto regarded as aggressors. Regional confrontation between Thailand and Vietnam was significantly reduced following 1989, when Vietnam decided to withdraw its army from Cambodia.

Reflecting such new features of the international environment, the US made new attempts to bring the parties to the negotiation table. It intensified its efforts to persuade the resistance groups to pursue negotiation more seriously, and it applied economic pressure by restricting its aid to nonmilitary support of the two noncommunist resistance factions. In addition, the US government also increased economic cooperation with Vietnam including approximately $11 million in US aid in 1990. China also became proactive in facilitating the four Cambodian factions' negotiations. In addition to accommodating most of the meetings between Cambodian factions from mid-1990 onwards, China's recognition of the PRK as a prominent actor in the Cambodian negotiation also served to increase its diplomatic pressure on the Khmer Rouge.

The mediators' efforts that headed in the same direction proved telling. Losing its largest military resource (the Vietnamese army) and seeing that Vietnam had more important national interests than supporting its Cambodian ally, the PRK began to work more earnestly towards the success of the negotiations. For the resistance groups, the withdrawal of the Vietnamese military forces meant that they had achieved their primary goal (the removal of Vietnamese imperialism). However, the concessions by Vietnam and the PRK did not result directly in a stable and productive negotiation. In contrast, believing that the PRK had been weakened, the CGDK conducted vigorous military operations during the rainy season of 1989–90. However, although these operations achieved relative success, the PRK recovered most of its lost territories in the next dry-season campaign, and all Cambodian provincial capitals, and all but two district towns, remained under PRK rule. It was obvious that the PRK's military strength was stronger than the resistance groups had estimated. After realising that the Vietnamese puppet regime was still strong despite Vietnam's withdrawal, two of the resistance groups – FUNCINPEC and the KPNLF – finally acknowledged the PRK as a negotiation partner.

Nevertheless, the Khmer Rouge remained a spoiler until the end of the peace process. Despite China's continued diplomatic pressure, the military party kept refusing to agree to the negotiations until early 1990. Although China's decision to discontinue all its military and economic aid to the Khmer Rouge eventually forced the latter to attend negotiation meetings following 1990, its commitment was half-hearted. Thus, even after the civil war was declared finished by signing the Paris Peace Agreements in October 1991, the Khmer Rouge's resistance against the implementation of the agreements continued until 1993.

Conclusion

This chapter considered the conceptual and theoretical issues relevant to conflict resolution. After giving an overview of five typical steps that many peace processes have followed (pre-talks, peace negotiation, signing of peace agreements, endorsement and implementation), the chapter introduced the strategies that many third-party mediators apply to facilitate successful peace negotiation. It then discussed contemporary academic debates regarding effective peace negotiation by focusing on four key terms: ripeness, spoiler, third-party strength and neutrality. Finally, the chapter demonstrated some of the issues involved by outlining how external mediators supported the Cambodian peace negotiations between 1985 and 1991.

The practices and debates presented in this chapter have indeed made significant contribution to international conflict resolution in the 1990s and early 2000s. As discussed in Chapter 3, more than a half of the armed conflicts were terminated by signing peace agreements or through nonviolent conflict resolutions. Nevertheless, in terms of the effectiveness of such measures, it should be noted that a large number of peace processes were followed by the resumption of violent conflicts within a few years. One prominent factor lying behind such limited success is major mediators' standardised understanding of peace and peacebuilding. In particular, the liberal peace – a perception of peace that is commonly shared in North America and Western Europe – has been criticised to direct most international peacebuilding programmes in a certain direction, ignoring the knowledge, skills and wisdom of the people in the war-torn societies. Hence, in contemporary peacebuilding, more efforts are being made to let national and local actors to take the lead in their peacebuilding programmes and to diversify the skills and measures for promoting peace.

At the same time, however, it should also be noted that conflict resolution is ultimately about people's conviction. As the case study of Cambodia demonstrates, the process of peace negotiation usually involves a long and complex process to reconcile the different interests and views of the immediate parties and other related actors. Spoilers may remain stubborn despite serious efforts of mediators. Sometimes none of the strategies described in this chapter seemed to work. Having dealt with such difficulties, many diplomats who were involved in previous peace negotiations commonly emphasise the importance of positivism. According to them, a peace process is a series of moments when the actors involved made the decisions relating to their next strategic behaviour. Thus, each of these moments can, in one sense, be a decisive point that determines the direction of the whole negotiation. At such a moment, it is the relevant actors' sincere, enthusiastic and constant attitude of support for the peaceful alternative to armed conflict that saves the negotiation from falling into failure.

Discussion questions

- Some people argue that dialogue is always the best way to deal with conflicts. Do you agree? Why/why not?
- Is the neutrality of intermediaries a necessary condition for successful conflict resolution?
- How can we make peace negotiation during the armed conflicts more inclusive and more reflective?
- In practice, how can external peace mediators judge the best timing to intervene?

Notes

1 Here, a 'game' refers to the conditions of interplay set by participants. The game largely determines the set of all possible utility payoffs. In a game, players make efforts to maximise their utility.
2 A contract zone refers to an area of common interest to the disputing actors that makes all the actors consent to a certain peace proposal.

Recommended reading

Bercovitch, J. and DeRouen, K. (2005) 'Managing Ethnic Civil Wars: Assessing the Determinants of Successful Mediation'. *Civil Wars* 7 (1): 98–116.
Bercovitch, J., Kremenyuk, V. and Zartman, I. (eds.) (2009) Chapters 16, 17 and 25, in *The SAGE Handbook of Conflict Resolution*. London: Sage.Crocker, C.A., Hampson, F.O. and Aall, P. (2004) Chapters 5–7, in *Taming Intractable Conflicts: Mediation in the Hardest Cases*, Washington, DC: USIP Press.

De Rouen, K., Bercovitch, J. and Pospieszna, P. (2011) 'Introducing the Civil Wars Mediation (CWM) Dataset'. *Journal of Peace Research* 48 (5): 663–72.

Greig, J. and Diehl, P (2005) 'The Peacekeeping-Peacemaking Dilemma'. *International Studies Quarterly* 49 (4): 621–46.

Jeong, H. (2010) Chapters 7–9, in *Conflict Management and Resolution: An Introduction*, London and New York: Routledge: 131–91.

Kydd, A. (2003) 'Which Side Are You On? Bias, Credibility, and Mediation'. *American Journal of Political Science* 47 (4): 597–611.

5   Post-conflict reconstruction

Although a successful conflict resolution may bring about the conclusion of an armed conflict, this is by no means the end of the peace process. By contrast, societies in the aftermath of armed conflict face even more formidable challenges that require support from solid peace processes. These may include a completely destroyed infrastructure, large numbers of war refugees, uneducated and untrained civil servants, lack of resources, inadequate medical facilities and so on. Moreover, the need to find ways to resolve the enmity can persist due to the atrocities committed by different social groups during decades of political oppression and the ensuing nationwide civil conflict.

Hence, post-conflict reconstruction is regarded as a critical part of peacebuilding in contemporary international peace-supporting activities. Most of the post-conflict reconstruction initiatives implemented in the post–Cold War period have tried to provide comprehensive solutions for war-affected societies, including

> disarming the previously warring parties and the restoration of order, the custody and possible destruction of weapons, repatriating refugees, advisory and training support for security personnel, monitoring elections, advancing efforts to protect human rights, reforming or strengthening governmental institutions, and promoting formal and informal processes of political participation.
>
> (UNSG 1992: para. 55)

Considering this, Chapter 5 aims to introduce the procedural aspects of and the practical issues related to the topic of postwar reconstruction by focusing on:

- Development of the concepts related with post-conflict reconstruction
- Different stages of post-conflict reconstruction
- Scope of reconstruction
- Challenges faced by actors in post-conflict recovery initiatives and operational principles as a tool for addressing some challenges.

As will be discussed later, the concept of post-conflict reconstruction has been developed in varied directions over the previous decades. Hence, the meaning of the term can be different according to the contexts, and post-conflict reconstruction and peacebuilding are frequently used interchangeably. However, in this particular chapter, reconstruction is used to primarily (but not exclusively) denote short- or mid-term peacebuilding programmes implemented in postwar societies, which focus on reconstructing political, economic and social institutions. In this sense, the programmes discussed in this chapter are typical examples of liberal peacebuilding introduced in Chapter 3, which reflect Western notions of and approaches to peace and peacebuilding.

Conceptual development of post-conflict reconstruction

The history of using post-conflict reconstruction as a major international peace-supporting process is relatively short. During the Cold War period, the United Nations (UN) and the broader international community paid most attention to humanitarian relief, peacemaking and peacekeeping activities. The term post-conflict reconstruction therefore rarely appeared in international security debates, except in reference to a few programmes implemented in the postcolonial, post–World War II and postcommunist eras. It was only at the end of the 1990s that the concept of post-conflict reconstruction emerged as a distinct activity. As the need for a more comprehensive understanding of peace-rehabilitation-development in post-conflict societies was recognised, this triggered active discussions on the theoretical and practical aspects of post-conflict reconstruction.

In particular, the World Bank's launch of the Post-Conflict Fund in 1997, and its publication of its framework for involving post-conflict reconstruction (*Post-Conflict Reconstruction: The Role of the World Bank*) in 1998, provided significant momentum for the emergence of post-conflict reconstruction as a core aspect of international peacebuilding. In the 2000s, post-conflict reconstruction became one of the central concepts in international intervention, and the UN Peacebuilding Commission was created, which proposes integrated strategies for post-conflict peacebuilding and recovery. Furthermore, the scope of post-conflict reconstruction has broadened significantly in the same period. In contemporary academic discussions, post-conflict reconstruction denotes "the rebuilding of the socioeconomic framework of society" (World Bank 1998: 4) and the "reconstruction of the enabling conditions for a functioning peacetime society" conducted in the post-conflict period (World Bank 1998: 14). As this definition implies, post-conflict reconstruction is a broad concept that has been used in contemporary discourse on peacebuilding without clear-cut boundaries as to its scope. Since post-conflict reconstruction supports the transition from war to lasting peace through the rebuilding of social and economic frameworks in the target countries, programmes can range in duration from short-term projects that deal with the immediate consequences of war to long-term projects that pursue the sustainable development of war-torn societies.

As regards its areas of focus, the purpose of international peace activities is to

> support people in rebuilding their lives, enabling them to regain a sense of hope, and in particular, for those who have been compelled to change their place of residence or work, to rediscover places where they can feel a sense of belonging.
>
> (Ikeda 2012: n.p.)

The social aspect of reconstruction therefore contributes towards the return to a 'normal' functioning of day-to-day life. Hence, postwar reconstruction covers a wide range of intervention activities and issues, ranging from the disarmament of ex-combatants to the development of social capital in rural areas, from restoring the relationships and support networks destroyed during the conflict to promoting justice, establishing the truth, reconciliation and so on.

Phases of post-conflict reconstruction

Implementing reconstruction programmes to revitalise the broad areas outlined earlier is a huge task, especially given that contemporary post-conflict reconstruction aims not only to provide short-term aid in war-affected countries but also to promote a more durable peace in these societies. The reconstruction process has thus become an increasingly long-term venture. Many previous studies identify such reconstruction processes as having four distinct periodical phases: the emergency relief phase, the rehabilitation phase, the reform and modernisation phase and the peace consolidation phase.

Emergency relief

Immediately after the end of hostilities, many peacebuilding programmes concentrate on meeting the need for emergency aid. The focus of emergency relief is to discourage the resumption of hostilities by providing the basic security necessary for the survival of people in war-torn societies. In cases where there is a high degree of violent instability, external actors may undertake military intervention such as dispatching peacekeeping forces or establishing an international interim authority. At the same time, international humanitarian agencies implement emergency relief programmes to provide basic necessities such as water, food, temporary shelter and urgent healthcare tools. For example, the International Committee of the Red Cross (ICRC) has operated emergency relief programmes in Mindanao, the Philippines, where a large number of people have been affected by the chronic armed conflicts between the government and insurgency groups. As of April 2015, the organization has utilized local trucks to deliver clean water and occasional emergency packages (consisting of half-month food rations, hygiene items, jerrycans and tarpaulins) to 16,000 internally displaced persons (IDPs) living in seventeen evacuation centres scattered throughout four local provinces (ICRC n.d.). In case emergency conditions extend for a longer period, more comprehensive aid is provided; this may cover community infrastructure, mine action, sanitation and hygiene and education.

Rehabilitation

The recovery and rehabilitation process for postwar society usually runs simultaneously with emergency relief or immediately after the emergency relief programmes have been successfully implemented. Since the internal actors in such war-torn societies are generally occupied with the issue of basic survival, the preparation in this period is normally implemented by external donor agencies. Implemented in this phase are the physical reconstruction of social infrastructure such as healthcare facilities, roads and schools, and efforts to restore basic public services such as governmental administration, policing and primary education. External interveners begin to support local initiatives aimed at restarting the economy and the recovery of broken social networks.

Regarding social security, for instance, protecting civilians from violence and maintaining territorial integrity are urgent issues in the aftermath of armed conflicts. In fact, security provides the foundation for the successful achievement of the goals of other reconstruction projects. Since the concept of human security was introduced in the late 1990s, the purview of this sector has been expanded to cover issues other than traditional state security issues. Enforcing peace agreements, disarming military forces and securing interim public order are some of the immediate security concerns. Sustaining and improving people's social and economic conditions is another important focus area. In the initial phase of reconstruction, measures to support the fundamental social and economic needs of the survivors of conflict include "restoration of essential services, provision of the foundation for a viable economy, and initiation of an inclusive, sustainable development program" (CSIS/AUSA 2002: 3).

The Cambodia Resettlement and Rehabilitation Program (CARERE I, 1992–95) of the United Nations Development Programme (UNDP) is one such example. The key goal of

CARERE I was to support the reintegration of the Cambodian refugees in Thailand and IDPs into four selected provinces in northwest Cambodia (Pursat, Battambang, Banteay Meanchey and Siem Reap). In the initial phases, the first priority was supporting the process of providing land and repatriation packages to the refugees and IDPs. However, this process was complicated by the lands contaminated by landmines and the local authorities or power elites who refused to share their land with new settlers. In the later period of the programme, CARERE I was involved a wide range of issues such as education (reestablishing schools, operating nonformal education), income generation (support for agricultural activities, development of irrigation systems, vocational training), infrastructure construction (roads, ports, governmental buildings) and health care (water, sanitation) (UNDP 2001).

Nevertheless, it can be difficult for peacebuilders to establish a comprehensive long-term plan for rehabilitation due to the unstable and highly changeable social environment; many of the previous programmes conducted during this phase have been adversely affected by the problems of inefficiency and lack of coordination. Moreover, since most state infrastructure, including the public administration, private sector mechanisms and public transport, have been completely destroyed and there is limited internal drive to take on new initiatives, reconstruction projects at this stage frequently require proactive assistance from external sources to meet technical, financial, logistical and social needs.

Reform and modernisation

The third phase of post-conflict reconstruction aims at the restoration of local people's capabilities to rebuild their societies. The programmes primarily focus on the reform of all aspects of the existing governance institutions – that is to say, their forms, procedures, structures, information management, capabilities of actors, patterns of performance and relations between actors. In terms of security, for instance, once the interim period has been successfully stabilised, longer-term security reconstruction programmes are put into place, including the restructuring of security forces, the reform of police institutions, border control, the protection of civil movements and public institutions, and modernisation of the security infrastructure.

Moreover, the mechanisms for transitional justice deal with past human rights abuses, creating effective law enforcement institutions and establishing mechanisms (formal and informal) for resolving disagreements. Some of the key projects in terms of law enforcement include the establishment of civil law, reorganisation of court institutions, reform of inappropriate laws and acts, and training/recruitment of legal professionals. Programmes for social reconciliation such as truth-finding projects and education for reconciliation are also usually initiated at this stage. With the gradual empowerment of the local community, the relationship between external peace supporters and local people gradually transforms increasingly into a more equal partnership and towards the handing over of responsibilities.

As will be discussed in more detail in Chapter 7, security sector reform (SSR) involves a frequently applied programme aiming at reform and modernisation of postwar societies. A key goal of SSR is transforming the security forces that had committed violent actions against civilians into a civilian institution that is more politically independent and accountable to constituencies. In post–civil war El Salvador, for example, three notorious security forces – the Treasury Police, the rural-oriented National Guard and the urban-oriented National Police – were completely dissolved and replaced by a new National Civilian Police (PNC). This new police agency was designed to be controlled only by civilian leadership, and the legislature could 'remove' PNC directors in cases where the PNC was involved in any type of human rights abuse. Moreover, all intelligence agencies that had been under the control of military leaders were redirected to report to the president only and be under the supervision of the legislature (Call 2003).

Peace consolidation

The final phase of post-conflict reconstruction is concerned with consolidating the transition initiatives with a view to ensuring sustainability. The initiatives in this category are normally applied in the final phase of peacebuilding and are likely to take place over a considerable length of time. In terms of social governance, many peacebuilding programmes at this stage aim to establish broad-based government and the participation of the private sector and civil society organisations in the formulation of public policies. The facilitation of social reconciliation and further development of socioeconomic reconstruction are also considered important in this phase. In the course of conducting these projects, the intention is that local people relearn how to balance their conflicting interests and opinions by contributing to and participating in social development programmes.

At this stage, the provisional security and social measures that had been applied in the earlier phases (such as deployment of UN peacekeeping troops, emergency humanitarian aid and interim governmental organisations) are withdrawn. Moreover, it is intended that the enhanced collaboration between local communities and international peace-supporting organisations will gradually lead to the empowerment of local institutions and pave the way for the roles and responsibilities of external actors to be transferred to indigenous people.

In relation to the exit of international aid, the timing of the transition from one post-conflict reconstruction phase to another should be carefully determined. As can be seen from UNHCR's Quick Impact Projects (see Box 5.1), a large number of peacebuilding agencies

---

Box 5.1 Linking relief and reconstruction: Quick Impact Projects

A key element of successful postwar peacebuilding is transformation of the programmes from phase to phase. In particular, linking emergency relief and longer-term reconstruction has been one of the most difficult issues in many peacebuilding processes. Quick Impact Projects (QIPs) are an important part of efforts by the United Nations High Commissioner for Refugees (UNHCR) for providing a bridge between UNHCR's short-term relief and reintegration programmes and more sustainable development efforts. In many contexts, QIPs provided benefits such as the rapid implementation of small-scale projects, only requiring a one-time allocation of resources; establishing institutional linkages between different actors; allowing communities to identify their local needs; contributing to the local economy by enabling an expansion of productive and commercial activities, and income-generation opportunities; making it easier for the community to market their produce; and fostering social cohesion between returnees, host communities and former political adversaries. Since the successful implementation of the first QIPs in Nicaragua in 1991, which comprised 250 microcredit projects for returnees in the areas of health, education, training, infrastructure, transportation, crop production, livestock and income generation, QIPs have been integrated into almost every UNHCR reintegration programme.

However, QIPs have not become as successful as anticipated, and the lessons learned from their implementation can be useful in gaining a better understanding of linking relief and reconstruction. Critically, they have not proved sustainable, either, and hence have proved incapable of making a lasting impact on the reintegration of returnees. In the first place, QIPs are essentially emergency development projects and not made to withstand the long-term problems of recurrent costs and sustainability. Donors were simply not interested in funding QIPs beyond the initial phase, while local governments were not committed to incorporating them into their national development strategies. In addition, the rush to complete QIPs without due consideration to community participation has resulted in problems with sustainability. Moreover, the burden of maintenance and repair has fallen on local governments who simply do not have the resources to handle them. There were also criticisms of QIPs for their mixed record in serving the needs of refugee women, their prevention of people's abilities to engage in more productive activities as a result of their focus on labour-intensive infrastructure-oriented projects, and the frequent lack of any significant community participation. Finally, QIPs have lacked sustainability because they suffer from another key consequence of being a programme of UNHCR – namely, the inability to address the structural economic problems that prevail in the country of origin.

Sources: Arafat, 2000; Ballard, 2002.

have developed strategies to promote effective transition. In principle, the transition is expected to be made gradually on the basis of whether the various goals set within each phase have been achieved and whether the level of engagement demanded by the participating actors has been met. In practice, however, judging the right time is always easier said than done due to various factors. For example, as the processes of reconstruction are multidirectional, the programmes that are carried out in the various phases coexist in the same reconstruction field. Moreover, since the social, structural and cultural conditions are dissimilar area by area, no general rules can be applied in determining good timing. Instead, a set of parameters for evaluating the development of peacebuilding need to be established according to the target society's situation. Furthermore, even in cases where suitable parameters are established, evaluation is frequently biased by evaluators' subjective views (Lee and Özerdem 2015a).

Challenges and operational principles

This section considers the obstacles that face contemporary post-conflict reconstruction programmes and the efforts made to overcome them. First, a number of the challenges that peacebuilding actors need to consider when planning their programmes will be outlined, including the issues of resumption of hostilities, the funding gap between donor pledges and actual disbursement, lack of local ownership and psychological war trauma. Then, it will identify the principles of operation that are currently applied in many projects. Based on the Cross-Cutting Principles of the United States Institute of Peace (USIP) and the US Army Peacekeeping and Stability Operations Institute (US Army), it will provide an overview of the significance of the following principles: political primacy, legitimacy, security, unity of programmes, host nation ownership, conflict transformation and engagement.

Challenges facing contemporary post-conflict reconstruction

The extent and the degree of post-conflict reconstruction may vary significantly depending on the particular contexts of the war-torn societies. For instance, the progress of social welfare reform in countries where severe violence and destruction have occurred (e.g. Rwanda in 1994) is generally slower than in countries in which relatively strong institutions remain (e.g. Kosovo in 1999). In post-conflict societies, a range of factors affect the progress of the implementation of postwar reconstruction: devastated economies, destroyed physical infrastructure, ineffective governance and corrupt legal and judicial systems. When these factors are combined, the following barriers to reconstruction are highly likely to emerge.

Unstable security conditions

Economic, social and political issues have often been cited as important factors in fomenting conflicts. Parties involved in conflict management therefore consider these factors when negotiating a settlement, and unless these underlying issues are addressed and survivors perceive a change in their situation, the likelihood of hostilities resuming is often very high. The issue of unstable security is particularly problematic in emergency relief programmes, as many of them need to be implemented during armed conflicts. Relief aiders usually work under various security threats, ranging from landmines to angry mobs, and their aid operations are frequently affected by security issues. For instance, a refugee camp for Somalis in Kenya was subject to seventy-seven cross-border attacks in one year (between October 2011 and October 2012), and the water, sanitation and hygiene programme operated by Médecins Sans Frontières (MSF) at the same refugee camp stopped for a long time after three staff were killed or kidnapped to Somalia (Munuve 2013).

Regarding institutional reconstruction, the signing of peace accords and the period following it are in most cases characterised by tension and insecurity. In countries with protracted political conflicts, negotiated settlements and plans for reconstruction have often been frustrated by the resumption of fresh hostilities. In fact, historical evidence reveals that there has been a recurrence of war in one-quarter to one-half of post-conflict countries (UNDP 2008). Examples include Sierra Leone, Liberia and Ivory Coast, where peacebuilding and recovery plans were abandoned due to ceasefire violations.

Funding gap between pledge and disbursement

Inadequate funding poses a major threat to speedy and successful reconstruction work in countries emerging from armed conflict. In the initial phases of post-conflict reconstruction, development partners of the country concerned generally host a donor conference to raise the funds required for the huge amount of reconstruction work. Such donor conferences are often well attended by donors, who make enthusiastic promises to support recovery efforts. In most cases, however, actual disbursements and the redemption of promises/pledges have been either too small or too slow. The donor pledge and disbursement gap has not only delayed reconstruction work but also led to the underfunding of reconstruction interventions, resulting in frustration for state officials and war victims. This situation has in some cases threatened the successful completion of reconstruction work and has increased the potential for the resumption of hostilities. Palestine, Afghanistan and Sierra Leone all experienced shortfalls in funding arrangements that caused considerable, and in some cases renewed, tension in those countries. Hence, swift and accurate identification of social needs and securing necessarily funding are considered a major challenge for conflict-affected societies.

Psychological war trauma

Although often ignored in academic debate, the psychological influence of war is frequently a barrier to post-conflict reconstruction. After surviving a protracted war, most people suffer from war trauma, symptoms of which include "insomnia, headaches, body pains, stomach discomfort and lack of appetite, in addition to their affective symptoms of depression, fear, feelings of hopelessness, loss of self-esteem, crying, irritability, and sexual anxiety/avoidance" (Leslie 2001: 52). Hence, reconstruction programmes frequently face difficulties in mobilising local participation and ownership. For instance, after having experienced the harsh labour mobilisation of the Khmer Rouge and a devastating civil war, it is widely reported that rural communities in Cambodia encountered difficulties with concentrating on skill-related training and tended to refuse to speak at/ contribute to open discussions. The impact of war trauma on children (both perpetrators and victims) is even more significant, as they have experienced and have been influenced by war culture from an early age. Although psychosocial healing projects such as community integration programmes, volunteer action and the training of professionals may improve the situation, severe psychological problems cannot be addressed within a short time period.

Lack of coordination

A challenge created by the proliferation of agencies in post-conflict settings is the lack of effective coordination between agencies. In some countries, the end of hostilities attracts a large number of players with genuine intentions to contribute to the reconstruction work. This influx of players can create two problems.

Multilateral institutions such as the UN and the World Bank emphasise shifting the focus of intervention from emergency and development programmes to peacebuilding and conflict transformation, and their position is usually based on the assumption that interventions that focus on preventing recurrence of the violent conflict could preclude the need for large investments in future development programmes. For these agencies, initiatives aimed at development assistance focus on the terms set out in peace agreements, elements of peacebuilding and building capacities for conflict prevention. International nongovernmental organisations (NGOs), however, have different priorities: some specialise in providing humanitarian relief, while others focus entirely on building local capacities through long-term development interventions. This clash in the priorities of peacebuilding actors and the subsequent lack of coordinated action is quite evident in post-conflict settings, and most practitioners agree that not enough has been done to improve the situation (Junne and Verkoren 2005).

Hence, a large number of issues are emerging, some of which include: duplication/overlap of project areas, competitiveness of responses (or even working at cross purposes), and spread of limited resources over many independent actors. Although some prominent international actors (e.g. UN Office for the Coordination of Humanitarian Affairs) have applied various strategies to address the issue, coordination still remains a challenging goal in international peacebuilding (Lee and Özerdem 2015).

Lack of local ownership

A number of major problems are caused or catalysed by the fact that reconstruction initiatives are too donor driven and rarely respond to the development priorities of the country concerned. Although the lack of local ownership is a common problem in many development programmes and is therefore not a problem unique to post-conflict reconstruction, the problems tend to be worse in war-torn societies owing to their fragility and the fact that the capacity of the state has been weakened by the conflict. Since multilateral organisations, which distribute a large portion of the resources for reconstruction programmes, prefer to work through private contractors and international NGOs, most programmes initiated by multilateral organisations and operated by international NGOs cannot avoid reflecting/perpetuating this donor-client framework. This biased approach not only serves to further weaken the capacity of state institutions but also undermines the sustainability of interventions, especially as the sense of ownership on the part of the state is likely to be minimal.

Politics of aid

Post-conflict reconstruction is greatly influenced by the attitude of donors and the resources they provide to address the aftermath of conflict. Ideally, allocation of resources for recovery interventions in the country concerned can have implications for the balance of power at all levels, be it national, regional or local. In reality, however, the aid is frequently determined by the partial interests of donor agencies, the stance of the media, or the rivalry between the donors. Moreover, although aid is meant to address inequalities and the legacies of conflict, the distribution of aid can actually cause or exacerbate inequality and improper use can undermine peace and recovery efforts. When agencies concentrate development efforts in one region while excluding others (often described by some agencies as remote and hard to reach), this can create imbalances, and if not handled properly can breed resentment and lay the foundations for future conflict.

Operational principles of post-conflict reconstruction

After two decades of extensive experience of post-conflict reconstruction projects, international peacebuilding actors became well aware of the challenges outlined earlier. Various methods for improving the situation have therefore been proposed and implemented to reduce the risk of these problems becoming insurmountable barriers. One of the most important efforts to meet these challenges has been setting the operational principles that all peacebuilding organisations in a society are expected to follow. Out of various principles applied in the field practice, the discussion in this section will be primarily on the Cross-Cutting Principles proposed by USIP and the US Army in 2009.

Host nation ownership and capacity

Post-conflict reconstruction in a war-affected country should be driven by the people in the country. It is important, therefore, to strengthen the capacities and capabilities of the national actors, including those of governmental employees, community leaders, civil organisations and private actors, so as "to mitigate and manage drivers of conflict" (USIP 2009: 13). The effectiveness of external actors' efforts to build ownership by the host nation may be improved when the peacebuilders (1) understand the local context well, (2) increase the inclusivity of participants (in terms of gender, ethnicity, religion and the private and public and civil and governmental sectors), (3) target resources towards local ownership building from the early phase of reconstruction and (4) utilise the host country's national processes and structures.

Political primacy

This principle assumes that everything done during post-conflict reconstruction is political. Although conflict resolution might bring about the end of violent actions, the root causes of the conflict remain, and these causes should be managed by political institutions. Moreover, effective political arrangements are essential if the performance of the state authority and local governmental agencies – the main actors facilitating peacebuilding projects and collaborating with international NGOs – is to improve. At the local level, the politics of local communities and regional municipalities can be a considerable barrier to the implementation of peacebuilding programmes. Bearing in mind their potential impact on the politics of conflict, reconstruction programmes therefore need to consider and take each step carefully.

Legitimacy

In post-conflict societies, reconstruction projects should be conducted not under conditions of enforcement but rather legitimacy. Three aspects of legitimacy need to be considered simultaneously: "the degree to which the host nation population accepts the mission and its mandate or the government and its actions"; "the degree to which the government is accountable to its people"; and "the degree to which regional neighbo[u]rs and the broader international community accept the mission mandate and the host nation government" (USIP 2009: 3/12). A number of strategies to gain legitimacy include a social contract between citizens and the government, transparent planning and implementation, management of expectations and communication, and proactive engagement by the international community.

Unity of effort

Coordination of reconstruction projects is a topic that has been long debated. Participants need to collaborate with each other in order to maximise the effectiveness of reconstruction projects. Such unity can emerge via common short- and long-term objectives, a shared understanding of the situation and past experience of collaboration. In field practice, peacebuilding organisations' efforts currently aim at three different levels of coordination. First, many international organisations like the European Union (EU) attempt to house participating actors under a common strategic management and promote a high level of collaboration that includes "common programming, strategic monitoring, vetting of agencies, disciplining of renegades and fund control" (Brabant 2001 cited in Strand 2005: 90). Second, there have been attempts for a minimal level of coordination that acknowledges aid organisations' independent positions and policies. In these cases, the core responsibility of participating organisations is to share information about their activities so that other actors do not duplicate them. Coordination activities by the United Nations Children's Fund (UNICEF) in South Sudan during the late 1990s provide a good example of such minimalist coordination. Third, other coordination efforts have presented positions that could be placed between the two contrasting approaches. For example, in 1994, the International Federation of the Red Cross

---

**Box 5.2 How not to do harm through reconstruction?
Špionića water supply reconstruction**

For external peacebuilding bodies, doing no harm to those involved is a first and most important step for gaining legitimacy of the programmes that they operate. The reconstruction of the water supply system in Špionića in the municipality of Srebrenik in northeast Bosnia-Herzegovina in 1997 is a good example of how not to do harm as a result of reconstruction. Interventions by the international community in such environments must not only be impartial, but must also be perceived to be impartial; this is often one of the most challenging aspects of the reconstruction process.

The ethnic distribution for a total population of 2,500 was approximately 55% Croats, 30% Muslims and 15% Serbs who lived in three separate neighbourhoods. An international NGO in 1996 managed to secure funds for a 1-kilometre pipeline which would only be sufficient for the partial completion of the reconstruction of water supply system in Špionića. In order to supply water to the whole population in these three neighbourhoods, the project required much larger funding, and subsequently the local authority faced the dilemma of either accepting this funding and getting its water supply partially rebuilt or refusing the funding altogether in order not to harm interethnic relationships. During the conflict in Bosnia-Herzegovina, interethnic relationships were already torn apart, and there were not many multiethnic settlements like Špionića left, where the country's three main ethnic communities could still live side by side in the immediate aftermath of the Dayton Peace Agreement in 1995. The local authority made the difficult but wise decision by not accepting the funding, as this would distribute benefits unequally among the three ethnic communities, and in such an environment it was critical that all ethnic communities felt they were being treated on an equal basis.

(IFRC) proposed and implemented a code of conduct for encouraging other humanitarian aiders to agree to general self-regulation of their activities.

Security

Security is a prerequisite of stable and sustainable postwar reconstruction. Where the resumption of military conflicts is highly probable, no reconstruction projects can be successfully undertaken. Although the USIP/US Army's Cross-Cutting Principles broadly adopt the concept of human security (the details of human security will be discussed in Chapter 6), as employed in these principles, security is limited to the physical security that "permits the freedom necessary to pursue a permanent peace" (USIP 2009: 3/20). Ensuring stable security, obtaining/sharing of good information, effectively controlling borders, managing violent crimes, demobilising ex-combatants and reforming the security sector are strongly recommended.

Conflict transformation

This principle emphasises that the means of promoting peace should also be peaceful. It intends to distinguish peacebuilding programmes from some of the early conflict resolution methods such as military intervention and economic coercion. For instance, from a short-term perspective, efforts to reduce the drivers of conflict and to mitigate the conflicts in the political, security and economic spheres are required. However, longer-term programmes based on the concepts relevant to conflict transformation may aim to enhance and support the ability of local people to manage conflict.

Regional engagement

Since no development issues are entirely domestic, the participation of neighbouring countries and other key states is imperative if post-conflict reconstruction is to be successful. In fact, various regional factors (e.g. political instability of a neighbouring country and the contamination of upper rivers) may provide important sources of further conflict in the target countries. The USIP/US Army principle proposes three components to encourage contributions from neighbouring states: comprehensive regional diplomacy aiming to prevent neighbouring countries from taking any destabilising actions; efforts to set a shared regional vision; and the formation or support of region-wide cooperation structures.

The importance of these principles is constantly reaffirmed in international conferences and academic/practical studies on developing effective peacebuilding processes. However, it is also frequently pointed out that one of the main problems in contemporary post-conflict reconstruction is that these principles are all too often neglected.

Case study: challenges to postwar reconstruction in Afghanistan

When the war in Afghanistan was declared over in 2001, the major peacebuilding organisations had three priorities in their endeavours for the post-conflict reconstruction: (re)building political/administrative/security systems, rehabilitation and relief, and a constant supply of funds for supporting other areas of reconstruction. Regarding institution building, there were five pillars: formation and training of a national army, reconstruction of the police force, creation of a working judiciary, drug control (eradication of the opium poppy) and demobilisation of private militias. As for emergency relief and rehabilitation, helping avert widespread famine and supporting displaced persons were key goals (GAO 2007).

The journey of the peacebuilding actors in pursuit of these objectives was hindered by various obstacles. This case study elaborates on three fundamental issues observed in Afghanistan. First, unstable political and security conditions themselves were the most formidable obstacles. The central government did not have supreme control over the country, which was divided into five or six regions, each of which was controlled by semiautonomous power groups. Subgroups of the Taliban were actively recruiting new forces while conducting frequent suicide bombings and guerrilla warfare. The unregulated circulation of weapons and the cultivation of opium were also considered threats to the country's security. Furthermore, apart from the vague 1964 constitution and the imposition of Islamic sharia law under the Taliban, the country had no concrete constitutional principles to support political reconstruction. Although a loya jirga (a traditional assembly of regional religious leaders) was used as a tool to consolidate power at the national level, Afghanistan's system of popular representation was underdeveloped.

Despite constant efforts to deal with the insecurity and political instability, these have been a major barrier to the reconstruction programmes in the country. For example, in the elections undertaken since 2004, people's participation was significantly discouraged by intense security threats from the Taliban. A striking example is the election in 2009, when only 4.6 million out of a voting population of 15 million managed to cast their votes. Local government institutions largely failed to be available to the local communities due to the power struggle between the central government and regional/local strongmen (including the Taliban).

Lack of a coordinated operational framework significantly prevented collaboration between different actors. Civil-military cooperation was a particularly important but challenging task. In the early phase of the Afghani reconstruction, military troops were dealing with the training and mentoring of local security forces, destroying Taliban forces and providing local population with reconstruction and medical services. Such security activities were highly important for the successful implementation of civilian actors' social reconstruction programmes, among them the US Agency for International Development (USAID), the Australian Agency for International Development (AusAID) and the Department for International Development (DFID), in addition to a large number of NGOs. Nevertheless, the two sides had few opportunities to interact with each other for coordination due to different organisational structures, working cultures and priorities of operations.

After operating reconstruction programmes for over ten years, the issue of civil-military cooperation still remained an unachieved goal. Although a number of frameworks were suggested and implemented, which included an Afghanistan National Development Strategy, an Afghanistan Compact and a Joint Coordination and Monitoring Board, the division between military actors and civilian practitioners was not significantly reduced. While humanitarian actors and small NGO practitioners were highly restricted by "the cooptation of the aid system by the international coalition," the International Security Assistance Force (ISAF) presented little success in facilitating the collaboration with NGOs (Hoffman and Dalauney 2010).

The Afghan people's perception of international actors was another challenge. Despite the good intentions of many international actors in supporting reconstruction in the country, a large number of people outside Kabul, the capital city, frequently presented their reluctance to collaborate with 'externals.' There are several key reasons for their negative perceptions. As a contextual issue, the preceding war was understood by many Afghans as an invasion by US imperialism. Hence, there was a strong suspicion among the Afghan people that the international humanitarian actors, as well as military troops, were the agencies of the imperialist power. The overdirection of post-conflict reconstruction that emphasised Western values such as democracy, accountability and market economy strengthened such suspicion further. Early-phase humanitarian aids frequently lacked consultation with local actors when planning and operating peace-supporting programmes, and such inconsiderate behaviour tended to galvanise local actors' anger and sense of humiliation (Minear and Donini 2005).

Due to such perceptual issues, a large number of reconstruction programmes failed to be integrated into local communities' daily lives. Instead, many programmes were ad hoc measures that were perceived as an extra burden by local residents. Moreover, longer-term capacity-building efforts gained limited successes due to the residents' lack of ownership, whilst the lack of good understanding of local contexts sometime caused new tensions between different tribes or religious groups. For instance, external aid in favour of an Uruzgan-based Pushtun leader caused the anger of other subtribe groups in the same area as well as non-Pushtun ethnic groups such as the *Hazaras* (Maley 2010). Under such circumstances, peace-building programmes faced strong resistance.

Conclusion

After reviewing conceptual development of post-conflict reconstruction, this chapter explored a number of the procedural and practical issues related to post-conflict reconstruction. First, the scope of post-conflict reconstruction projects was presented by focusing on four thematic areas: security, justice and reconciliation, social and economic well-being, and governance and participation. Then, the details of the reconstruction process were examined by dividing the process into four phases and looking at the goals and implementation strategies of the projects undertaken in each phase. From a more practical viewpoint, some of the most significant barriers to effective postwar reconstruction as well as operational principles applied for overcoming such challenges were introduced. Finally, the case study of Afghanistan reviewed how the challenges of unstable political and security conditions, lack of coordination and local people's negative perception of external aid have hampered the reconstruction process in the country.

The overview of these challenges and recent efforts to deal with them also highlights the fact that postwar reconstruction is not a technical matter of (re)establishing physical infrastructure. Instead, it should deal with various issues embedded in the political, social, economic and psychological dimensions of the society. Hence, a successful post-conflict reconstruction requires the long-term commitment of peacebuilding actors in order to address various structural, social and psychological issues.

Nevertheless, until the early 2000s, the majority of international humanitarian organisations and nation states involved in post-conflict reconstruction processes had only short- or mid-term plans for implementation (usually with a time frame between five and fifteen years). The primary goal of these programmes was setting up the institutional foundations on which national actors of the conflict societies could nurture further peace and development. Thus, many scholars in this period emphasised the importance of well-planned exit strategies that had minimal impact on the conflict-affected societies. However, with such preset mid-term plans, it was well beyond the capacity of any single body to look into the complex and interrelated social issues discussed in this chapter.

Gradually, the limitations of conventional programmes for post-conflict reconstruction have come to be taken more seriously. Moreover, such institution-oriented reconstruction programmes are gradually being replaced by more long-term and inclusive peacebuilding processes with more flexible, nuanced and comprehensive programme design. Chapter 6 will pay more attention to this new trend of peacebuilding under the theme of conflict transformation.

Discussion questions

- Is making reconstruction assistance conditional an effective tool for post-conflict reconstruction?
- Some people argue that (re)building of state institutions is a prerequisite of a sustainable peacebuilding. Do you agree? Why/why not?
- Under what conditions should external peace supporters terminate their aid to war-affected societies?
- Due to the aid dependency of the war-torn societies, the international peacebuilders usually wield stronger power than their local partners in reconstruction programmes. How can this asymmetric power relation be addressed?

Recommended reading

Barakat, S. (ed.) (2010) *After the Conflict: Reconstruction and Development in the Aftermath of War*. London: IB Tauris.

Cockell, J. (2003) 'Conceptualising Peacebuilding: Human Security and Sustainable Peace', in *Regeneration of War-Torn Societies*, edited by Pugh, M. London: Macmillan: 15–34.

David, C. P. (1999) 'Does Peacebuilding Build Peace? Liberal (Mis)steps in the Peace Process'. *Security Dialogue* 30 (1): 25–41.

de Coning, C. (2007) *Coherence and Coordination in United Nations Peacebuilding and Integrated Missions*. A Norwegian perspective NUPI Report on Security and Practice No. 5. Hambrosplas: Norsk Utenrikspolitisk Institutt.

Gamba, V. (2003) 'Managing Violence: Disarmament and Demobilisation', in *Contemporary Peacemaking: Conflict, Violence and Peace Processes*, edited by Darby, J. and Mac Ginty, R. London: Palgrave Macmillan: 125–36.

Kingma, K. (2002) 'Demobilisation and Peacebuilding in Africa'. *International Peacekeeping* 9 (2): 181–201.

6 Conflict transformation

In response to the shortcomings of a large number of peacebuilding operations carried out in the 1990s, the international community gradually came to recognise the limitations of conventional methods that were based on conflict resolution frameworks. Despite the huge amount of aid and investment in postwar reconstruction, most peacebuilding operations of this period failed to achieve their goals. While some countries experienced a resumption of military conflict within a few years of reaching ceasefires (e.g. Sierra Leone, Angola and Cambodia), other countries struggled due to concomitant issues such as corruption, unregulated violence, ongoing repression of social minorities and the like (e.g. Guatemala, Afghanistan and Rwanda).

Therefore, since the late 1990s, a number of efforts have been made to break from the conventional path of conflict resolution by reflecting on the new characteristics of warfare and the complexity of postwar reconstruction. Conflict transformation is one prominent strand of these new attempts. If the reconstruction of institutions and infrastructure was at the centre of conventional post-conflict reconstruction, the new type of peacebuilding pays more attention to social capacity building and self-sustaining human development. Although there is little consensus on the concrete concepts of conflict transformation as it is a relatively new (and still developing) theoretical perspective, the programmes adopting this new approach are making a significant impact in contemporary peacebuilding.

Out of various conceptual and theoretical issues relevant to conflict transformation, this chapter will pay its particular attention to:

- Core concepts of conflict transformation, including the dimensions of transformation;
- Significance of the conflict transformation paradigm in peacebuilding practice;
- Human security as a conceptual foundation of contemporary peacebuilding;
- Gender and peacebuilding.

Concepts of conflict transformation

Conflict transformation is a relatively new term and both its definition and procedures are still evolving and being refined. Various debates on the theoretical and practical applicability of conflict transformation are ongoing. Nevertheless, a number of the key features present within a broad definition of conflict transformation – the intentional, relationship-centred, long-term efforts to de-escalate violent conflicts by addressing the cultural, contextual or structural causes of the conflicts – are accepted by many academics and practitioners.

Lederach's (2003) definition of conflict transformation – an attempt "to envision and respond to the ebb and flow of social conflict as life-giving opportunities for creating constructive change" – forms the broad conceptual grounds upon which different researchers and practitioners have developed their own definitions. For instance, Bush and Folger (1994) analyse conflict transformation at the interpersonal level and identify it as a process of empowerment and recognition of the transformation of the individual. By contrast, Francies (2004) places emphasis on structural transformation within war-affected countries, which includes changes to power asymmetries, gender inequalities and cultural differences. Fischer and Ropers define conflict transformation as "the structure of conflicts and the process of moving towards 'just peace'" (Fischer and Ropers 2004: 13). Yarn (1999: 121) views conflict transformation in terms of "change[s] in the characteristics of a conflict" and the efforts "inducing change in the parties' relationship through improving mutual understanding."

In general, however, conflict transformation broadly denotes a group of approaches towards conflict and conflict resolution rather than a single specific idea or theory. Studies that employ a conflict transformation approach are founded on the fundamental assumption that conflict is "a normal and continuous dynamic within human relationships" (Lederach 2003: 15). Although conflict can be more or less active, rather like the ebb and flow of the sea, eliminating conflict is impossible. Moreover, conflict may be a useful source of constructive change. However, these assumptions do not mean that conflict transformation simply accepts conflict as a natural and insuperable phenomenon. Instead, a conflict transformation approach aims to make more fundamental changes to human relations and the structural environment in a war-affected country by addressing the root causes of the conflict.

In addition, conflict transformation suggests that a transformation can be achieved only by a gradual process in which interveners engage with local communities to propose solutions aimed at mitigating the destructive effects of conflicts. Conflict transformation is not about seeing disputants as the problem and interveners as the solution; rather it is a long-term goal aimed at changing people's attitudes and building the capacity of local institutions to manage resources for the benefit of all while minimising those factors that lead to incompatibilities (Lederach 2003). Conflict transformation also emphasises that the process of 'transformation' necessitates a systemic change. Since most conflicts are deep-rooted parts of the social system in the countries concerned, it is believed that transforming the society from a conflict-habituated system into a peace-desiring system is key to successful peacebuilding (Notter and Diamond 1996). In this regard, conflict transformation comes about only when "violent conflict ceases and/or is expressed in nonviolent ways and when the original structural sources (economic, social, political, military, and cultural) of the conflict have been changed" (Clements 1997: 8).

Dimensions of transformation

Under the concept of conflict transformation, the 'transformation' of conflict-related factors is central to the promotion of successful peacebuilding. What factors, then, do we need to

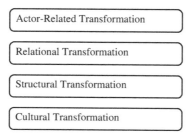

Figure 6.1 Dimensions of transformation

transform and in what ways can we transform them? Although recent studies have suggested different approaches to bringing about transformation, most of them take the following dimensions of transformation into consideration.

Actor-related transformation

Groups of actors are held together by a common purpose, interest and, in most cases, a leadership that determines the direction of the group. Actors have a sense of identity, emotions and goals, factors that usually motivate them into action. Actor-related transformation aims to change people's perceptions of these factors. During the period of peace negotiation, for example, a change in the goals of actors may lead to new proposals or goals that satisfy the needs of all disputants, thus reducing the level of incompatibility between them. Since conflict has destructive effects on personal well-being at the physical, emotional, intellectual and spiritual levels, psychological healing and redevelopment of community networks are frequently applied to alleviate the impacts of the conflicts.

Relational transformation

Although relational transformation might not change the fundamental issues underlying social violence, it is important because a large number of violent acts are caused or catalysed by the issues related to interpersonal relationships. The affectivity, power and interdependence of human relationships are important in this type of transformation. For instance, in order to transform an aggressive relationship into a more neutral or positive one, respect for the position of others and the willingness and ability to establish and maintain an equal power relationship is highly desirable. In this sense, Yarn (1999: 121) argues that "inducing change in the parties' relationship through improving mutual understanding" should be a central part of conflict transformation.

Apart from religious programmes pursuing transformation of people's inner spirituality, the programmes for actor-related transformation and relational transformation frequently overlap, broadly aiming at the facilitation of positive mutual understanding between different social units. For instance, while nationwide programmes for social reconciliation between former perpetrators and victims are emphasised as key elements of postwar reconstruction, more local-level initiatives such as religious rituals, mediation for dialogue and transmission of information are also widely applied.

Moreover, the importance of peace education is frequently emphasised by international organisations or donor agencies as a useful programme for actor-related and relational transformation. The education programmes developed by the United Nations Educational, Scientific and Cultural Organization (UNESCO) are a representative example. Based on multiple pilot tests and the participation of experts from different cultural backgrounds, UNESCO has developed various manuals and toolkits for peace education, which are adopted by various governmental and nongovernmental organisations (NGOs). Key elements of such peace education programmes include conflict resolution skills, knowledge of conflict dynamics, human rights, democratic values and people's inner peace. In some cases, national governments facilitate their own training or education programmes for social reconciliation.

Nevertheless, mismanaged peace education may negatively impact on a society. An example of this is Rwanda's Ingando camps that were established in the aftermath of the genocide in 1994, to provide people (i.e. youths, ex-combatants and students) with intensive education on Rwandan history, social reconciliation and unity within the country. They initially attracted international attention as a peace education programme that presented creative modes of delivery. Reflecting their cultural tradition, they adopted jamboree-like campfires, collaborative labour work and informal conversation as key delivery modes. Nevertheless, as they have become more institutionalised by the government, many Ingandos are now being criticised as being utilised to disseminate political propaganda for the ruling party, the Rwandan Patriotic Front (Purdeková 2011).

Structural transformation

Structure refers to the pattern of relationships between the various disputants (e.g. social power structures and the international or regional environment), and these relationships are often affected and determined by the local sociopolitical arrangements and institutions. Social interactions, norms, rules, dominant patterns of discourse, distribution of resources and so on are important factors that can either foment or reduce conflict in a group. Hence, many contemporary peacebuilding programmes have attempted to address the social conditions that give rise to violence by changing the way that social resources are distributed (Burton 1990; Harrington and Merry 1988). For example, in the postwar period, the redistribution of land, which used to be considered a part of a rehabilitation programme, is now getting widely accepted as an important method of structural transformation (redistribution of productive wealth). In other cases, peacebuilders are making efforts to achieve their goals by enhancing the participation of local constituencies in the governance decision-making process. A large number of 'social democratisation' processes are in line with such efforts. However, since institution-focused programmes have demonstrated only limited utility in bringing about structural transformation, these projects have gradually adopted longer-term and more comprehensive methods that rely on the concepts of conflict transformation.

Cultural transformation

The cultural environment frequently affects the dynamics of conflicts in terms of initiation, mobilisation, deterrence and resolution. For instance, an overarching culture can be utilised to justify the violence or oppression against certain social groups (e.g. women, ethnic minorities or inhabitants of a particular region) and so may be an important root cause or catalyst of violent conflicts. In addition, the culture of human interaction (e.g. deal making, religious rituals and community activities) may influence the methods used to resolve conflicts. Therefore, identifying and responding to the cultural patterns that contribute to violent conflicts is important.

'Culture of violence' is an especially prominent cultural factor that prevents progress in peacebuilding in most postwar societies. Chronic conflicts usually lead to pervasive mutual mistrust and the disappearance of cultural traditions. In addition, prolonged and extreme violence in civil wars bring about two contradictory psychological symptoms: leaderships' tolerance of violence and a tendency towards passive obedience among the constituencies.

Transformation of culture usually requires a long-term commitment, with the role of external mediators or peacebuilding being less significant. However, previous studies confirm that war culture at local levels has occasionally been addressed with support from external actors within a relatively short time period. For instance, the intertribal conflicts over water in South Kordofan, Sudan, which had long been marked by a chain of attack and revenge, were significantly reduced by a series of workshops between the stakeholders. In this case, based on a common understanding of the negative impact of continued violence, representatives of the local tribes agreed with the demarcation of agreeable migration routes and to respect local administrative power (Oxfam 2014).

The practical utility of conflict transformation

The concept of conflict transformation has been widely welcomed by international donor agencies and peacebuilding practitioners as "a process that will make up for the inadequacies of mere resolution" (Mitchell 2002: 1). In fact, many contemporary peacebuilding initiatives adopt conflict transformation as their "central political objective" (Goetschel 2009: 98). Although there are various issues surrounding conflict transformation that could be discussed here, its utility is highlighted because conflict transformation addresses new characteristics of contemporary conflicts that conventional approach could not have dealt with.

First, many of the contemporary intrastate and interstate conflicts occur between actors whose power relations are asymmetrical, which is problematic for traditional concepts of conflict management and conflict resolution as they generally consider symmetric power relations only. For instance, the Israeli-Palestinian conflict could be described as one characterised by domination and resistance. While minority groups often adopt several strategies, including rebellion, to maximise their power, dominant groups can in return use repressive measures to maintain the status quo. Conflict transformation acknowledges such inequalities and uneven distribution of resources. It further argues that in such an environment, peace processes should aim at transforming the relationships characterised by domination and resistance into ones based on empowerment and cooperation (Maney, Ibrahim, Higgins and Herzog 2006).

Moreover, since interventions based on conflict resolution or conflict management approaches failed to address the root causes of conflicts, many civil conflicts developed into chronic conflicts. However, as a transformational approach understands that conflict resolution involves a series of ongoing processes in which people respond to the conflict, innovate and change, the concept of conflict transformation has been adopted as a more useful tool for promoting sustainable peace in war-prone countries. Conflict transformation theory contends that actors and interests are continuously changing according to the social, economic and political dynamics of societies and that the relationships and structures pertinent to particular conflicts can move towards being "honest, alive, and dynamically responsiv[e] to human needs, aspirations, and growth" (Väyrynen 1991: 4). In a sense, the purpose of conflict transformation is about minimising poorly functioning communication and maximising mutual understanding to promote positive changes. From this viewpoint, conflict resolution is not about terminating conflict through a single peace agreement but about gradual transformation (Lederach 2003).

The other contribution of conflict transformation is that it places emphasis upon the social context within which a conflict arises and escalates. Elements of the particular social context such as grievances (the root and immediate causes of conflict), relationships (interactions and networks) and structures (e.g. institutions, policies that govern people) are important factors affecting conflict situations, and peacebuilding approaches to contemporary conflicts therefore require comprehensive and systematic frameworks that leave behind the traditional "reframing of positions and the identification of win-win outcomes" (Miall 2004: 3). The aim of conflict transformation is therefore to modify relationships and social structures such that they eliminate the consequences of conflict and improve social cohesion. More specifically, approaches that aim at transforming the underlying causes of conflict tend to focus on two major areas, namely, changing power relations and reducing the level of uncertainty (Maney et al. 2006).

In addition to the contribution that conflict transformation has made to addressing the new characteristics of contemporary conflicts, it should be noted that it also produced a new peace intervention approach: conflict prevention. As the root causes of conflicts are embedded within the relationships between individuals and within the social and cultural contexts of society, some of the advocates of conflict transformation argue that violent conflicts might be prevented if we identify and transform these relational or social issues. The studies that have been undertaken by advocates of this approach discuss three main types of preventive action: early prevention aimed at addressing the situations that underpin the emergence of violent conflict; last minute prevention in pursuit of deterring the onset of violence; and post-conflict activities that aim to prevent the outbreak of further violence.

Human security

Since the late 1990s, the concepts relevant to human security have provided a highly important theoretical basis for exploring new directions of peacebuilding. Although the term 'human security' has been intermittently used in political debates since the 19th century, it was not until the 1970s that human well-being was considered as an element of security. Until this period, security referred to national security, where it is solely concerned with the interests of states. However, as a number of development planners began to pay more attention to local capacities and strategies for empowerment, discussions focusing on the factors associated with human development, economic growth and democracy became more prominent in the study and understanding of security. After Huhbubul Haq included the concept of human security in the 1994 UN Development Report, it has been adopted as a core security concept in the international security arena.

What are the core components of human security and how different is it from traditional security concepts? Most fundamentally, human security transfers the subject of security from the 'state' to the 'individual.' In other words, while protection of state territories and sovereignty had been the dominant objective of international security since the 19th century, human security shifts the focus to persons (Alkire 2003; Richmond 2007). In line with this perspective, the 1994 UN Development report states:

> The concept of security has for too long been interpreted narrowly: as security of territory from external aggression, or as protection of national interests in foreign policy or as global security from the threat of a nuclear holocaust. It has been related more to nation-states than to people . . . who sought security in their daily lives. For many of them, security symbolizes protection from the threat of disease, hunger, unemployment, crime, social conflict, political repression and environmental hazards.
>
> (UNDP 1994: 22)

Accordingly, a wide range of issues were included as security issues, including financial crisis, HIV/AIDS, crime, inadequate health care, water shortages and pollution (McIntosh and Hunter 2010; UNDP 1994: 22). Sen summarises the scope of human security issues as follows:

> The insecurities that threaten human survival or the safety of daily life, or imperil the natural dignity of men and women, or expose human beings to the uncertainty of disease

and pestilence, or subject vulnerable people to abrupt penury related to economic down-turns demand that special attention be paid to the dangers of sudden deprivation.

(Sen 2003: 8)

In order to address such security threats, human security concepts call for institutionalised (not episodic), responsive (not rigid) and preventive (not reactive) responses. While traditional security debates focus on the management of interstate relations, human security focuses constructing peace through the introduction of social, political and economic reforms. Although the state remains the primary security provider, the human security approach demands the participation of more diverse actors at various levels to ensure security protection. In addition, through its appreciation of the interrelation that exists between various threats, it demonstrates the necessity for more comprehensive, interdisciplinary and holistic approaches towards security issues (Kerkkänen 2009).

The fundamental concepts of human security underpin its three core assumptions on post-conflict reconstruction planning. First, conflict analysis frameworks based on human security regard local people not only as the objects of security issues but also as the subjects. The idea is that although externally imposed institutions may play strong roles for a short period, social changes can be made only when local communities perceive that the changes are beneficial to them. Moreover, it is held that local people have the best knowledge of what should be achieved and how to pursue these goals. As a result, activities based on local participation are central to human security approaches. Second, human security pays attention to the root causes of conflict embedded in the society, such as social exclusion, horizontal inequality and structural violence, rather than the immediate sources of the violence. Thus, human security emphasises the importance of promoting preventive actions, the removal of structural repression and social reconciliation. Third, while it recognises the contribution of the liberal peace institutions (e.g. the state, democracy and the market economy) to securing stable peace, human security regards such institutions (and their strength) as a means of protecting citizens rather than the end goal of peacebuilding. These changes have had a major influence on contemporary peacebuilding operations. A statement made by the UN in 2005 summarises these elements well: "We will not enjoy development without security, we will not enjoy security without development, and we will not enjoy either without respect for human rights" (UNSG 2005).

Over the past ten years, however, a number of criticisms have been raised on the comprehensiveness of the concept of human security. While some academics argue that "once anything that generates anxiety or threatens the quality of life in some respects becomes labelled a 'security problem,' the field risks losing all focus" (Freedman 1998: 53), others point out that its definition is too expansive and vague to be applicable in practical programmes and academic discourse (Paris 2001). Furthermore, a review of past discourse on human security reveals that academics have been arbitrary in setting the criteria for human security threats (Alkire 2003).

The significance of human security in peacebuilding

What does human security mean to us? What changes have been made in peacebuilding processes since the concept of human security was introduced? This section will explore these questions by considering the following three contributions that it has made.

In terms of conflict resolution, it provided an important normative basis for coercive third-party peace intervention. Until the middle of the 20th century, UN peace operations adhered to traditional principles of peacekeeping, which aimed to separate disputing parties by pro-viding physical buffer zones between them, to intervene only when all disputants agreed and not to use its military forces in aggressive ways. However, such passive interventions have been criticised for their ineffectiveness. The UN's inactivity on (or its inadequate reaction to) the massacre in Rwanda in 1994, in which at least 800,000 Tutsis were killed, is a good example. Since then, there have been calls for more active involvement by the international community in such cases.

Nevertheless, proactive military intervention sometimes caused normative problems as well. For instance, NATO's bombing of Yugoslavia in 1999 led to arguments about the legiti-macy of military intervention in a sovereign state. In fact, the principle of 'non-interference or non-intervention' in intra-sovereignty issues has traditionally been seen as a key principle of international relations, at least in the Western world. Since the 1648 Treaty of Westphalia, sovereign states have been respected as the fundamental units of international relations, have been deemed free to exercise absolute control over their internal affairs and have been viewed as enjoying equal status in the international arena.

It has been difficult, therefore, for supporters of international peace to find normative grounds to justify coercive peace intervention. However, after the concept of human security had been widely accepted, antihumanitarian actions began to be recognised as a security issue that is the concern of other sovereign states, and that the international community has the rights and responsibility to respond to major human rights violations. For instance, the Inter-national Commission on Intervention and State Sovereignty (ICISS), which was proposed by the UN and sponsored by the Canadian government, released a comprehensive report in 2001 called *Responsibility to Protect* that marked another milestone in the changing direction of international peace-supporting operations. The report argued that cross-border interven-tions on genocides or near-genocidal actions should not only be permitted, but are morally obligatory. The main arguments contained in the report were adopted as UN Security Council Resolution No. 1674 in 2006 (McIntosh and Hunter 2010).

Second, as regards post-conflict peacebuilding and long-term development, human secu-rity has transformed the ways in which peacebuilding projects are perceived, conceived, planned and implemented. Human security effectively adopted the various strands and dis-courses of peacebuilding programmes, which had traditionally been treated as humanitarian assistance measures delivered on the basis of good will, as 'security' issues – the core agenda for the international community. Although the provision of security and stability is still rec-ognised as a priority, the achievement of welfare goals ranging from immediate basic needs and public service delivery to job security through employment creation and poverty allevia-tion have emerged as a core part of peacebuilding. For instance, the UN declared eight humanitarian issues as its most important Millennium Development Goals in 2000. In addi-tion, to address the erosion of social trust, peacebuilding programmes emphasise the impor-tance of reconciliation and coexistence.

The roles of nonstate actors in the implementation of peacebuilding have been significantly widened. As there is a wide range of security issues that postwar states or failed states are unable to cover, states increasingly regarded nonstate actors such as humanitarian actors, NGOs, private corporations and individual activists as their peacebuilding partners. Further-more, in cases where humanitarian intervention by states was likely to raise the issue of legitimacy, the deployment of nonstate actors was considered a useful alternative.

Third, human security opened a new window of opportunity to address the weaknesses of the peacebuilding programmes based on the liberal peace ideas. Human security has become accepted as a core element of 'donor-centred' approaches due to its stress on the importance of focusing on the local context, reflecting local needs and strengthening local capacity. Thus, in many recent post-conflict recovery programmes, the local population is encouraged to take the lead in the 'planning' process rather than relying on external models. As regards 'institution-based' projects, new analytical frameworks that put individuals and communities (not institutions) at the centre of the analysis have been suggested. In terms of coordination, since previous liberal peace projects focusing on individual mandates demonstrated significant coordination limitations, recent programmes recognise the interconnectedness of the issues and attempt to incorporate intersectoral integration based on coherence and the needs of local contexts.

Gender in conflict transformation

New approaches towards peacebuilding from 'transformative' perspectives enable contemporary postwar reconstruction programmes to respect and reflect the interests and views of various social actors that have long been marginalised in such procedures. In particular, integration of gender perspectives in peacebuilding has emerged as a crucial agenda, and both academics and peacebuilding practitioners have attempted to achieve this objective.

First, a group of studies highlights that the needs and interests of women that are distinct from those of men should be integrated into peacebuilding programmes. Although violent conflict and political insecurity affect all social groups, their impact on women in most conflict-affected societies is usually stronger and longer than on men regardless of "the context-relevant peculiarities of each post-war situation" (Schnabel and Tabyshalieva 2012: 13).

For instance, during conflicts, sexual violence against women may seriously impact on women physically, psychologically and socially (Porter 2007). In countries like Kosovo and Rwanda, rape was utilised as a tool in ethnic conflict, while many young girls in Angola and Sierra Leone were forced into 'jungle marriages' or 'AK-47 marriages.' Moreover such violence had cultural consequences that including being "shunned, ostracized and considered unmarriageable" (Schnabel and Tabyshalieva 2012: 13), and women were frequently subject to 'crimes of honour' (Welchman and Hossain 2005). In many more cases, even if women manage to avoid being the subjects of direct violence, they are still likely to be in full charge of the survival of their families if the men were dead or wounded during the conflicts.

Even after the termination of violent conflicts, challenging social conditions such as insecurity, normalised violence, poverty and economic deprivation usually have more impact on women than men. For instance, women are generally considered easier targets for paramilitary groups that continue to terrorise civilians; women are also forced to be involved in prostitution or subject to human trafficking. Moreover, many traditional institutions and societal structures that grant women lower social status restrict their chances for managing their economic and social life. Accordingly, more gender-sensitive approaches toward peacebuilding are called for, in order to develop more appropriate responses to the social needs in the aftermath of conflicts.

Second, another important strand of discussion considers the unique roles of women in peacebuilding operations. Although women have always been the central figures in nurturing peace in their families, communities and societies, several studies argue that their potential to play critically important roles in peacebuilding have been largely neglected in contemporary peace operations (Olonisakin, Barnes and Ikpe 2011; Sherriff and Barnes 2008).

There are numerous examples of women peacebuilders' contributions. For example, Porter (2007) and Anderlini (2007) highlight prominent roles of women in bridging social divisions/

polarisations, enabling political arrangements to be more inclusive and nurturing restorative justice and social reconciliation. To present a more concrete example, the Women in Peace-building Network (WIPNET) in Liberia has been involved in the implementation of the Accra 2003 Comprehensive Peace Accords. WIPNET's activities focused on dissemination of detailed information on the accords to the public who did not have proper mechanisms for information sharing, hosting workshops to discuss how to implement the agreements, moni-toring the progress of peace implementation, and campaigning for accelerating the disarma-ment process in the country. Moreover, because many women were not interested in participating in the election in 2005, WIPNET organised volunteer groups to encourage women's voting (Bekoe and Parajon 2007). In addition, the Cambodian Women's Develop-ment Agency (CWDA) in Cambodia focuses on addressing the challenges facing women in their societies by undertaking vocational training, microcredit lending, campaigns against domestic violence, projects related to women's health (HIV/AIDS in particular) and other public advocacy activities. The Cambodian Prostitute Union established by CWDA offered services that the women involved in the sex industry can use to protect themselves from human rights abuses and improve their lives generally (CWDA n.d.).

However, much larger numbers of women's peace-advocating activities have been con-ducted in informal, unofficial, less visible (in public), less tangible ways; these have not been properly integrated into mainstream peacebuilding activities. Moreover, various social restrictions and traditional/cultural limitations on women's social participation have pre-vented such women's peacebuilding from mobilising wider social interest and developing into more institutionalised movements (Olonisakin et al. 2011; Porter 2007). Hence, the question, "How can peacebuilding programmes encourage and support women in conflict affected countries to play bigger roles in peacebuilding?" has recently been explored in many academic discussions and international organisations' seminal documents.

Third, more recent studies have begun to revisit somewhat simplistic assumptions that many discussions were built on. For instance, gender in peacebuilding should not be tied to "simplistic dichotomies of men as perpetrators and women as victims" (Myrtinnen, Naujoks and El-Bushra 2014: 8). In relation to this, there is a gradually increasing number of seminal documents that recognises sexual violence victimising men and the challenges to gender minorities (UNSC 2013a). Other studies emphasise that 'women' are by no means a homog-enous group and women's challenges vary according to socioeconomic and cultural con-texts. As Myrtinnen, Naujoks and El-Bushra (2014: 9) mention, the social conditions of "a middle-aged, married, urban, upper-middle-class, high-caste woman in Nepal" will be sig-nificantly different from those which "a young, unmarried, rural, low-income Dalit woman" has to deal with.

Furthermore, studies also warn of the risk of automatically identifying women as innocent victims, pacifists or carers. In fact, women in many conflict-affected societies have played diverse roles that range from victims to primary perpetrators, material supporters of soldiers, justice executers and social healers (Alison 2006; Bouta 2005; Sjoberg 2010). Thus, such simplified identification (frequently based on unproven assumptions) may strengthen con-ventional stereotyping of women's roles. For instance, the narrative of "men are patriots, and the women are mothers; the former bear the national duty of defense, the latter that of pro-creation" are commonly found in early debates on gender-related issues (Rosenberg-Friedman 2003: 121). Moreover, although the identification of women as pacifists was utilised to increase women's roles in many peacebuilding activities, such narratives may restrict women to a limited range of social roles, mainly as domestic carers, informal social organisers or passive supporters of male-oriented peacebuilding programmes (Dogra 2011).

Reflecting these concerns, more recent peacebuilding activities pay more careful attention to gender issues. A particularly important impetus for improving field practice was provided by the UN Security Council Resolution 1325, which was adopted in 2000. The resolution was one of the earliest official documents endorsed by the UN that recognised women's security concerns in situations of armed conflicts and called for women's needs to be better reflected in resettlement programmes. Moreover, the resolution acknowledged the important role of women in all stages of peace-supporting activities, from conflict prevention to post-conflict reconstruction, and called for the equal participation and full involvement of women in peacebuilding. It highlighted that women's roles should be increased in the 'decision making' process as well as in field implementation (UNSC 2000). Resolution 1325 was followed by other Security Council Resolutions that supplemented it. For instance, Resolution 1820 (UNSC 2008) officially acknowledged sexual violence as a key issue of international security while Resolution 1888 (UNSC 2009) clarified the measures for addressing the problems recognised by Resolution 1820. Specifically, it called for enhanced systems for monitoring sexual violence and applying legal responses to the identified violence.

In response to this, the UN Department of Peacekeeping Operations adopted new guidelines for gender-based operations in their military peacekeeping actions in 2004, and a UN system-wide action plan on gender issues was released in 2005. Regional organisations like the EU, the Organisation for Security and Cooperation in Europe (OSCE) and the International Conference on the Great Lakes Region (ICGLR) were particularly active in implementing and supporting gender-balanced policies (Barnes 2011). One example is the EU Guidelines on Violence against Women and Girls and Combating All Forms of Discrimination against Them that was adopted in EU-funded programmes since its publication in 2008.

Nevertheless, although gender-sensitive approaches are emphasised in most internally driven peacebuilding operations implemented since the mid-2000s, the reflection of gender issues in actual field practice is still far from the goals proposed in UNSC Resolution 1325, (i.e. advocating gender equality, women's empowerment and women's human rights). Although the limitations in legal and institutional provisions for gender-based peacebuilding need to be addressed (Olonisakin et al. 2011), it should be noted that a large number of women's empowerment programmes implemented during the late 2000s failed due to local operators' ignorance or misunderstanding of gender mainstreaming (Sherriff and Barnes 2008).

For instance, while the absolute majority of the field practitioners are male, they were requested to operate or support women's empowerment programmes without having any particular education or practical training on gender issues. Moreover, although mainstreaming women in many conflict-affected societies cannot be achieved without enthusiastic support from the societies' male leaders, international organisations tended only to target women's groups. In this sense, the development of gender-sensitive peacebuilding at this stage needs a dual approach that involves institutional supplements for overcoming social hurdles as well as practical measures to help field practitioners. Reflecting this view, most recent discussions in the UN call for deployment of gender expertise from the early phase of postwar reconstruction onwards, and for constant consultations with women (UNSC 2013b).

Case study: promotion of locally driven peacebuilding in Colombia and Kenya

Reflecting the themes of conflict transformation, a large number of programmes recently implemented in conflict-affected societies attempt to address more fundamental issues that caused violence. Moreover, as the limited abilities of external interveners in handling such fundamental issues have become evident in many early models of peacebuilding, efforts to encourage local actors to develop their own ways of peacebuilding are increasing in field practice. This section examines the promotion of local ownership in a few peacebuilding programmes in Colombia and Kenya.

Since there is no clear-cut definition of local ownership that all peacebuilding actors agree on, various versions of local ownership programmes exist in contemporary peacebuilding programmes. While some programmes pursue autonomous power/exclusive control by local actors, the majority aim to have the full involvement of local actors in post-conflict governance programmes. In this section, three representative examples of general trends are presented.

In many conflict-affected and/or fragile states, promotion of local ownership is much easier said than done. A large number of technical, structural and cultural barriers discourage local actors from taking more proactive peace initiatives which include risk of conflict resumption, lack of human resources, demolished infrastructure, severe war trauma and dependence on external aid. Hence, it is more common for external aiders to initially make plans for nurturing local capacity and then to transfer ownership in a later period. Due to this tendency, some critics argue that local ownership is empty rhetoric or just another 'buy-in' principle to justify the dominance of international actors (Chesterman 2007; Donais 2009; Krause and Jütersonke 2005).

Nevertheless, there certainly are a large number of examples that show something close to the ideal type of local ownership. The case studies from Colombia and Kenya are two of these, although there are a large number of challenges that these initiatives have yet to overcome.

The Peasant Farmer Association of the Cimitarra River Valley (ACVC) in Colombia represents an example of a locally owned peace initiative with the 'accompaniment' of external supporters. These peasants had been the victims of Colombia's sixty-year armed conflict. As, for various reasons, they were targeted by both left-wing guerrilla groups and the government, in the mid-1990s the peasants organised their own associations to protect themselves from such violence. ACVC is one of the associations and it carries out a number of social, political and community works in nearly 120 small rural communities in the Magdalena Medio region of Colombia. It has approximately 25,000 members who are small-scale farmers (*campesinos*).

The most urgent issue for them is surviving such physical violence perpetrated mainly by the paramilitary group – United Self-Defence Forces of Colombia. ACVC has been facilitating the sharing of the information between peasants, organising collective actions for self-protection and negotiating with the government regarding future actions. In addition to community networking, the association also focuses on education, respect for human rights and the improvement of the lives of traditional small farmers, as well as creating favourable conditions for structural changes needed in the Colombian countryside. Apart from these issues, the Peasant Reserve Zone (PRZ) is a key initiative of this association. The primary goal of the PRZ is to make land transfer much harder in reserve zones so that the inhabitants of these areas are protected from land grabs and are able to benefit from rural development efforts. Land transfer to a small number of wealthy people, as well as relocation to escape from guerrilla groups, has been a big issue in this area. Hence, by organising an association, the peasants decided not to leave or sell their lands. Instead, they are determined to share information on the potential risks and skills on cultivation in order to stabilise the peasant economy.

Although a number of external actors, such as UK-based Peace Brigades International (PBI), have acted as advocates for this association, their roles are limited to accompanying people or organisations under threat, making regular visits to conflict zones, distributing information about the evolution of the conflict, lobbying and public relations work with representatives of the international community as well as with civil and military authorities, and campaigning for international support. In other words, while PBI supports ACVC's peace activities, they do not really become involved in the process of making decisions.

Their programmes are still far from being altogether successful, although ACVC won Colombia's National Peace Award in 2010. However, initiatives such as ACVC have eventually become part of more national-level organisations, such as Development and Peace Programmes and Laboratories of Peace.

Kenya's adoption of traditional justice forms in their judicial systems is an early-phase attempt that shows how local people can utilise their own traditions for advocating human rights and fostering sustainable peace. In Kenya, just as in many other countries, all citizens are in principle entitled to access the state law systems as a fundamental human right. However, due to geographical and financial constraints, many people in rural areas cannot access the formal justice systems due to high costs, distances to courthouses, complicated court procedures, language barriers and understaffed judicial officers. Thus, traditional community justice systems (TJS) are being utilised as alternative methods of conflict resolution in many areas of the country.

The forms of TJS vary from community to community and have various names. In most of the communities, however, TJS members are predominantly elders drawn from the community and the members are mostly elected by the community, but in some cases they are appointed by the chiefs. Usually, the members are men only, although there are a few exceptions. Moreover, at the village and community levels, TJS mostly deal with family and neighbourhood disputes: marital conflicts, parental misconduct, juvenile misconduct, abusive behaviour and boundary disputes. They also hear petty criminal offences such as theft and assaults. Although proceedings themselves are not very different from what we generally find in the law court, one key distinction is its speed and simplicity. Usually, the decision is made within a day of the hearing. Moreover, people do not refer to the specific legal provisions. The decisions are made based on the common sense that is widely accepted within the communities.

The contemporary case studies present both strengths and limitations. TJS provide local people with opportunities for accessing justice within a short period of time, in forms that they are more familiar with, and with less practical barriers like language and financial costs. Nevertheless, they tend to present biased views against women and poorer people and apply inappropriate measures for enforcement or punishment (e.g. the beating of the offender by community people) (FIDA-Kenya 2013).

A number of Kenyan and international organisations like the Open Society Initiative for Eastern Africa (OSIEA) have supported a large number of people involved in traditional justice. One key activity is sharing information on human rights and gender equality with elders in local communities who usually take the roles of judges in traditional justice. However, their roles are limited to information sharing and giving consultancy services rather than proposing the direction in which to operate such justice systems.

Conclusion

In summary, conflict transformation differs from previous approaches in that it emphasises the importance of transforming the unequal relationships between social actors, regards the promotion of peace as a process of gradual transformation of conflicts rather than merely their termination, and acknowledges the importance of social contexts in peacebuilding. As associated concepts, this chapter introduced the concepts of human security, focusing on its definition and its contribution to the development of contemporary peacebuilding. Human security differs from traditional security in that it includes 'the individual's well-being' as a core item of the security agenda. Finally, the chapter discussed how gender issues are being raised and reflected in both academic discourse and field practice in the context of conflict transformation.

As discussed earlier, conflict transformation pursues the changes of both individuals and social systems and emphasises the interrelatedness of all social elements. The peacebuilding programmes undertaken based on this approach tend to deal with social issues comprehensively. This approach indeed expanded the scope of peacebuilding to develop more sustainable peace and to increase justice and equality in war-torn societies. Nevertheless, from a practical viewpoint, recent peacebuilding programmes tend to be massive in size, require the involvement of a large number of participants, and most importantly demand more resources. Since the national or local actors in the war-affected societies do not possess such material and human resources, these changes unavoidably make contemporary peacebuilding more reliant on external actors.

Observing the discourse of different approaches towards peacebuilding and their critiques, some people may consider contemporary peace-supporting activities involve too many problems. It is true, in a sense, that there are a large number of issues to be addressed. However, in another sense, it is a sign of the constant development in the fields of practice and academic research to seek more effective methods for peacebuilding. International peace activities have rapidly expanded both quantitatively and qualitatively within a short period of time. The conceptual shifts from conflict management to conflict resolution and conflict transformation that have been made in the last twenty years are a striking example of this. It should be noted that such expansion was made through many trials and errors, and that vigorous reflection on previous errors as well as sustained efforts to identify new types of challenges have produced extensive critical exchanges in the associated academic discourse. Based on the resultant critiques, new directions for building sustainable peace in conflict-affected societies are being sought. In the near future, people may observe another exciting moment within which the latest conceptual foundations like conflict transformation and peacebuilding are replaced by a new theme for further effective innovation.

Discussion questions

•   What types of practical programmes can be implemented to promote relational transformation in intergroup conflicts?
•   Some studies argue that the concept of 'human security' is useful to criticise conventional peacebuilding but unrealistic as a means to forming alternatives. If you agree, why is this so? If not, why not?
•   What are the major obstacles to women's participation in peacebuilding processes?

Recommended reading

Du Toit, A.M. (1998) 'Building Cultural Synergy and Peace in South Africa'. *Journal of Social Development in Africa* 13 (1): 9–21.

Fischer, M. (2006) *Civil Society in Conflict Transformation: Ambivalence, Potentials, and Challenges.* Berlin: Berghof Research Center for Constructive Conflict Management.

Miall, H. (2004) *Conflict Transformation: A Multi-Dimensional Task.* Berlin: Berghof Research Center for Constructive Conflict Management.

Paris, R. (2001) 'Human Security: Paradigm Shift or Hot Air?' *International Security* 26 (2): 87–102.

Porter, E. (2007) *Peacebuilding: Women in International Perspective.* London: Routledge.

Part III

The practice of peacebuilding

7   Political and security peacebuilding

Based on the analysis of peacebuilding from theoretical and procedural perspectives presented in Part I and Part II, the three chapters in Part III will provide more detailed information on how field practice in contemporary peacebuilding is currently undertaken. After a short overview of the scope of relevant peacebuilding sectors, each chapter will introduce a few selected programmes detailing the key goals of operations, specific projects implemented pursuing these goals, the roles of external actors in the process and the programmes' major achievements and limitations.

First, Chapter 7 examines the issues relevant to political and security peacebuilding. The two key words that define peacebuilding in these sectors are stabilisation and legitimacy. Reform initiatives in this arena are conducted based on the assumption that weak and ineffective state institutions can pose a serious obstacle to lasting peace and development. Most conflict-affected countries experience various problems related to security and political issues that increase the risk of conflict resumption, such as unstable state borders, illegal arms trade, poor political leadership, high levels of corruption, insensitive budget controls and the like. Hence, one of the primary objectives of postwar peacebuilding is the transformation of political (governmental) and security systems to make them more effective, accountable and professional, and so enable more stable and inclusive public activities to prosper.

Such stable security and accountable governance have been considered a prerequisite for durable peace and further economic development since the progress in other peacebuilding sectors cannot be expected without having a reliable and stable security and political environment. For instance, long-term economic investment cannot be encouraged unless the risk of the resumption of hostilities is minimised. Moreover, social reconciliation is inconceivable in cases where there is ongoing oppression from government military forces. Hence, throughout the history of international peacebuilding, the stabilisation of security and political governance in war-affected societies and the improvement of the effectiveness and accountability of the military sector have been recognised as a core part of the peacebuilding process from the early period.

This chapter will explore more details of the reconstruction programmes in security and political sectors and focuses on:

* The scope of contemporary peacebuilding in security and political sectors
* Disarmament, demobilisation and reintegration of ex-combatants (DDR)
* Security sector reform (SSR)
* Electoral assistance
* Public administration reform
* New forms of security and political peacebuilding.

Moreover, of the various issues that create limitations for contemporary peacebuilding, this chapter will pay particular attention to peacebuilding's primary focus on institutional and technical assistance.

The scope of security and political peacebuilding

It was not until the mid-1990s that the complexity of political reform and security reassurance in post-conflict societies attracted the attention of the international community. Prior to this, the scope of political and security peacebuilding was very limited to the measures for border control, demilitarisation of ex-combatants and the promotion of a prodemocracy political structure.

Nevertheless, the challenges in the post–Cold War era became more complex as nonmilitary issues such as political, economic, societal and environmental problems increasingly threatened people's security and safety. Alongside this, globalisation and the emergence of many 'failed states' weakened the role of states in both the security and political sectors. In order to respond such new conditions, the concepts relevant to human security that emphasised the protection of individuals and social groups in addition to states were proactively adopted from the mid-1990s. Since then, the reform of political and security sectors was understood as an integral part of the conceptual framework of international peace and the scope of peacebuilding has steadily increased.

Security peacebuilding

Traditional forms of security peacebuilding are based on more narrowly defined state-centric concepts of security and primarily concern the management, oversight and supervision of military forces. Specifically, they can be categorised into four areas:

1   Traditional projects related to controlling armed elements, which include upholding ceasefires, disarming military forces and demobilising troops;
2   Programmes for constructing or reforming national security institutions, including the national police, the army, intelligence agencies and nonstate armed elements;
3   Projects for protecting civilians, such as disposal of small arms and landmines, the regulation of state power and the construction of a poverty relief system;
4   Programmes for the protection of external security such as those dealing with controlling state borders, combating human trafficking and screening the drug trade.

Successful implementation of these programmes is particularly important in the earlier phases of peacebuilding. As a key direction of security peacebuilding, the UN set its goal so as to let the security sector "be subject to the same standards of efficiency, equity and accountability as any other [public] services" (Kofi Annan, cited from Hänggi 2010: 80).

In practice, the operation of security peacebuilding programmes can be highly complex due to the nature of national security. The challenges to security stabilisation in conflict-affected societies are frequently affected by four interrelated issues: chaos in postwar societies, long-extended authoritarian and military rule, an underdeveloped economy and high criminality. Moreover, the performance of security sectors is directly connected to the wider governance system in the concerned society such as judicial institutions, private industry, local communities and civil society. Hence, a plan for security peacebuilding needs to reflect a variety of concerns and issues at the same time and many programmes have failed to achieve their intended goals due to such complexities.

To address this complexity properly, an increasing number of security peacebuilding programmes have become more comprehensive and lengthier. For these programmes, the goal is "the provision of security in a fragile environment which could be characterized as no longer being in the throes of conflict" (Hänggi 2010: 81). They include less formal dimensions of security such as power structures at local levels, relationships between informal traditional authorities, sustainability of the justice system, and community-based security-assurance systems (in addition to the traditional security reform).

Political peacebuilding

Political peacebuilding aims to facilitate political processes that accommodate more inclusive dialogue between different social actors, promote social reconciliation and nurture local actors' conflict management capacity. To achieve this goal, the programmes implemented in many war-affected countries include:

1   Interim measures for stabilising political apparatus in the aftermath of armed conflicts, such as arrangements for power sharing, establishment of transitional authority, inclusion of former military factions into political activities;
2   Provision of institutional and procedural support for building more legitimate and democratic political system which include implementation of regular election, reform of the decision-making systems within central/regional/local governments;
3   Programmes supporting administrative reform to make the governmental administration more professional, transparent and accountable, such as downsizing, centralising policy-making systems, decentralising delivery systems and coordinating contradictory and redundant interdepartmental relations;
4   Material and advisory support for developing civil society, including human rights advocacy mechanisms and civil education programmes.

Many of these traditional programmes, however, have paid attention to the institutional dimensions only. For instance, the promotion of democracy in the earlier UN peacebuilding programmes in El Salvador and Cambodia mostly focused on conducting the first postwar elections without serious interruption and violence. Thus, the primary focus on them was made on technical aspects of 'election,' which include identification of electorates, education of election process and security arrangements for supporting people's voting. Although the follow-up political reforms concerned a wider range of issues, the issues that these reforms attempted to address were mainly about the governmental institutions such as ineffective organisational structure, unprofessional civil servants, political influence on judicial bodies and the like.

In case there had been a mediated peace agreement with a third-party intervention such as was the case with Bosnia-Herzegovina, constitutional reform can easily prolong the process and become a new platform for the politics of war (see Box 7.1). In such an environment the

---

Box 7.1 Lessons learned from international post-conflict governance and administration experiences

Based on Richard Caplan's review of four international administrations – Eastern Slavonia, Bosnia-Herzegovina, Kosovo and Timor-Leste – Box 7.1 identifies a number of lessons learned from these experiences. Governance in post-conflict environments

would include a wide range of interventions: constitutional design, democracy and elections, the establishment of watchdogs and local governance structures. In a classical tripartite division of power – executive, legislature and judiciary – the challenge is to structure a governance system that can function sustainably by providing democratic accountability between different levels of decision making, ensuring a system of checks and balances over decision makers and protecting the rights of all in the country. Constitutional reform tends to be the most important challenge in initiating the reconstruction of governance as this forms a guiding framework for all other governance related initiatives.

The most critical issues for constitutional reform concern when to start the process, how much time can be allowed for its completion, and how this process should actually take place. In many cases, constitutional reform needs to be started as early as possible. As this process requires time, however, interim administrations have been formed in a number of recent cases such as Kosovo, Timor-Leste, Afghanistan and Iraq, so that there would be an executive to run the country until the organisation of the first parliamentary elections. However, it is at this point that different post-conflict scenarios prove quite decisive in the restructuring of governance. If the peace accord was signed at the end of a decisive victory by one of the belligerent groups, as in the cases of Eritrea or Timor-Leste, then the reconstruction of governance and constitutional reform should proceed without any major difficulties.

Compared to others, the mission in Eastern Slavonia was modest in size and scope. The mission in Timor-Leste was a nation state – building exercise, and while both the Bosnian and Kosovo cases had the same element, they were politically much more ambiguous. The case of Bosnia was plagued by factionalism, while the Kosovo case had to rely on an unclear framework in terms of the future of the province. For a number of different reasons, all faced great difficulties in establishing functioning post-conflict governance. For example, in Timor-Leste a low level of human resource and institutional capacities at local level meant that although there was an active 'Timorization' process for handing over the administration to local authorities, the governance actually resides with the international community.

Partisanship was a factor in the way Kosovars were selected for their posts in the joint administration. At a more general level, the interim administration in Kosovo was slow overall and ineffective in responding to the governance needs of the province. While the interim government had to establish the entire governance process from scratch and to achieve this in a multipillar organisational system, few government officers or international advisors had previous administration experience in post-conflict environments and did not know much about Kosovo. There were also great variations in the achievements under different pillars. For example, while the return of displaced populations under the guidance of the United Nations High Commissioner for Refugees (UNHCR) took place relatively smoothly, the economic revitalisation which has been under the responsibility of the European Union is yet to be resolved.

In the case of Bosnia-Herzegovina, the international administration suffered from a series of contradictory policies. For example, while the international community was a great advocate of democratic governance in the country, its high representative took a series of unilateral policy decisions and then forced the governing bodies to adopt them, with the threat that these democratically elected representatives would be dismissed from public office if they failed to comply. It should be noted that some of those decisions had to be made in order to overcome stalemate and political bickering among Serbs, Croats and Bosniacs on such important matters as adopting the use of nonethnic licence plates, currency, restructuring constitutional commissions and so forth.

These experiences also show that tight timetables designed according to external prerequisites do not reflect the reality faced by many post-conflict reconstruction initiatives. For example, the return of refugees and internally displaced persons (IDPs) to their homes of origin was mandated by the Dayton Accords. However, this did not succeed in its objective according to the timetable envisaged by the international community, as those populations were simply not prepared to take the risk of going back 'home,' in most cases as a minority return. Some of the other lessons learned from these experiences were the lack of coordination among international actors, limited means of resources for tasks undertaken, shortcomings in training local capacities and limited means of accountability to local populations.

Source: Caplan (2002).

international community needs to assist local actors closely, as there would always be some spoilers who are prepared to derail the peace process for their own ends. In contrast, a war can be terminated with no peace agreement signed by all belligerents, as was the case with Afghanistan. This scenario is also a highly sensitive environment for constitutional reform, and the situation can be much more complex because the third-party intervention occurs by means of occupation which has been the case for Iraq.

Although there are major variations among the preceding scenarios, it is interesting to note that in almost all recent constitutional reform experiences, the process was rapid and did not involve extensive negotiations among the parties concerned. For example, the case of Timor-Leste proved to be straightforward, as expected, and took around a year to complete. In the Timorese case there was a great desire from local actors to take control of governance from the UN interim administration as quickly as possible. In the Afghan case, the process of less than a year involved the participation of traditional decision-making structures – the loya jirga – in order to bring a certain level of legitimacy to the interim administration, which was placed and funded by the US and its allies after the 2001 Bonn Agreement. Although both cases represent a rapid process of constitutional reform, having a good level of social consensus in Timor-Leste helped to compensate for the lack of participation, but the process in Afghanistan had to turn a blind eye to a wide range of deep-rooted sociopolitical conflicts.

In other words, recent peacebuilding experiences indicate that the determination to complete the constitutional reform process as quickly as possible, in order to increase the legitimacy of the initial governance structures being installed by the international community, represents a major opportunity loss for war-torn countries. If dealt with properly and given adequate time, the constitutional reform process can be a great opportunity for deliberative participation which can address the deep-rooted divisions of a war-affected country. One of the most critical issues in this process would be the protection of minority rights through constitutional and other legislative guarantees. In the case of South Africa, the reform process took more than seven years and involved comprehensive and intensive negotiations. As a result, the country now benefits from a constitution that is one of the most progressive and inclusive constitutions in the world, which provides an important guarantee for the sustainability of peace.

Disarmament, demobilisation and reintegration of ex-combatants (DDR)

The laying down of arms by former belligerent groups and their acceptance of the terms of peace accords are considered the "minimum conditions of a peaceful transition" (Arnson and Azpuru 2003: 200) and the importance of DDR has been emphasised in many previous peacebuilding processes due to the following reasons. First, successful DDR is essential to prevent a return to conflict. Ineffective control of weapons can provide important tools for further military combat or general crimes. In addition, demobilised soldiers might cause serious social problems and jeopardise the entire peace processes if they are unable to be effectively reintegrated into society (Özerdem 2008). In such cases, employment and vocational training can help to disconnect former soldiers from potential peace-spoiling activities. In fact, various post-conflict economic and social insecurities in El Salvador, Nicaragua and Timor-Leste can be traced to inadequate reintegration efforts (Buxton 2008).

From a positive viewpoint, successfully reintegrated ex-combatants can make important contributions to sustainable development in war-affected societies. In many cases, the early implementation of DDR can also be utilised as a litmus test for the sincere commitment of all ex-belligerent parties participating in peacebuilding programmes (Jeong 2005). Moreover, well-organised vocational training programmes can help to turn former fighters into a source of new skilled labour. Additionally, reintegration is a way of achieving 'compensatory justice' through the acknowledgment of ex-combatants' belief that they 'had performed their duty' to society. This is particularly relevant in cases of civil conflicts in which the fighting was largely about opposing repressive and authoritative governments. Reintegration is also understood as a form of humanitarian assistance to former warlords, based on the assumption that they too are a group of war victims.

DDR is a complex process that combines multilateral action programmes such as political negotiations, weapon disposal, humanitarian relief and the provision of training and a means to secure a livelihood. From a procedural perspective, it consists of three significant phases: disarmament, demobilisation and reintegration.

Disarmament usually takes place in the initial period of post-conflict peacebuilding. The programmes in this category pursue the systematic control and disposal of military weapons and deal with processes of collecting, documenting and removing various arms. In specific, it involves gathering armed forces at specified assembly areas and registering them (*encampment*) and collecting weapons from the soldiers. Effective security guarantee for disarmed combatants, control of personnel and verification of weapons are vital for successful DDR implementation. For instance, in Nicaragua, approximately 20,000 square kilometres (equivalent to the size of Slovenia or El Salvador) that had effectively been occupied by the resistance group was set as a 'security guarantee' area between 1990 and 1994.

Demobilisation of military troops is the formal and controlled discharge of active combatants and is often conducted alongside disarmament. After collecting arms from the combatants, a demobilisation process usually provides support packages that help the combatants resettle into society. Such support packages may include the provision of food, clothing and agricultural tools. In Nicaragua, every combatant who voluntarily disarmed received approximately US$50 in compensation. In addition, short-term literacy classes, social reinsertion education or cultural activities may take place during the demobilisation process.

Finally, once disarmament and demobilisation have been completed, the longer-term reintegration process begins. While disarmament and demobilisation are relatively short-term projects that mainly aim to remove armed forces, the reintegration process normally focuses on ways of assisting demilitarised ex-warlords and ex-combatants to settle into civilian life and reintegrate into communities. The reintegration programmes implemented in many contemporary peacebuilding processes can be categorised into three groups. First, vocational training and employment creation are longer-term strategies. Governments, international organisations, the private sector and nongovernmental organisations (NGOs) may collaborate in initiating local- or national-level industrial or commercial projects that may offer new jobs. Furthermore, bringing about reconciliation between former perpetrators and victims within local communities requires lengthy and constant efforts. Traditional or religious reconciliation rituals and workshop-styled collaboration programmes are employed in many peacebuilding processes. Finally, medical and rehabilitation services to disabled people are also provided as an important part of the reintegration process. As disabled ex-combatants normally have more limited opportunities to get jobs and to engage in public activities, carefully designed support packages are required.

Security sector reform (SSR)

The restructuring of security institutions is carried out with the intention of building up an accountable and effective security sector by forming a unified national army, adjusting the size of military forces and redesigning their internal structure. In addition to the provision of better security, the restructuring of the armed forces can provide a good opportunity to address issues of security performance. Successful reform of security institutions can also support social reconciliation, develop democratic governance and enhance political legitimacy. Hence, in contemporary security-sector reform, "an integrated, holistic system that encompasses related civilian structures and capacities" is being increasingly emphasised (Sedra 2013: 213). Although the approach to the restructuring of security institutions may differ according to the contexts of military conflicts and peacebuilding processes, the armed forces and police are two major objects of reform.

In terms of the restructuring of military forces, the main purposes are placing military forces under effective control of the national civilian leadership, creating and enhancing loyalty to the state and responsibility for the people, and reducing insecurity among social minority groups that had been underrepresented during or before the military conflicts. In order to achieve these goals, three types of programmes are frequently implemented.

The most common form is the integration of opposing military forces into a single national army. Such integration may reduce the possibilities of remobilisation and armed conflicts because the influence of former factional leaders is significantly reduced once troops have been relocated and placed under different commanders. However, since these units have fought against each other, overcoming the deep mistrust that many former opponents harbour towards each other frequently becomes a formidable barrier to the successful integration of forces.

Reducing the overall size of the national army is also frequently attempted. This is particularly common in countries where the governmental forces had committed war crimes (killings, kidnappings, ethnic cleansing and the like). For example, in El Salvador and Guatemala, the army's brutal human rights abuses were an important factor in encouraging many people to join the rebel movements. Thus, the reduction (or the purging) of notorious governmental forces is a fundamental goal of opposition movements in many countries. Nevertheless, the power wielded by the military in such cases tends to be considerable, and overcoming their resistance is a difficult challenge.

The recruitment of new soldiers from various cultural, social and economic backgrounds is another way of restructuring military forces. As many violent conflicts are caused by the oppression of certain groups by others, the recruiting of previously underrepresented groups (such as those defined by their ethnicity, geographical region, religion and political association) may ease social tensions by ensuring social diversity in a nation's armed forces.

Since the police may have had a negative influence on social stability and law and order in many war-affected societies, reform of the police force is considered another key aspect of security reconstruction. However, the reform of civilian police institutions frequently involves different priorities. Accountability is usually a primary concern of police reform. In many conflict-affected countries, the police force overtly serves and protects the interests of certain social groups (primarily the incumbent government leaders). Moreover, it frequently plays the role of a paramilitary group in the fight against rebel movements and commits anti-humanitarian acts. To address this problem, police reform attempts to 'civilise' the police force. In societies where violence has severely affected the lives of civilians, the establishment of a civil police force is important because it offers greater security for citizens and demonstrates an institutional commitment to the fostering of respect for human rights. It is therefore considered a precondition for democratic transition. The establishment of a national community-based police service brings the focus of attention to social policing issues rather than military-related operations.

A more frequently observed problem, however, is an underqualified policing service. For instance, the police forces in most sub-Saharan countries are "understaffed, underequipped, poorly trained, lacking modern administrative procedures, and corrupted" (Conflict Prevention Forum n.d.), and war-affected societies often need to professionalise the police force to improve its quality of performance. Methods commonly employed to restructure the police institution include the recentralisation of local police forces and the creation of appropriate administrative structures. Moreover, a range of measures to enhance human resources capacity, establish training programmes and institutions, and improve equipment, transportation and communication systems are also implemented in many peacebuilding programmes (see the case study later in this chapter for more details of security sector reform).

Electoral assistance

As discussed in Chapter 3, promoting a neutral political environment in which all people are free to choose their leadership has been a core agenda item of international peacebuilding. Moreover, a free and fair election is considered an important step in facilitating such an environment. Since many intrastate conflicts are caused or exacerbated by the lack of a participatory political system, facilitating free, fair and inclusive elections in which all constituencies, without discrimination, can participate fully is a necessary condition for stable peace in war-affected societies. By allowing constituencies to select their leadership based on individual, free and fair voting, the new authority can gain more legitimate power and people can have stronger influence on the authority's policies. In this line, the UN confirmed that "democrati[s]ation is central to a state-building and peace-building exercise if peace is to become sustainable and post-conflict reconstruction and development is to succeed" (UNGA 2007).

There are three important issues that should be borne in mind in this process: the timing of elections, sociopolitical and security conditions for elections, and the electoral system. The timing of elections is significant because this will depend on whether or not the particular post-conflict environment in question is ready for free and fair elections. The decision concerning timing ideally should be based on local indicators, but unfortunately it is often the case that they tend to be decided according to the political agendas of external actors. For example, a forthcoming general election in the intervening country is likely to result in rushed elections, in order that the electorate of the intervening country can be provided with a 'success' story. For example, this was the case with the organisation of the first post-Dayton elections in Bosnia-Herzegovina, which were determining by elections facing the Clinton administration in the US. Subsequently, the poor timing of the elections meant that nationalist politicians and warlords from the conflict were elected and thereby legitimised as representatives of conflict-affected populations.

In regard to the conditions for elections, there are a number of factors to be considered, such as: whether or not the security environment is conducive to the organisation of free and fair elections; and whether the process involves the participation of other elements of democratic governance, such as political parties based on societal groups and interests, strong civil society, free media and rule of law. It is clear that for many post-conflict environments it would be unrealistically wishful thinking to ensure all these components of democracy in a short span of time, particularly if that country does not have a tradition of democracy, and if democracy has been 'imported' as part of the external intervention 'package.' It is in such environments that 'democratisation' programmes take a central role in the governance and constitutional reform process, as if those societies can be democratised as long as they are guided by intervening 'democratic' countries. The so-called democratisation programmes seem to view the process as more of a technical than sociopolitical and cultural one, in which democracy can actually be transferred from country to country – an approach which contradicts all the major lessons learned in a variety of post-conflict environments.

Since its first deployment of electoral assistance teams to Namibia (1989) and Nicaragua (1990), the UN and its special agencies has completed at least 400 electoral support projects (Borzyskowski 2015). There are a few measures commonly employed in many contemporary peacebuilding processes. First, there are programmes aiming to guarantee the credibility of the electoral process which include monitoring of the process by representatives from all political parties, preventing pre-electoral period campaigning, ensuring transparent voter registration, training election personnel and detecting fraud. For instance, while the international interveners led by the UN took a lead in organising the entire processes of the postwar elections in Cambodia (1992–93) and Timor-Leste (1999–2002), external actors played relatively less significant roles as coordinators and observers in Ethiopia (1992) and Armenia (1995).

In many other cases, international observers are involved in the election processes with the purpose of verifying the transparency and accountability of the elections. Rather than being involved in as key promoters, external actors limit their commitment as neutral and external verifiers. In such cases, these actors may produce monitoring reports with suggestions for future elections as happened in Angola (1992) and South Africa (1994).

Voter assistance measures are another important part of a good electoral process. Efforts are made to promote the participation of social minorities and ensure that their interests are reflected in the electoral process and system. In societies where one of the sources of the violent conflict was the marginalisation of certain social groups from central politics, these are essential projects. While establishing electoral districts that incorporate different ethnic, religious or social groups is attempted in some countries, affirmative action for parties representing minority groups is pursued in others. In many Central American countries, for example, it is frequently observed that a large number of people are unable to participate in elections due to a lack of transport or the money to get to the ballot points.

In such cases, programmes aimed at providing voter education and transport or other necessary services for people with special circumstances (e.g. those who live in remote areas or have an extremely low income) need to be implemented (Lee and Mac Ginty 2012).

Finally, the way that the electoral system is structured would have profound implications for the outcome of elections, as representation would depend on the electoral formula. For example, if political parties can send representatives to parliament based on their small pockets of regional power bases, regardless of their overall representation in the country, then this would not encourage parties to opt for societal groups and interests; instead political representation would be based on ethnicity or religion. Alternatively, if the system requires an absolute majority to win a seat, then this would lead political parties to form alliances. However, this might in return create a limited representation of minorities in decision making. Although proportional representation can be enabling for broad-based government, it may result in abuses of power-sharing systems among colluding elites.

The reform of public administration

Public administration institutions are key bodies in the peace process, and weak and ineffective state institutions can prove to be a serious hindrance to lasting peace and development. Hence, it is imperative to strengthen the effectiveness of these institutions in order to achieve the fundamental goals of post-conflict reconstruction. In the contemporary peacebuilding process, a variety of efforts to implement administrative reform are taken in an attempt to rectify the past decisions and actions that affected relationships and subsequently provoked the conflict.

The administrative reform programmes can be categorised into the following three types. First, the restructuring of government organisations is a key programme pursued mainly by the national authority itself. While going through chronic armed conflicts, the government structure in many countries becomes distorted to enable the authority to mobilise and utilise resources for conducting warfare. Hence, interdepartmental division of labour within the government is frequently unclear, and political or military figures can easily intervene in judicial performance. Moreover, sound communication between the central government and substate governmental units may have been replaced by one-way communication of order/ obedience. Hence, downsizing, centralising policy-making systems, decentralising delivery systems and coordinating contradictory and redundant interdepartmental relations are the main goals of this type of restructuring.

Moreover, the government and supporting external agencies frequently provide various forms of training to improve the capacity building (or professionalisation) of government officials. In addition to technical skills such as administrative organisation, finance and budgeting, leadership skills and conflict resolution skills, these training programmes frequently focus on improving the accountability and responsibility of civil servants. In the early phase of postwar recovery, peacebuilding agencies have sometimes become directly involved in the operation of the governments. For example, in Gulu, Uganda, the Northern Uganda Rehabilitation Programme (NUREP), funded by the European Development Fund, provisionally installed a cluster system where the representatives of external actors made executive decisions and drafted detailed plans for peaceful recovery in the province (Gerstl 2015). Nevertheless, once a minimal level of governance system exists, external peacebuilding agencies pay most attention to operating ad hoc intensive trainings for the governmental civil servants and the representatives of local communities, rather than intervening in domestic administrative activities.

Another important institutional reform in a post-conflict environment should be the establishment of 'watchdogs' so that the tripartite elements of governance can be checked against abuses and inefficiencies. These watchdogs can be categorised under three main headings: those for rights, reform and audit. The rights watchdogs are particularly important for the protection of human rights in the volatile sociopolitical environments found in post-conflict countries and play a significant role in building trust and confidence, especially in scenarios where there was no clear winner of the war, or in which the peace agreement was secured through third-party intervention. From El Salvador and Bosnia-Herzegovina to Afghanistan, a number of post-conflict countries have benefited from the formation of a human rights watchdog. The second type of watchdog – reform – can carry out an essential role particularly during highly sensitive reform processes such as security sector reform. Finally, audit watchdogs can be an important actor in the fight against corruption which tends to be a major challenge in almost all post-conflict environments. However, it should be remembered that watchdogs can only be effective as long as they are equipped with the necessary power to carry out their mandates and while there is a political will to implement their recommendations.

Finally, in many peacebuilding processes, particular attention is given to strengthening the performance of local governments. Since it is local institutions that deliver the decisions of central authorities, their role is crucial to successful peacebuilding. International donor agencies and NGOs provide a wide range of support, from training on the basic functions of local institutions, such as food security, human resources and disaster prevention, to advisory assistance on improving communications between local officials and constituencies and dividing responsibilities between mayors and elected councils (Evans 2005).

Nevertheless, externally driven administrative reform projects faced unexpected challenges in many countries. In a nutshell, many international peace-supporters wanted to transplant their skills and knowledge of government performance without careful consideration of the social and cultural contexts of the local societies. For instance, in many multiethnic/religious countries including Sudan, emphasis on local governance was utilised for alleviating the tensions between different ethnic groups or tribes, even though there was little governmental capacity to promote close collaboration between the central governments and local authorities. In such cases, the central governments have to rely on the legitimacy and power of traditional local authorities or local power elites. Hence, further promotion of decentralised governance caused a stronger patron-client relationship within the local governance system. Moreover, the skill development programmes of the United Nations Development Programme (UNDP) for governmental officials (1993–2010) gained only partial success, primarily due to frequent staff turnover. Under the central government's strong financial control, civil servants at substate levels struggled to implement the programmes that they wanted and the salary was too low to convince them to stay with the government. Hence, once they had earned good enough administrative skills to be employed by foreign NGOs or private companies, they immediately left their governmental positions (Lee and Park 2015).

New forms of security and political peacebuilding

As discussed earlier, the limited scope of contemporary peacebuilding, which was primarily based on Western standards of good governance, has been criticised by both academics and field practitioners. It should be noted that taking state-centric approaches toward security and political problems is in a sense both unavoidable and effective at early stages of postwar peacebuilding: without making the essential state function workable, little achievement in peacebuilding could be made.

Nevertheless, the criticisms made the point that the traditional forms of international peacebuilding have offered little more than institutional measures, which should be a foundational method for further political transformation rather than an end. In security sector reform, for instance, a lack of holistic approach has been pointed out as a key problem of recent peacebuilding activities, while many electoral assistance programmes have been criticised for their focus on technical assistance. Moreover, these programmes were designed to complete their operations within limited time spans (normally within three years). When the priority of peacebuilding processes is given to 'speed' rather than 'quality,' the measures essential for nurturing credible and solid participation of the constituencies cannot take place.

Reflecting such concerns, alternative/supplementary initiatives began to emerge in more recent peacebuilding programmes, highlighting the importance of civil participation. Many of them adopt a more inclusive process when forming security and political arrangements to reduce the violence in the societies. In terms of political peacebuilding, in order to develop more democratic governance in conflict-affected countries, an extremely large number of NGOs across the globe have developed human rights advocacy programmes, education for community residents (women in particular), activities for monitoring governments' performance, and organisations of civilian associations or for local development. Moreover, institutional decentralisation of government structure to make local governance more accountable to constituencies is frequently followed by regular meetings of all stakeholders (government officials, NGO representatives and community residents), village-level workshops for women and inclusion of feedback from the communities as key requirements for operating government policies.

However, regarding security sector peacebuilding, this section highlights recent civilian security measures that challenge the Weberian understanding of security, which assumes that state should dominate the violence. These civilian activities, frequently referred to as unarmed civilian peacekeeping (UCP), aim "to create a safer environment, or a 'safer space,' for civilians to address their own needs, solve their own conflicts and protect vulnerable individuals and populations in their midst" (Furnari, Oldenhuis and Julian 2015: 3). Examples including Peace Brigades International (PBI) and Witness for Peace have developed key strategies for advocacy programmes for vulnerable local communities in Latin America since the 1980s; and the Nonviolent Peace Force, which has attempted to transform structural issues in Africa, Asia and Europe.

A primary aim of such initiatives is protecting people's human rights from an underdisciplined army and police force. The following are some examples of the methods used by these civilian organisations to protect human rights. First, *accompaniment and international presence* denotes the strategy for reducing the risk of violence occurrence by making frequent visits to threatened human right activists or by being a constant and visible presence at activists' offices or in their communities. Many reports confirm that the presence of international activists significantly reduces the frequency of violence committed by local militia groups or gangs. UCP operators also conduct *citizen diplomacy*, a method that is closely related to accompaniment and international presence. To make the government understand the purpose of their use of accompaniment and international presence, civilian actors can maintain contact and have regular meetings with civil and military authorities and institutions. The *production of monitoring reports* is another important method. By disseminating regular reports on the performance of the security sector, they attract international attention to the issue. Finally, UCP programmes frequently make efforts to promote *self-protection networks* among local communities. They carry out training sessions for local NGOs and community leaders on the topics of protection and security and organise night patrol networks or emergency warning systems within the local communities (Checa Hidalgo 2008).

Despite its limitations, the civilian-led UCP has been relatively successful in supplementing the mainstream security projects implemented at local areas. Since traditional security programmes normally aim to deal with armed groups and exclude unarmed or demilitarised groups, they do not effectively cover the political violence or general crimes caused by unarmed groups, and UCP is often effective in filling the gap. Moreover, when the UN's peacekeeping operations are taken over by succeeding rehabilitation programmes, the transition usually creates security areas that are not well covered by subsequent operations. In such cases, community residents continue to suffer from human rights violations committed by a corrupt police force, uncontrolled local violent groups or military guerrilla groups.

Although previously implemented UCP programmes have addressed such gaps by constantly engaging in various community groups, the effectiveness of UCP is determined largely by whether it can be accepted as a neutral and reliable initiative by all relevant actors including the government, direct parties of armed conflicts, local power elites and community residents. Civilian organisations operating UCP adopt working principles such as nonpartisanship, independence, civilian-to-civilian partnership and nonviolence; however, many of them confirm that 'acceptance by the local communities' is one of the most challenging issues (Furnari et al. 2015).

Case study: security sector reform in El Salvador and the US intervention

Security sector reform, particularly the demilitarisation and demobilisation of ex-combatants, is considered one of the most crucial issues in the post-conflict reconstruction period, in that its progress determines the security conditions in the post-conflict society and ultimately affects the success of a peace process. At the same time, demilitarisation is frequently the most difficult and controversial part of reconstruction because it is a process that involves removing a fundamental means by which actors conduct their activities. At the elite level, core political powers or military leaders tend to present strong opposition to the process of the reform or apply deceptive actions to avoid losing their power ground. At the lower level of armed groups, soldiers try to retain possession of their weapons to protect themselves from any potential threats or to gain financial benefits by selling them. Thus, there is great need for constant efforts on the part of external actors to provide military actors with the motivation to disarm and to verify the process of implementation.

The security sector reform process in El Salvador demonstrates how the tensions between national military leaders and external peace-supporting actors have been transformed in the post-conflict peacebuilding procedures. When the civil war was ended by the signing of the Chapultepec Peace Accord in 1992, it was agreed that both governmental armed forces and the military factions of the rebel group, the Farabundo Martí National Liberation Front (FMLN), would be dismantled and reintegrated into civil society. Regarding the demilitarisation of the governmental forces, although the core leadership of the national army was granted the opportunity to remain in place, the military and political power of the national military forces (Armed Forces of El Salvador, or ESAF) were significantly reduced. In addition, all paramilitary agencies, including the Rapid Deployment Infantry Battalions (BIRIs), the National Directorate of Intelligence (DNI) and the national police were to be disbanded or completely reformed.

Nevertheless, although President Cristiani had liberal ideas on military power and agreed with the provisions, purging the army was an extremely difficult issue, because this did not involve reducing the size of the military but rather eliminating the power group that had controlled the country for decades. Two external actors provided constant support with the implementation of this process. In terms of keeping national actors' motivation high, the United States pressed both the Cristiani government and the key military leaders to fulfil the provisions in the peace accords whilst the UN Observer Mission in El Salvador (ONUSAL) played key roles in monitoring the process of implementation.

In particular, the US managed to direct the Salvadoran leaders to carry out the dispersal of their key military forces using three measures. First, it applied various material and non-material pressures on both the Cristiani government and the ESAF High Command to persuade them to become more flexible. Second, the US initiated direct talks with the FMLN in order to improve the circumstances surrounding the negotiations. Third, the superpower also began to cooperate more closely with the UN and other regional supporting countries.

During the early stages of the demilitarisation of the National Guard, the BIRIs and the death squads in February and March 1992, the ESAF leadership's resistance was extremely strong, as expected. They frequently sabotaged the process and faked implementation causing serious delays in the overall process. Hence, the US's diplomatic and material pressure in this period became focused on persuading the top military leaders to abide by the accord. The US provided incentives to secure the implementation of demilitarisation, announcing to the Cristiani government that it would provide resources such as funds for demobilisation, facilities for training new military organisations, and other support that Cristiani needed. Moreover, in order to increase its diplomatic pressure, the US also held direct meetings with the ESAF leadership to persuade them to abide by the peace process. The US also linked its military and economic support to the progress of the implementation of the peace agreement. For instance, then Secretary of State, Warren Christopher, warned El Salvador in February 1993 that military assistance and funds for the Department of Justice would be withheld unless the Salvadoran government demonstrated its resolve to implement the accord.

Consequently, the combined effects of ONUSAL's diplomatic pressure on the Cristiani government, the repeated promises of financial support for the implementation process from other external actors as well as the US, and the latter's continuous assertion of its determination to complete the demilitarisation succeeded in changing President Cristiani's attitude.

A good example of this pattern can be observed in the retirement of core military officers who had perpetrated human rights abuses against the Salvadoran people. Although the UN Ad Hoc Commission recommended the immediate dismissal of approximately one hundred officers in September 1992, the Cristiani government was unable to take swift action because the removal of fifteen top leaders was a particularly sensitive issue for the ESAF. Thus, there was little sign of implementation until February 1993. Nevertheless, as the Clinton government made it clear in February that no more military support would be given until the military leaders accused of human rights abuse were dismissed, the government was able to overrule the ESAF resistance. Thus, between March and April 1993, all the military leaders listed in the Ad Hoc Commission's report were forced to retire. Moreover, the government announced a revised target date for the completion of the commission's recommendations: 30 June 1993.

As a result, although the process extended beyond the originally proposed deadline, all missions of ONUSAL were declared complete in September 1993. Moreover, as Licenciado Rodriguez, who took the lead in the demilitarisation as the Ad Hoc Commission's chairman, stated, only the US had the effective power to enforce the commission's recommendations, and its pressure was the most important (and, in reality, the only) factor in compelling the Salvadoran military leaders to cooperate with the demilitarisation process.

Conclusion

Thus far, several major programmes employing insecurity and political sector reconstruction have been reviewed regarding their scope and a few key areas of the process. In particular, core implementation measures in each of the key areas were the main foci of the discussion. Although the range of programmes in the security and political reconstruction arena may involve different specific goals, the peacebuilding efforts in both areas generally attempt to improve the effectiveness and accountability of institutions in their respective areas of interest. During the build-up to the onset of conflict in the war-affected countries, the poor quality of performance of these institutions and the fact that they served the interests of elite groups and helped to consolidate their power at the national level meant that they were major factors in oppressing constituencies, galvanising opposition and bringing about conflict. As a result, many peacebuilding projects consider improvement in the effectiveness and accountability of security and political institutions to be one of their main goals.

Moreover, the limitations of contemporary peacebuilding programmes primarily caused by their institutional and state-centric approaches were discussed, as well as recent endeavours to address these problems. Nevertheless, although they were not covered in this chapter, it should be noted that the process of reforming security and political institutions faces various sorts of challenges. One of the most formidable is the resistance from the institutions that are targeted to be reformed, as presented in the case study of El Salvador. As most of the actors in the political and security sectors have wielded strong power before and during the armed conflicts, forcing them to transfer their power to other civil actors, to change their modes of practice and to cut out unofficial sources of financing and personal gain tend to cause strong resistance. Unstable security in the aftermath of conflicts offers a further challenging environment, since the state authorities and external advocates cannot promote many substantial changes while significant security threats exist. Moreover, divergent understandings of fundamental assumptions such as 'accountable security,' 'democratic governance,' 'financial transparency,' and 'institutional effectiveness' between external and internal actors frequently cause serious failings in implementation.

A significant number of studies have sought ways through such difficulties and suggested a wide range of proposals. Apart from technical and practical ideas, three suggestions are outstanding. First, considering the institutional tendencies and power politics within security and political agencies, the reconstruction in these two areas is likely to take particularly long period of time. Hence, plans for political and security reform should be made from a long-term perspective with flexibility and resilience. Second, provision of clearer security reassurance and practical incentives is highly useful at an early stage of the reform. Since, at this stage, most political and military elites are worrying about the negative consequences of losing power, specific efforts by the new authorities to reassure them in regard to their (physical and political) survival as well as their potential to gain other benefits are recommended. Third, capacity-building processes for governmental civil servants and security units should be constantly promoted. In fact, a large number of problems caused by the security forces and governmental agencies are created by unprofessional and undereducated lower-rank officers and soldiers.

Discussion questions

- What are the major challenges to cooperation between civilian and military actors in the postwar recovery process?
- How can social actors supplement the limited scope of state-centric security systems?
- External military interventions for building the capacity of security forces in conflict-affected societies tend to make the security actors be more reliant on external support. What can be done to address this dilemma?
- What ethical issues should be taken into consideration in the reintegration of ex-combatants into civil society?

Recommended reading

Caplan, R. (2012) 'Exit Strategies and State Building', in *Exit Strategies and State Building*, edited by Caplan, R. Oxford: Oxford University Press: 3–20.

Kingma, K. (2002) 'Demobilisation and Peacebuilding in Africa'. *International Peacekeeping* 9 (2): 181–201.

Neild, R. (2001) 'Democratic Policing', in *Peacebuilding: A Field Guide*, edited by Reychler, L. and Paffenholz, T. Boulder, CO: Lynne Rienner: 416–27.

Oberschall, A. (2007) *Conflict and Peace Building in Divided Societies: Responses to Ethnic Violence*. London: Routledge.

Online resources

For more information about unarmed civilian peacekeeping, please see:

http://www.nonviolentpeaceforce.org/
http://www.peacebrigades.org/
http://www.witnessforpeace.org/

8 Socioeconomic peacebuilding

In this chapter, the areas of social and economic peacebuilding will be presented. While security and political peacebuilding mainly focus on the protection of people's human rights and safety, the primary concern of socioeconomic peacebuilding is the well-being and livelihood of the population. Since most of the root sources and catalysts of violent conflicts relate to dissatisfaction with social and economic conditions, reconstruction in these areas is considered a fundamental part of peacebuilding. Moreover, the key directions of this aspect of peacebuilding frequently determine the nature of postwar social development (Addison and Brück 2009). In order to identify key objectives and practical aspects of socioeconomic peacebuilding, Chapter 8 will focus on the following issues:

- The scope of social and economic reconstruction
- Rehabilitation of industrial infrastructure and refugee repatriation
- Employment generation
- Development of sustainable communities.

Over the last two decades, the discussions over socioeconomic peacebuilding have faced two fundamental questions related to the direction of future development:

1. Does peacebuilding pursue the 'reconstruction' of the prewar societies or the 'transformation' of the social contexts?"
2. In the case where 'peace,' 'democratic governance' and 'development' do not go along with each other, how can such different social values be accommodated in peacebuilding programmes?

As for the first question, previous experience of contemporary peacebuilding made it relatively clear that simple reestablishment of prewar conditions (in terms of income levels, social tensions or social capital) cannot address complex social issues in war-affected countries. The precedent social conditions in many of the countries that experienced armed conflicts during the 1990s were marked by "extreme inequality, poverty, corruption, exclusion, institutional decay, poor policy design and economic mismanagement" (UNDP 2008: 5). For instance, prior to its independence from Indonesia, Timor-Leste did not have a self-sufficient economy. Although 90 per cent of its population worked in labour-intensive agricultural production, most of its food and other essential products were imported from Indonesia. Thus, most contemporary peacebuilding processes pursue the creation of more prosperous and sustainable social and economic conditions and strive for a structural break with the past.

Nevertheless, the second question, regarding the tension between peacebuilding programmes pursuing different social values, is still controversial. As the economic policies advocated by international financial institutions and private industry give priority to economic growth, their negative impact on other social aspects such as social equality, protection of the environment and balanced social development have become more evident. Although the criticisms of such growth-oriented peacebuilding are gaining more academic attention, the theoretical and practical criticisms have not delivered significant correctives to the dominant development debates or policy agendas. Hence, in evaluating the achievements and limitations of contemporary peace-supporting activities in economic and social sectors, the discussions in this chapter will pay more attention to such programmes' priority in market-based economic development, in addition to various practical challenges.

The scope of socioeconomic peacebuilding

Economic peacebuilding

Together with security instability, poverty is one of the most important issues that determine the challenges in postwar societies. According to a macro-level analysis, a few typical economic consequences of armed conflicts are falls in gross domestic product (GDP) per capita, high inflation, displacement of human resources, decrease in foreign investment and an overvalued currency exchange rate (Haughton 1998). From a more micro-level perspective, conflicts disrupt people's main form of activities (agriculture, in many countries), destroy assets, remove their shelters and undermine social conditions for maintaining economic lives. A large number of social issues, such as human trafficking, narcotics crimes, piracy and illiteracy, are directly and indirectly related to the economic instability and poverty of the concerned societies. Moreover, as discussed in Chapter 2, many civil conflicts are either caused or catalysed by poverty or economic polarisation.

Therefore, economic reconstruction programmes that aim to (re)generate economic activities and increase wealth within the target societies have been proactively promoted by a large number of international organisations or donor agencies. Examination of the reconstruction programmes implemented in the post–Cold War period indicates that these can be categorised into these four areas:

1   Physical (re)construction of infrastructure as well as establishment of economic and financial institutions;
2   Public policies for eliminating the war economy and promoting long-term economic development;

Table 8.1 Examples of economic peacebuilding

Construction of infrastructure	Market buildings, government offices, roads, ports, airports, electricity power stations, industrial complexes
Polices for long-term development	Restructure of legal framework, national development plans, construction of credible financial system, establishment of fair customs and immigration policies
Income generation	Labour-intensive construction projects, vocational training services, control of cash flow within/between industries, invitation of foreign investments, strengthened border control
Empowering local communities	Support of basic agricultural materials (seeds, tools, fertiliser), restoring irrigation facilities, microfinancing for small business operators

3   Material support for promoting income generation and revitalisation of industry;
4   Efforts aimed at empowering local communities and encouraging local ownership in economic activities.

Social reconstruction

Chronic armed conflicts have devastating physical and nonphysical impacts on society that include destruction of infrastructure, breakdown of social relations, displacement of people, elimination of the social health system, extreme poverty, lack of social trust and psychological trauma. These social issues affect people's well-being and undermine rapid economic recovery. Hence, a large number of social reconstruction programmes are implemented, aiming to foster a social condition in which people can achieve "a level of tolerance and peaceful co-existence," gain "social cohesion through acceptance of a national identity," develop peaceful measures of conflict resolution, and address "the legacy of past abuses" (USIP n.d.b.).

Since extremely large numbers of programmes are conceptualised as social peacebuilding, it is impossible to generalise the types of these activities. However, a few frequently utilised categorisations include the following:[1]

1   Rehabilitation projects pursuing social security;
2   Programmes for strengthening civil society;
3   Efforts for supporting people's access to various social services;
4   Activities for redevelopment of social cohesion and community solidarity.

Compared to security and political reconstruction, socioeconomic peacebuilding programmes normally take much longer to achieve their goals as the issues of concern are associated with fundamental social structures. For instance, building social cohesion in societies that have gone through identity-based civil wars requires addressing preexisting stereotyping, structural discrimination against certain social groups, economic inequality, establishment of mutual trust at individual levels and so on. Hence, most social peacebuilding programmes require the transformation of social, structural and relational factors of such societies, which can be achieved only through peacebuilding actors' constant and lengthy commitment (Jones 2005). Furthermore, socioeconomic issues in conflict-affected countries have extremely various dimensions; moreover, many of these issues have not been included in core agenda of state-level peace processes. For example, the education of citizens about democratic values was regarded as a second-tier agenda by many new authorities that primarily focused on institutional peacebuilding. Hence, socioeconomic peacebuilding required the participation of a wide range of civilian actors including local elites, grassroots

Table 8.2 Examples of social peacebuilding

Social rehabilitation	Social reintegration of ex-combatants, resettlement of refugees, essential medical care services
Civil society	Skill training, education on democratic values, monitoring government policies
Access to social services	Nationwide affordable healthcare system, compulsory education, free access to independent media
Social cohesion	Reconstruction of religious institutions, revitalisation of cultural traditions, organisation of local associations

organisations, foreign nongovernmental organisations (NGOs), private entrepreneurs, humanitarian aid agencies and the like.

Early-stage rehabilitation: construction of infrastructure and refugee repatriation

In the early phases of peacebuilding, socioeconomic reconstruction can be defined as rehabilitation. Since societies in the aftermath of armed conflict usually have various problems that put people's livelihoods in danger, it is important to implement urgent rehabilitation programmes to meet people's basic needs and to set the foundation for further social activities before (or together with) the initiation of longer-term socioeconomic peacebuilding. Using representative examples of peacebuilding at the rehabilitation phase, this section looks at the (re)construction of social infrastructure and refugee repatriation.

Reconstruction of infrastructure – Since sustainable economic development cannot be achieved without industrial infrastructure such as electricity generation and distribution, public transport (e.g. ports, airports, roads, railways), a water supply system and telecommunication facilities, the development and/or rehabilitation of such infrastructure is considered a first step towards economic peacebuilding. In many war-affected countries, including Bosnia-Herzegovina, Cambodia, Haiti and Sri Lanka, the governments and international development organisations began to repair or reconstruct industrial infrastructure immediately after the cessation of violent conflict.

Sometimes the benefit of reconstructing infrastructure goes beyond its positive impact on economic growth. In Uganda, for example, the construction of a dam contributed to the resolution of long-term disputes between communities over land and water, and the reconstruction of the Old Bridge in Mostar in Bosnia-Herzegovina contributed to reconciliation between Bosniacs and Croats (Calame and Pasic 2009; Preti et al. 2010). In addition to increasing the movement of goods and human resources in general, road reconstruction in Liberia created considerable job opportunities for the local population; in Nepal, it enabled the government to implement more effective development support in rural areas.

In terms of implementation procedures, since physical reconstruction is a 'straightforward' and highly visible project, it has been considered a less controversial and troublesome part of peacebuilding. Nevertheless, in many cases physical rehabilitation projects have faced the following challenges. First, the reduction in funding due to diminished international attention on certain reconstruction projects can be a critical obstacle to efforts at reconstruction. For example, since the early 1990s, many major international development agencies have prioritised structural adjustment programmes rather than physical reconstruction (UNDP 2008). Second, a lack of local human resources with the necessary technical capabilities may also be a significant challenge. In Timor-Leste, for instance, most managers and technicians working prior to the civil conflict were from Indonesia, and the country had few people capable of leading reconstruction projects. Although external supporters might provide some project managers or technical personnel, such support is generally insufficient to manage all programmes effectively, and this external dependency is not sustainable in the medium to long term (UNDP 2008). Third, corruption is often a serious issue. As reconstruction projects require the influx of huge sums of money, dishonest government officials, local companies, transport agencies and community leaders may regard them as good opportunities for increasing their personal wealth and influence.

Refugee repatriation – Considering social rehabilitation, refugee repatriation is considered as the first priority in many peacebuilding processes. The influx of a huge number of refugees or internally displaced persons (IDPs) is a challenge common to many post-conflict societies. For returning refugees, the overall social conditions in their home country often do not provide sufficient social, economic, physical and psychological security and their new quality of life is sometimes worse than it was in refugee camps. Furthermore, the impact of this refugee population influx on the society exacerbates existing social problems such as low incomes, food insecurity, scarcity of shelter, the lack of the rule of law and disputes over land ownership. Nevertheless, in some cases (such as Cambodia and Guatemala), refugees may be important human resources with the knowledge and skills to contribute to the recovery of post-conflict societies. Hence, a well-organised repatriation plan is essential if durable peace and development are to be achieved.

Until the late 1980s, the programmes implemented by international organisations and humanitarian agencies for refugee repatriation were reactive, exile oriented and refugee specific. These programmes normally focused on the provision of individual or family-based repatriation packages that typically included food and other aid, transport to their countries of origin and diplomatic lobbying for amnesties. During the 1990s, nevertheless, the international community's thoughts on repatriation began to turn towards pursuing more proactive, homeland-oriented and holistic programmes, and most contemporary repatriation projects adopt a comprehensive approach that includes the reintegration of refugees into their countries of origin and rehabilitation and development of these societies. For instance, the UNHCR implemented around 250 microprojects that dealt with the issues of "health, education, training, infrastructure, transportation, crop production, livestock, and income-generation" in Nicaragua (Crisp 2001: 11).

The key challenges faced by contemporary repatriation programmes are related to the competition and conflict between local residents and returnees over resources, social services, employment and education opportunities, a representative example of which is restoring the property rights of returning refugees (primarily restoring the rights related to land ownership). Moreover, as seen in the repatriation process in Bosnia-Herzegovina, the return of ethnic minorities to their previous 'home' can be highly tricky as the ethnic majorities who have committed various harm on those minorities still live in the same place. In such cases, in addition to setting clear and fair principles for dealing with disputes over property rights, peacebuilding authorities need to engage in constant dialogue regarding return and repatriation with all stakeholders at national, regional and local levels. Moreover, when repatriation to their homeland is unrealistic, financial or alternative compensation to returnees should be provided (UNDP 2008).

Employment generation

Since economic disparity and a lack of economic opportunities may encourage violence and social tensions – as evidenced by events in Mozambique and Guatemala, for example – employment generation contributes to the stabilisation of war-torn societies and to the deterrence of violence in varied ways. For instance, it offers people a source of income and opportunities outside the established war economy. Employment also helps to reintegrate conflict-affected groups (both perpetrators and victims) into civil economic activities and to prevent other post-conflict issues such as criminal activity and the alienation of certain social groups from emerging as serious issues. In fact, in the early period of postwar economic development, the competition for getting jobs can be extremely intense and young ex-combatants tend to face more barriers in finding gainful job opportunities due to their lack of education or practical skills. Hence, former warriors frequently end up involved in gang violence or other daily crimes to manage a minimal level of economic life. In this sense, 'employment generation' has been singled out as one of the most critical but challenging issues of social peacebuilding (McLeod and Dávalos 2007).

In an effort to encourage the design and implementation of more effective and systematic job creation projects, the UN introduced a multitrack approach in 2009 that set out the necessary features of contemporary job creating projects; this approach summarises contemporary strategies for generating employment well (UN 2009). First, labour-intensive public work programmes are initiated in order to provide those affected by or vulnerable to violent conflicts with temporary jobs. Regarding former combatants, employment opportunities are provided in the ways that can utilise their previous experience or expertise. For instance, the HALO Trust, which has remained as the third-largest employer in nongovernmental sectors, employs more than 600 ex-combatants to operate its mine clearance programmes (HALO Trust 2012). Second, vocational training is implemented in order to improve job-related skills and to rebuild economic and social infrastructures. In postwar Sierra Leone, the government supported approximately 3,000 displaced blacksmiths by providing tools, materials and space for opening workshops that later participated in the country's rehabilitation programmes. Seeing the need for more blacksmiths, the government then operated the Sierra Leone Work Oxen Programme, which trained new skilled workers, for approximately ten years (Greene 2009). Under such programmes, organisations may also offer conflict-affected individuals some temporary job-seeking support, including emergency employment schemes and basic start-up grants.

Another part of this approach deals with issues at the community level. By reconstructing the target country's socioeconomic infrastructure and restoring its natural resource base, the intention is to create more job opportunities for a larger number of people. For example, between 2008 and 2013, the EU funded the Liberia Community Empowerment Project (LACE), which conducted 265 subprojects to reconstruct infrastructure essential for the local community's livelihood (i.e. schools, medical clinics, water supply facilities, bridges and market buildings), which primarily employed community members. As these projects do not create intense personal competition for employment and provide a common work environment, they also frequently contribute to the development of a sense of community and unity. Since private sector investment is essential for such programmes, collaboration between international organisations and private corporations is key to the success of such programmes.

Since neither of the two previous strategies can provide long-term job security, however, many contemporary peacebuilding activities aim to create jobs at the macro level as well. In addition to implementing large-scale economic reconstruction programmes that aim to establish/transform the industrial structures of a society or foster the private sector and labour markets, programmes are also launched to initiate and foster social dialogue towards the economic actors' consensus on the 'rules of the game.' Hence, a coherent national economic strategy (for example, the 3×6 approach adopted in the peacebuilding in Burundi)[2] based on a comprehensive analysis of the local market and social resources is necessary (Preti et al. 2010). In Cambodia, the government implemented low-interest land concessions to attract foreign investment. Through these, international companies were able to occupy state lands for up to ninety-nine years with extremely low costs. Consequently, since 1993 more than 270 foreign companies have initiated labour-intensive industries (i.e. plantation agriculture and garment production).

Although these nationwide income-generation programmes created new work opportunities, they have created various social and economic problems due to the combined effect of the imposition of neoliberal agenda of foreign investors and the corrupt and unprofessional governance of the national authorities. The land concessions in Cambodia, for instance, enforced the evacuation of a massive number of people from where they had lived (although the exact number was never released yet), destroyed the natural environment in 2.1 million hectares (forests and water resources, in particular) and negatively affected the livelihoods of the people living nearby the foreign factories (LICADHO 2015).

Building sustainable local communities

Another key element of socioeconomic peacebuilding is fostering solid and collaborative communities within societies. From external supporter's viewpoint, nurturing local capacity so that social stability and sustainable development can be promoted and maintained by the 'owners' of the society is an important goal. For the national actors within the conflict-affected societies, community development is the first step toward all other types of peace-building, such as economic development, local governance and social reconciliation.

Microfinance

Regarding economic measures, microfinance is frequently utilised to support local community residents' economic self-help ventures. It denotes a wide range of financial services provided to the poor and to war-affected people, which include microcredit, micro-insurance and micro-savings (Hulme 2008). In order to reduce their dependence on humanitarian aid, local people need to secure employment or start their own income-generating businesses. Nevertheless, for people with low-income and little access to mainstream financial institutions (this includes most war-affected people, the displaced, returning refugees and ex-combatants), raising the capital required to (re)start a business is a major challenge, and many humanitarian agencies and local NGOs therefore run microfinance or local credit programmes to help such people. A 2008 report by the United Nations Development Programme (UNDP) claimed that approximately 500 million people have benefited from these programmes (UNDP 2008).

In addition to economic benefits, microfinance sometimes contributes to the de-escalation of conflicts. For instance, by bringing together mixed ethnic groups of ex-combatants and local farmers under common microfinance arrangements and utilising joint repayment liability for loans secured, the microfinance programmes in Afghanistan provided new opportunities for promoting interethnic collaboration. In Indonesia, microfinance provided one of the rare opportunities for meaningful interaction between Christians and Muslims. In attempting to secure microfinance and invest it more effectively, many members of these two religious groups established joint ventures (Marino 2005). In Papua New Guinea, the workshops hosted by the Bougainville Microfinance Scheme promoted the recovery of trust between people (Newsom 2002). In Bosnia-Herzegovina, it was reported that microcredit organisations brought people from two ethnic/religious groups together in common enterprises and that this helped to reduce mutual prejudice (UNDP 2008).

Nevertheless, various challenges have been identified in the provision of microfinance in war-affected countries, the first of which is the risk of 'losing money.' Micro-entrepreneurship in war-affected societies, especially in businesses run by a single individual, runs a high risk of failure, and debtors normally do not have alternative resources for repaying loans if their business fails. To overcome this difficulty, some microfinance institutes encourage group lending, which tends to have better rates of repayment. Another challenge is the high transaction costs of microfinance. As microfinance involves loaning small amounts of money to a large number of people, the service requires significant human and material resources to maintain the transaction system. Moreover, staff and volunteer training has been reported as a significant difficulty. As microfinance is a new sector that combines the concepts of traditional finance and local empowerment, microfinance staff need to understand both sides of the equation. However, acquiring suitably qualified people or training them in war-torn societies can sometimes prove extremely difficult.

Strengthening social cohesion (social capital)

Social cohesion refers to the bonds between the members of a society and local patterns of cooperation (Chipkin and Ngqulunga 2008; Fearon, Humphreys and Weinstein 2009). Although the detailed concepts of social cohesion and social capital may differ, a definition of social capital as the connections within and between social networks is frequently used interchangeably with the concept of social cohesion.[3] Since a society with strong internal unity has less of a possibility of armed conflicts occurring between its members, building interpersonal or intergroup networks and trust are the most effective ways of preventing and de-escalating intrastate conflicts (Colletta and Cullen 2000). Social cohesion is also frequently portrayed as a key contributor to poverty reduction and sustainable development (Ferroni, Matteo and Payne 2008).

The efforts for strengthening social capital normally focus on the reestablishment of a civil society that encourages wide participation in planning and decision making on the issues related to local societies, shares common future goals, recognises the interconnectedness between social groups, and accepts the dissimilar or contradictory interests and ideas that exist between different social groups as a normal phenomenon and deals with them in peaceful ways.

One direction taken by these programmes is the revitalisation of traditional sources of solidarity, such as the *MatoOput* system[4] of the Acholi in North Uganda and the *Ubuntu* culture[5] in East, Central and Southern Africa (Murithi 2006). Another direction taken is the development of democratic civil relationships though education on democracy and community-based collective activities (Haider 2009). The major targets of these programmes include traditional associations, village leaderships, community-based organisations (CBOs), local NGOs, trade unions, youth organisations and the like.

Nevertheless, the development of social cohesion tends to be slow and problematic because many war-affected societies have lost traditional social bonds such as norms, culture, religion, organisations, networks and even family and do not easily develop new sources of social cohesion. Moreover, the prevalence of extreme poverty in post-conflict societies can prohibit internal solidarity in a society.

Education support

Education support is one of the most widely accepted strategies for building local capacity. It is believed that the provision of good-quality education services to children and war-affected people makes a positive contribution to the peace process and creates an incentive to maintain peace. For a long time, however, the reconstruction of education systems was not afforded a high priority on the post-conflict reconstruction agenda, and in many peacebuilding projects the resources allocated for education services were either limited or nonexistent (UNESCO-UNEVOC 2007). Since large-scale military conflicts seriously degrade the physical and structural environment for education, educational institutions (e.g. formal schools, colleges and universities, and traditional or religious education systems) are left significantly weakened and damaged (if not completely destroyed) at the end of chronic military conflicts – precisely the point at which the contribution of good education is most needed, particularly if meaningful progress is to take place in the immediate post-conflict environment (UNDP 2008).

Hence, instead of improving the quality of formal education, development agencies and NGOs have paid more attention to providing education and training programmes that improve employability and develop local capacity, such as skills training, vocational education, leadership training and technical consultancy. Despite some common obstacles, such as the lack of coordination between these informal education programmes and the disparity between training and employment opportunities, these informal education systems have made significant contributions to developing human capacities, promoting further employment and sustaining peace (UNESCO-UNEVOC 2007).

In addition, the number of long-term programmes for developing formal education has also been on the increase in recent years. The core parts of contemporary post-conflict reconstruction efforts in the field of education take place in the following four areas. First, to address the shortage of qualified teachers, development agencies and NGOs deliver a range of short training courses. Second, curricula and textbooks are revised, with a focus on redressing bias, prejudice or distorted interpretations of social, cultural and political issues. Third, efforts are made to improve education governance, which is usually marked by corruption and under-transparency. Last but not least, in addition to addressing the initial financial shortages and supporting one-off projects, international organisations provide ongoing funding to keep the education system running (e.g. constructing school buildings and publishing textbooks).

Addressing development-driven peacebuilding

Contemporary peacebuilding developed many useful strategies for fostering more consolidated peace and sustainable development in postwar societies. Nevertheless, many programmes related to socioeconomic peacebuilding have, at the same time, also presented serious limitations, such as imposition of Western values, support of preexisting power structures, and minimally regulated economic activities. In relation to these issues, this section pays attention to the problems caused by growth-oriented socioeconomic policies.

Many aspects of socioeconomic peacebuilding are beyond the capacity of weak states' functions in post-conflict societies. Moreover, due to the limited scope of most conflict resolution processes, these socioeconomic issues are rarely reflected in peace agreements signed by direct participants in civil wars (see Joshi, Lee and Mac Ginty 2014). Hence, socioeconomic peacebuilding in the early periods tends to be directed by a large number of external aiders and investors without centralised governing bodies. Hence, the influence of major financial organisations such as the International Monetary Fund (IMF) and the World Bank can be very strong. Moreover, these financial organisations generally support liberal market economics and are reluctant to apply any restrictive interventions to economic activities.

The new governments in postwar countries also tend to give priority to economic development in order to deal with various social issues caused by extreme poverty and the destruction of their basic social systems. In order to attract foreign investment and to encourage inter-border trade, the governments reduce regulations on economic activities and leave other social agenda aside. Under such circumstances, private industry tends to pursue relatively quick profit rather than invest their capital in long-term development.

As many previous empirical studies confirm, it is fair to say that economic growth is highly important as the economic foundation for poverty reduction and sustainable development (e.g. Dollar and Kraay 2002; Easterly 1999). Nevertheless, the negative long-term impact caused by the dominant influence of growth-oriented programmes has become more obvious as time goes by.

One of the most frequently discussed issues is exacerbated social inequality. Market based liberal economic policies tend to provide more benefits to those social actors that have a more liberal orientation, richer financial resources and stronger social networks. In more serious cases, such growth-oriented policies propel economic polarisation by deterring the poor from accessing the increased social wealth. As discussed in many studies on the roles of social/economic inequalities in violent conflicts (Cobham 2005; Langer 2005; Mancini 2005), the consequent sense of marginalisation from certain social groups is likely to be a trigger for further social violence. Hence, many studies call for provisional affirmative actions (i.e. pro poor expenditure on health care and primary education for poorer sectors of society) to enable previously excluded or marginalised groups to gain equal economic standing in terms of access to land and natural resources, economic opportunities and standard of living (Langer and Brown 2007).

Another frequently observed issue is the unregulated destruction of nature and resources. Without having serious legal or institutional regulations on their commercial activities, private entrepreneurs (national or foreign) in many conflict-affected societies attempt to reap the highest profit through "natural resource-rich sectors, commercial property in major cities, importing high-value consumer goods to supply urban elites, food-markets supplying major urban areas, and rehabilitating large commercial farms" (Addison and Brück 2009: 264). This tendency has usually resulted in overexploitation of natural resources such as forests, fisheries, minerals and water. The deforestation in the Democratic Republic (DR) of the Congo is a representative example. DR Congo possesses approximately half of the Congo Basin, the second-largest rainforest in the world; nevertheless, approximately 2,854,000 hectares of the forest were destroyed in the first ten years of postwar reconstruction by private companies in road construction to access more mineral resources, peasants' unregulated 'slash and burn' methods, the timber industry and artisanal logging (Butler 2013).

Moreover, the balanced development of different economic and social sectors has been undermined by such economically driven peacebuilding. Being influenced by the examples of economic development and progress in democratisation in East Asia (i.e. Taiwan and South Korea), many postwar governments made their social plans based on the unproven assumption that economic growth would go hand in hand with other social development. Furthermore, through engaging in corrupt practices with private industry, many power elites found good opportunities for strengthening their profits (Addison and Brück 2009). Hence, other social values that are highly important for balanced socioeconomic development, such as the protection of human rights, advocacy of indigenous cultural traditions, recovery of social unity and promotion of social reconciliation, are frequently neglected. The eviction of social minorities in order to host a new business complex in Cambodia, as described earlier, is a clear example of this.

Recently, various attempts have been made to address the dominance of growth-oriented agendas in socioeconomic peacebuilding, from both theoretical and practical perspectives. One noteworthy theoretical strand is the livelihood approach to development. Escaping from economy-focused concepts of development, the livelihood approach understands that development involves political, cultural and ecological dimensions as well as economic growth (Kaag et al. 2004). Moreover, people's poverty and sense of deprivation are dependent on their opportunities to access capital that includes financial, natural, human and physical capital. According to such studies, policies that focus entirely on short-term profit will eventually remove key sources of sustainable economic development (Bebbington 1999; Chambers and Conway 1991; Mullen 2008; Sen 1981).

Case study: social capital development in Mozambique

In the aftermath of the civil conflicts in 1992, the development of social capital in Mozambique existed more in principle than in reality. After going through long-term colonialism from Portugal, fifteen years of foreign-influenced civil war and a prolonged period of serious drought, people had no space for collective action pursuing development. The impact of a lack of economic and civil infrastructure, chronic poverty and the rapid spread of HIV/AIDS was devastating as well.

Nevertheless, a significant number of initiatives have emerged for enhancing social capital in the country since the early phase of the post-conflict reconstruction process. At the national level, the reform of institutions has been attempted by both domestic and external actors to make the process of policy making more inclusive. It was intended to reflect more diverse opinions and interests of people and create a strong sense of cooperation between different groups of people. For instance, the Foundation for Community Development (FDC, following its Portuguese abbreviation), which was the first endowed grant-making foundation in the country, shows a typical direction of such efforts. The FDC was founded in 1994 by a widow of the country's first president, Samora Machel, and a group of politicians to support the activities of NGOs and community-based organisations. In addition to mobilising funds for supporting these organisations' activities for education, health and disaster recovery, the foundation's key goal was bridging the gaps in the network between local NGOs and community actors. For example, in order to provide HIV/AIDS vaccinations to more people, the FDC facilitated a network of different healthcare aiders in northern Mozambique, linking the central government and local organisations, educating community residents' for participation, and establishing a logistical system for effective delivery of vaccines.

A more recent example was the creation in 2002 of the UNDP's long-term development strategy, Agenda 2025. This strategy, adopted by the Mozambique government, immediately proposed a number of important provisions for enhancing the governments' interaction with civil society organisations and the private sector (Fred-Mensah 2004). More importantly, a focus group called the Committee of Counsellors was organised to propose the long-term plans for development based on their consultation to a wide range of social groups. The members of the committee, who were themselves selected from different social groups, continued to meet with various segments of Mozambique society, such as academics, political party representatives, doctors, science researchers, veterinarians and community leaders.

Whilst national-level activities for social capital development focus more on institution building, projects at the community level pay more attention to education, poverty reduction and the establishment of local associations. It is believed that the capacity building of the community members and the trust and collaboration between them can be strengthened at the same time. Such activities are particularly important in the country as the ritualistic use of violence by the rebel group, the Mozambique National Resistance (RENAMO), for controlling rural communities left many parts of the country with a severe sense of mutual distrust, fear and incapability. Child aid and adult literacy campaigns that ADPP-Mozambique operates are good examples of this. By organising approximately 3,000 households in Maputo Province as key members, the organisation operates community development projects and education services in rural areas where the electricity supply is either unstable or nonexistent.

Traditional rituals played important roles in healing people's war trauma and in enabling them to engage in public life with their former enemies. *Mpfhukwa* is a spiritual ceremony to capture spirits that have died inappropriately and to appease their anger and grief. While a large number of *Mpfhukwa*s took place at community levels for both RENAMO solders and civil victims, people in the community commonly prayed that there would not be a return to war. Meanwhile, former soldiers tended to be taken to *ndomba* (a family's house of spirits) to purify their guilt (Honwana 1998).

Conclusion

This chapter has explored a number of the programme areas of socioeconomic reconstruction. As regards the economic dimension, it considered the reconstruction of industrial infrastructure, the provision of microfinance, and the creation of job opportunities. Within the social dimension, it discussed the repatriation of refugees, the promotion of strengthened social cohesion and the provision of formal and informal education. Based on information gathered from peacebuilding practice, this chapter also discussed the influence of a growth-oriented agenda in socioeconomic peacebuilding.

Related to the previous discussion, it should be noted that all the aspects of peacebuilding discussed in Chapters 7 and 8 are interconnected. For instance, while security stabilisation is a key requirement for enhancing the effective performance of the government, good government performance is necessary if security sector reforms such as (disarmament, demobilisation and reintegration of ex-combatants [DDR]), reconstruction of the armed forces and border control are to be carried out. Similarly, the DDR programmes implemented in Sierra Leone, Kosovo, Liberia and Cambodia demonstrate that the reintegration of ex-combatants can succeed only when it is well supported by growth in the employment market (economic reconstruction) and continuing re-education and resocialisation programmes (social reconstruction). Likewise, whereas a poorly functioning central/local government is a barrier to a rapid recovery in economic activity, the rebuilding of state capacity, including the creation of a professional public administration and civil service, cannot be sustained without the support of the economic sector.

Therefore, effective reconstruction programmes require a holistic approach that takes a wide range of (interlinked) issues into consideration. A policy for economic development, for example, needs to be aware of the reciprocal impact between the rehabilitation of basic services, the reconstruction of physical infrastructure, establishing human livelihoods and national reconciliation. Moreover, in terms of time frame, possible ways to (re)activate the economy and social activities in the short term and, at the same time, make sure of sustainable development in the long term should be considered. In fact, as external actors, international peacebuilding entities should respect their obvious limitations in addressing structural and social issues. Overall, such holistic considerations can provide a useful method for reducing the harmful impact of misjudged or less careful implementation of programmes.

Discussion questions

- Do democratisation and development necessarily bring about durable peace? Why and why not?
- How can peacebuilding projects gain popular legitimacy and acceptance in the context of a war-affected country?

- In what senses do culture and sports contribute to the enhancement of social cohesion in post-conflict societies?
- Some state actors argue that, although economic distribution is essential for preventing the recurrence of poverty-based conflicts, such distribution can be made only when sufficient growth has been made. Do you agree?

Notes

1 Although the programmes pursuing rule of law and administrative reform are frequently undertaken in the name of social peacebuilding, these programmes were discussed in other chapters.
2 The 3×6 approach adopts three principles to reintegrate conflict-affected people into fruitful economic activity: inclusiveness (inclusion of ex-combatants), ownership (local ownership) and sustainability (continued support to successful associations).
3 Although a great variety of definitions of social capital have been presented, 'social capital' is generally understood as "social structure and its facilitation of certain actions of actors – whether personal or corporate – within the structure" (Fred-Mensah 2004: 440). A few key words that penetrate different programmes of social capital development at the micro level are 'trust,' 'social relationships (ties),' 'network' and 'collective action,' while the core concepts defining macro-level policies pay attention to social, environmental and political structures.
4 A traditional conflict resolution system based on consensus building.
5 Although the version of *ubuntu* may differ according to the geographical area, *ubuntu* generally emphasises interdependence and trust between people.

Recommended reading

Appleby, R.S. (2003) 'Retrieving the Missing Dimension of Statecraft: Religious Faith in the Service of Peacebuilding', in *Faith-Based Diplomacy: Trumping Realpolitik*, edited by Johnston, D. Oxford: Oxford University Press: 231–58.
Du Toit, A.M. (1998) 'Building Cultural Synergy and Peace in South Africa'. *Journal of Social Development in Africa* 13 (1): 9–21.
Harris, G. and Lewis, N. (1999) 'Economic Reconstruction and Recovery', in *Recovery from Armed Conflict in Developing Countries: An Economic and Political Analysis*, edited by Harris, G. London: Routledge: 52–64.
Kumar, K. (1997) *Rebuilding Societies after Civil War: Critical Roles for International Assistance.* Boulder, CO: Lynne Rienner.
UNDP (2008) *Post-Conflict Economic Recovery: Enabling Local Ingenuity.* New York: UNDP Bureau of Crisis Prevention and Recovery.

Online resources

For more details of *Agenda 2025* explained in the case study in this chapter, please see http://www.portaldogoverno.gov.mz/docs_gov/outros/agenda2025.eng.pdf
For more details of ADPP in Mozambique, please see http://www.adpp-mozambique.org

9   Transitional justice and reconciliation

One of the most crucial issues faced by post-conflict or post-authoritarian regime societies is the challenge of handling dark chapters of their history. While improving stability is a prerequisite for sustainable peace and development and for prevention of further violent conflicts, it is difficult to achieve stability without proper recognition of war crimes, especially crimes against humanity, and the reconciliation of enemies within/outside borders. Psychological war trauma, people's lack of confidence in managing public lives, heavy reliance on patron-client relationships, and extreme distrust/antagonism between different social groups are a few typical issues that are caused by insufficient actions to promote justice and reconciliation in conflict-affected societies.

Hence, efforts to overcome the issues related to past crimes have been implemented in many previous peacebuilding processes. In societies where appalling human rights abuses have taken place (e.g. the genocide in Rwanda and ethnic cleansing in the former Yugoslavia), such processes are an essential element of efforts towards achieving sustainable peace. The previous efforts of the international community and the governments of war-affected countries to deal with the past were constructed on the basis of two closely interrelated but sometimes contradictory values: justice and reconciliation. While transitional justice pursues stable peace in war-affected countries by identifying past injustices and punishing the perpetrators, reconciliation aims to achieve the same goal via perpetrators' confession of past crimes and encouraging forgiveness from victims.

This chapter will explore the concepts of justice and reconciliation in war-affected societies and some of the major issues that peacebuilding programmes need to address based on these two values. Specifically, it will examine:

- Goals and core features of transitional justice and reconciliation programmes;
- Major methods of justice and reconciliation – truth-telling, trial and prosecution – as well as reparation and compensation, and reconstruction of the legal and judicial systems;
- Academic debates on the utilities and weaknesses of punitive justice and social reconciliation.

Transitional justice

Transitional justice refers to "the set of judicial and non-judicial measures that have been implemented by different countries in order to redress the legacies of massive human rights abuses" (ICTJ 2013) and aims to allow the affected nation and its people can put the past behind them and move on towards sustainable peace. Typically, the measures are intended to identify states' legal responsibility, to punish the human rights violators, to address victims' needs and demands, and to reconstruct society "in such a way that it is recognized by the entire population" (La Rosa and Philippe 2009: 369).

Transitional justice is believed to contribute to durable peace in war-affected countries in the following ways. First of all, by implementing justice, all members of the society as well as the international community confirm the grounds of morally acceptable human behaviour and make sure that violations will be punished. This confirmation is an important factor in deterring the potential of future violence. Moreover, transitional justice acknowledges the suffering of victims in conflict and post-conflict situations. Recognition and compensation of victims is important in that it can contribute to the political, social, economic and psychological aspects of building peace and stability in post-conflict societies.

More specifically, punitive justice in war-affected societies pursues social justice by addressing the following dimensions (see Figure 9.1). Regarding victim-related issues, justice needs to address and protect the right of victims to know what happened in the past and

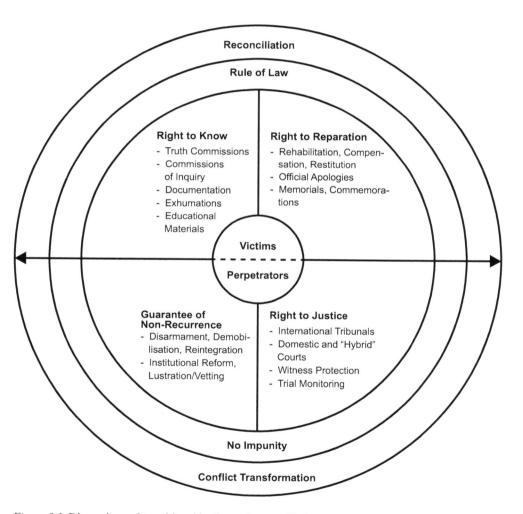

Figure 9.1 Dimensions of transitional justice and reconciliation

Source: Servaes and Birtsch (2008: 3). Reproduced with permission of the Working Group on Development and Peace (FriEnt) and KOFF Swisspeace.

to provide reparation that suitably acknowledges and reflects their sufferings. It is widely accepted that the victims and survivors of violent conflicts have both the moral and legal right "to see perpetrators brought to justice" (Gloppen 2005: 22). With regards to the perpetrators, justice should make sure that the human rights abusers receive appropriate punishment and that mechanisms are put in place to ensure that antihumanitarian crimes are curbed in the post-conflict society.

To address these dimensions, transitional justice frequently employs a number of methods. The capture and prosecution of perpetrators is a foremost method. Revealing the truth about past crimes is regarded as one of the most important parts of prosecution because it leads to both perpetrators and victims acknowledging and confirming past issues. Successfully establishing the truth is key to the implementation of further steps. Another popular method is the administration of reparation to victims of war-related crimes, especially as material, financial and institutional reparation has become more common in recent programmes. Reforming state institutions is also pursued to address the structural and systemic factors behind war crimes. Although crimes may be committed by individuals or groups, in many societies such violations are supported or enforced by state structures (van Zyl 2005).

Each of these methods has merits and disadvantages, and their utility in addressing war legacies usually depends on the local context, including the nature of the conflict, the government in power, the available resources, the goals of national reconciliation and the involvement of third-party interveners. Hence, comprehensive and cautious strategies should be employed in attempts to deal with truth-finding and the punishment of aggressors.

Nevertheless, imprudent application of punitive justice can risk causing further social tensions. For instance, methods of punitive justice could be used by new regimes in post-conflict societies to punish the individuals and groups that had fought against them. According to some observers, this is precisely what happened at the Nuremberg Trials, when those who had emerged victorious from World War II presided over the trials of their former enemies. In addition, the biased or hasty application of trials or prosecutions might cause serious social tensions or, in extreme cases, a reemergence of violent conflict. The risk of biased trials is relatively high, since punitive justice is frequently pursued in early phases of the post-conflict period, when peace is fragile and perpetrators still hold strong power. The fear of new regimes using war crimes tribunals to punish former enemies becomes a particularly serious issue in nations where the judiciary is weak and corrupt, creating the ideal situation for manipulation by politicians. Hence, the goals of justice should be more than simple punishment for past war crimes, and the measures that are taken in pursuit of justice should include a focus on social reconciliation and reparation, which will be discussed next.

Reconciliation

Reconciliation is a process of "restoring broken relationships and learning to live non-violently with radical differences" (Ramsbotham, Woodhouse and Miall 2011: 246), and it seeks to promote a more peaceful society through forgiving perpetrators and recognising the sufferings of victims at the same time. More specifically, social reconciliation "redefine[s] the relationship between former enemy groups, and, fundamentally, to re-humanize former enemies" and modify "individual and collective identities and, subsequently, the representations of oneself and of others" (Hazan 2009: 260). Reconciliation can help to ensure that the victims will not suffer the same abuses again and that the relationship between social groups can escape from a cycle of revenge and retaliation. If the individual and collective traumas are not addressed, residual grievances can provide the basis for self-perpetuating cycles of violence among future generations.

The promotion of social reconciliation is a comprehensive process that includes a wide range of programmes, from small encounter group–level rituals for forgiveness to high-profile truth commission projects for fact-finding. When reconciliation was initially proposed as a component of peacebuilding, it was assumed that workshop-type dialogue would be the most effective form for accommodating reconciliation (Fisher 2001; Montville 1993). However, as ideas on reconciliation became more specific, more diverse forms of programme began to be included.

More recently, the reconciliation programmes undertaken in contemporary peacebuilding processes pursue more varied values and themes that contribute directly to fundamental reconciliation in war-affected societies. First of all, truth-finding is regarded by many people as the first step towards reconciliation. The programmes that are typically undertaken to address this requirement include recognition of past social injustices, public telling of victims' experiences, sharing the pain of other people, apology or reparation. 'Identity' is another theme that penetrates a number of programmes, involving more inclusive social policies that pursue unity within society as well as activities aimed at raising awareness of mutual interdependence, acknowledging the humanity of others, and accepting the identity and autonomy of others. Moreover, many programmes attempt to promote forgiveness through one or more of the following: amnesia,[1] unearthing and identifying the pain of the other, cultural healing rituals[2] and sharing pain. Justice is also considered an essential part of reconciliation, and this includes all programmes discussed in the justice section. Last but not least, reconciliation at the individual or group level is pursued as a part of the reconciliation process. Projects aimed at restoring broken relationships and recreating/rebuilding local communities are representative examples of those used in contemporary reconciliation programmes (Lambourne 2004; Rigby 2001).

Nevertheless, in many cases, the process of reconciliation is not as straightforward in practice as it might appear to be in theory. In the first place, many victims are at the same time perpetrators. Violent conflicts are usually marked by mutual aggression, and many victims of war crimes have actually been involved in perpetuating human rights abuses and war crimes as well. Furthermore, people's prejudices and the tensions between social groups make the process of reconciliation more difficult. In societies where there have been serious tensions between various social groups, strong psychological prejudices exist and tend to predetermine people's ideas, perceptions and actions, and many perpetrators do not have a sense of guilt over what they have done. Moreover, even in cases where people admit their past crimes, they frequently refuse to apologise due to equally strong pressure from their own political or social groups. As a result, it is often the case that reconciliation is interpreted by the constituencies of the society as a politically biased process and further catalyses social tensions.

Meanwhile, the reconstruction process can also be a means for healing societal wounds caused by armed conflicts. This could be achieved in a variety of ways, by using the reconstruction of key lifelines such as water supply systems, education and health services as opportunities for those conflicting communities to work towards an improved infrastructure or service beneficial to all. For example, Leslie (1995: 29) points out that one of the most important lessons learnt from the involvement of the United Nations Centre for Human Settlements (UNCHS, or UN-Habitat) in Afghanistan during the mid-1990s was "the value of encouraging a process that helps bring communities and institutions together in pursuit of a common goal, in the face of the upheaval of the conflict." The example of the project – '216 Steps to Reconciliation' in Kabul, which was initiated by UN-Habitat provides a good example of how post-conflict reconstruction projects can be implemented with the aim of facilitating reconciliation between conflicting communities (see Box 9.1 for further information on this project).

Box 9.1 216 steps to reconciliation

This project, which was carried out in the mid-1990s, focused on securing and repairing a steep path for a Panjshiri housing area on a hillside against flood and mudslides. When Hazara workers were asked to work on this project, they were suspicious about the Panjshiris (a community they had fought against during the conflict). After being assured by UN-Habitat, they agreed to work alongside Panjshiri workers, although an uneasy feeling of mistrust remained in the group for the first couple of weeks. For example, on one occasion they were suspicious about drinking water provided by a Panjshiri family. They wanted to see the Panjshiri workers drinking this water first, as they had thought it might have been poisonous. After seeing that it was safe, they also drank the water. In the following days, there were more examples of rebuilding trust and confidence, which led to their realisation that they could actually work together. After the completion of the project, as the residents of the area were highly satisfied with the work carried out by Hazara workers, the Panjshiris had asked them to continue to work as water bearers.

Source: SAFE (1996).

Methods of justice and reconciliation

Until the early 1980s, there were only two reactions to human rights crimes: trials or amnesty. However, after a number of truth commissions were established in Latin American countries in 1983, various methods of realising these two goals have been developed, including amnesia, criminal prosecution, truth-telling, judicial process reform, cultural rituals of healing and the like. From among these, this section will discuss three of the methods that have been most commonly utilised in previous transitional justice and reconciliation programmes. While truth-telling is discussed as a core method for bringing about social reconciliation, trial and reparation are presented as key measures for transitional justice.

Truth-telling

Truth-telling is an accountability mechanism that enables survivors (both victims and perpetrators) of a conflict to recount their experiences and actions in the aftermath of violent conflict or authoritarian rule. Truth-telling is seen by most peacebuilding practitioners as a prerequisite for forgiveness, reconciliation and returning society to the coexistence and high levels of trust that existed before the conflict. In its simplest form, truth-telling can be described as a confession or a process of dialogue in which an individual accounts for past actions (and decisions) and takes responsibility for wrongdoing.

This act of confession psychologically enables those who have suffered injury to accept loss, let go of the pain and eventually draw a curtain on the past, thus laying the foundation for healing and reconciliation. More specifically, truth-telling provides vital information about violations and therefore helps victims (and society at large) to know the truth about their suffering and loss, missing relatives or circumstances surrounding their death, and possibly where remains can be found for reburial. In addition to shedding light on what happened in the past, such initiatives are important for reconciling people and groups who in the past have been in competition and conflict. However, since such truth-finding activities refresh the victims' painful memories, the programmes should be supported by projects that serve the psychological healing process. Moreover, confessions provide an opportunity for victims to put the past behind them and move on, thus laying the foundation for healing and for reestablishing social support networks that were destroyed by the conflict. This has been the case in some countries, especially Sierra Leone and South Africa, where symbolic reconciliation exercises were held in public.

In an ideal setting, confession is followed by forgiveness, a commitment from the victim to let go of all bitterness, resentment, anger and so on against a wrongdoer. Forgiveness is a personal decision and is seen as an act capable of mitigating the harmful effects of decisions and actions in the past. From this perspective, truth-telling reduces mutual hate and is capable of transforming the relationship between the perpetrator and the victims, enabling the two to move into the future without fear (Rigby 2001).

In post-conflict situations, especially after gross human rights violations, third-party interveners work with the concerned governments to establish the truth about violations. This has resulted in the establishment of truth and reconciliation commissions (TRC), which generally give individuals who have suffered violation an opportunity to communicate their experiences to people in authority and to receive collective acknowledgement of their suffering. Truth commissions are nonjudicial bodies that intend to support victims by listening to, recording and acknowledging their stories of human rights violations. These temporary commissions examine a defined period of the past, and their mandate ends with the submission of a report (Ramsbotham et al. 2011).

Since the first truth commission was created in Argentina in 1983, more than twenty truth-telling bodies have been formed (e.g. in Bolivia, Uruguay, Uganda, Nepal, Chile, Chad, Germany, Haiti and Burundi). Although several agencies (e.g. the UN, nongovernmental organisations [NGOs] and churches) have set up fact-finding initiatives, a truth commission usually requires a strong mandate to enable it to access sensitive information, question powerful individuals to testify and protect people involved in the commission's work. As a result, most truth commissions have been established by either a presidential decree or parliamentary order, although there were exceptions to this rule in El Salvador, Guatemala and Timor-Leste, where commissions were sanctioned by the United Nations (Weissbrodt 2005).

Previous truth commissions demonstrate varied characteristics in terms of their scope and modes of operation, composition and resources. As part of their mandate, commissioners involved in establishing the truth about abuses are always required to produce a report on their findings, with recommendations on how to address the legacies of the past. Such reports have been closely linked with consolidating the collective memory of the nation concerned. Collective memory, in turn, has been found to be useful in post-conflict societies, as it acts as a social glue that promotes cohesion in divided communities (Miller and Bunnell 2011).

Nevertheless, a number of limitations have been associated with these truth commissions. One example is that when commissions applied a general blanket amnesty to former war criminals, they left the new authorities little power to reveal the truth. As their impunity was not always assured, many war criminals refused to publicly acknowledge their human rights violations. High-ranking officers, who have the biggest responsibilities for such crimes, presented particularly reluctant attitudes. As new governments tended to acquiesce to this reluctance in the interest of preventing potential future conflicts, a large number of victims became disappointed and resentful about the outcomes of these commissions. Moreover, the activities of truth commissions tended to be seriously limited by the restrictions in their mandates. A frequently occurring issue was too narrowly defined areas of investigation. For instance, whilst truth commissions in Latin America dealt with cases of killings and kidnappings, issues like torture and sexual abuses were neglected. In regard to this problem, Rigby (2001: 126) states that "there was too little justice, too little truth, and hence, although social peace was maintained, there was no solid foundation for reconciliation."

Trial and prosecution

The trial and prosecution of the perpetrators who conducted antihumanitarian actions such as genocide, ethnic cleansing, war crimes, murder, torture and rape comprise a core element of transitional justice in post-conflict societies. As described earlier, prosecution is expected to contribute to the justice system in war-torn and post-conflict societies by deterring future crimes, reducing the sense of marginalisation felt by victims, building trust between victims and the state, and reflecting a new set of social norms. Moreover, the trial 'individualises' guilt. By distinguishing the actual perpetrators of misdeeds from the wider group to which they belong, it can prevent the potential risk that a society will express its anger against an entire social group (Williams and Scharf 2002). In addition, the punishment of former war criminals through legal trials can serve to demonstrate the higher morality of the new authority in the war-affected country and the international community in dealing with perpetrators of antihumanitarian acts (Rigby 2001).

In order to achieve these goals, various forms of trial have been undertaken since the 1990s (see Table 9.1). First, one of the most common mechanisms utilised in post-conflict societies is the domestic justice system where war crimes are judged under domestic law. Many contemporary cases such as Argentina, Timor-Leste and Iraq adopt such formats for prosecution of war crimes. The prosecutions in Argentina and Uganda provide striking examples of contrasting outcomes from similar mechanisms. Both cases had strong links with institutions whose principal objective was to establish the truth about human rights

Table 9.1 Institutionalisation of transitional justice

	Permanent institutions	*Temporary institutions*
Domestic judicial system	Existing national judiciary system (Ethiopia, Argentina, Rwanda)	National temporary tribunals (Iraq, Rwanda, South Africa)
Hybrid forms	National courts with international actors' administration (Timor-Leste)	Joint tribunals of both domestic and international actors (Rwanda, Sierra Leone, Cambodia, East Timor, Kosovo, and Bosnia-Herzegovina)
International initiatives	International Criminal Court (Central Africa, DR Congo, Uganda) The courts in foreign countries (Chile, Rwanda)	International temporary tribunals (former Yugoslavia, Rwanda)

Sources: Adapted from Gloppen (2005: 24) and Chetail (2009: 23).

violations with a specific focus on identifying perpetrators and witnesses. Facts were then passed on to the courts in order to prosecute individuals identified as perpetrators.

In Argentina, the democratic government that replaced the military junta worked in collaboration with the National Commission for the Disappeared (CONADEP) to prosecute individuals who were responsible for gross human rights violations. CONADEP was established in 1983 after democracy had been restored in Argentina and was mandated to investigate the fate of the thousands of people who disappeared during the rule of Emilio Eduardo Massera. On completion of the investigation, CONADEP presented its findings to the court, which prosecuted five people for violations. Although many Argentines were angry at the court for prosecuting such a small number of people, the effort of the government was applauded internationally as an impressive local effort aimed at addressing abuses committed in the past.

In Uganda, the Truth and Reconciliation Commission that operated between 1986 and 1995 passed on some of its findings to the police and courts in support of prosecutions. Although thousands of cases backed by evidence were passed on, very few individuals were prosecuted, and even when they were, it was in most cases for more minor offences such as kidnapping and conspiracy. Although the attempt made by Uganda at trial and prosecution was not very successful, it serves to raise some of the challenges faced by nations coming out of conflict. Due to the absence of witness protection programmes, very few people appeared in court to provide a reliable account of the crimes committed by armed men. Uganda's experience is similar to that of Haiti, where witnesses, lawyers and judges expressed fear of retaliation by armed gangs and therefore distanced themselves from trials of individuals connected with the regime of General Raoul Cedras.

Second, in cases where the domestic judicial system cannot find a route to justice, trials in foreign courts or in international tribunals may be initiated. For instance, in permanent international courts, all justice issues are dealt with by international third parties; the International Criminal Court (ICC) is representative of this form of permanent body. Moreover, a number of ad hoc courts have been established to prosecute war crimes. The International Criminal Tribunal that was established in former Yugoslavia in May 1993 under Chapter VII of the UN Charter was the first post–Cold War international court to deal with war crimes. Since then, approximately 160 people, including former heads of state, have been charged, and an additional sixty people are still awaiting judgement (ICTY 2012). Another example is the International Criminal Tribunal for Rwanda (ICTR), which was established in November 1994 to deal with the genocide in Rwanda.

Finally, there are other hybrid forms of trial that combine the legal systems of national authorities and international assistance. In order to respond to the need for domestic ownership and legitimacy, both national and international actors participate in the trials on past war crimes. In Sierra Leone, Kosovo, Timor-Leste, Cambodia and Iraq, for instance, the courts on war crimes were composed of both domestic and international justice actors (Chetail 2009; La Rosa and Philippe 2009).

Due to the complex range of benefits and limitations that previous trials and prosecutions have demonstrated, extensive discussion on the usefulness of these methods has taken place since the early 1990s. First of all, many normative discussions criticise previous international tribunals for being the tools of victors' justice. As most rules and related settings in these mechanisms were mainly determined, implemented and funded by Western actors, the judgments made in these mechanisms tend to reflect these actors' values. Consequently, many cases were decried as biased against the people who were not allied with the Western countries (Costi 2006).

Moreover, in terms of practice, research suggests that these mechanisms are neither effective nor efficient. For instance, the international tribunal on the Rwanda genocide spent $245,295,800 and recruited approximately 650 staff for the 2010–12 budget year alone. Nevertheless, the combined outcome of trials over the last twenty years was the conviction of twenty-nine criminals. Furthermore, as many of the trials set up by international tribunal took place far from where the conflict occurred, the victims had very limited opportunities to get involved in the process.

From a longer-term viewpoint, inadequately structured judicial mechanisms and lack of human resources prevented many conflict-affected countries from developing sustainable justice systems that could promote social justice and democratic governance. For instance, many sub-Saharan African countries like Zambia, Zimbabwe, Mozambique and Uganda commonly suffer from formidable problems at all phases of their justice systems, from policing to punishment. Some examples include shortages in policing forces, lack of investigative capacity, minimal prosecution structures, limited numbers of legal courts (most of which are concentrated in cities and towns) and high rates of corruption (Chikwanha 2009).

Reparation and compensation

Reparation is concerned with restoring the situation that existed before the conflict "by returning things to their original state or by providing compensation for the damage sustained" (Sassòli 2009: 279). Most fundamentally, many studies argue that improving the victims' well-being and financial situation is a requisite for social reconciliation (Gloppen 2005). From the perspective of the rule of law, many international laws indicate that a state should guarantee the individual rights of all its citizens and be responsible for antihumanitarian acts committed by previous regimes (IDEA 2003). From a normative perspective, acknowledging the past suffering of victims is a means to acknowledge them as human beings. From a more practical viewpoint, moreover, it is sometimes important to help them overcome their suffering by providing various levels of social support.

Although the most common form of reparation is material or financial assistance (e.g. individual reparation grants, pensions and scholarships), a wide range of measures are conducted as parts of compensation and include medical support (e.g. trauma treatment and the building of local treatment centres), community rehabilitation programmes (resettlement of displaced people, stabilising community-based social activities), satisfaction regarding immaterial harm (e.g. verifying of facts, offering public apology and searching for missing people) or symbolic projects (e.g. national days of remembrance, monuments and parks, and renaming buildings and clearing criminal records) (Minow 2000; Sassòli 2009; van Zyl 2005). Ideally, the choice of appropriate methods should be made based on the victims' cultural background, their post-conflict socioeconomic position and the length of time since the violations occurred.

Formulating the terms of compensation is always complex and frequently problematic because there are various competing types and degrees of perpetration and various forms of victim. In terms of financial compensation, for instance, it is frequently questioned whether compensation should be made only to victims who experienced critical human rights abuses, such as killings, torture, rape and disappearance, or to a wider range of people who experienced systemic social discrimination. In the case of South Africa, victims were defined as those "who were not only tortured, maimed and ill-treated but who also witnessed the destruction of whole families and communities" (Truth and Reconciliation Commission of South Africa 2000). Although calculation of reparation is based on the extent of the suffering that was experienced, the need for access to services and daily living subsidies are common criteria and usually cause various controversies during the implementation process.

Moreover, in cases where national authorities have provided a services package that included access to health, housing, education and other basic services as reparation, the high administrative and logistical costs and less flexibility to adapt to victims' changing needs have been major problems. It should also be noted that providing a privilege in the form of constant access to social services that are necessary but costly for other constituencies might cause further tensions between social groups.

Reconstruction of the legal and judicial system

In many contemporary intrastate conflicts, poorly functioning or biased judicial systems have contributed to the emergence of human rights abuses and exacerbate the tensions between social groups, by supporting the arbitrary wielding of political and economic power by certain social/political groups. Hence, from a long-term viewpoint, rebuilding and strengthening the system of justice and law enforcement to provide constituencies with fair and equal treatment before the law is an essential foundation for realising social justice and more fundamental reconciliation. The reconstruction of legal and judicial system are ultimately intended to ensure that "all persons, institutions and entities, public and private including the state itself, are accountable to laws that are publicly promulgated, equally enforced and independently adjudicated and which are consistent with international human rights norms and standards" (UN 2004).

The various programmes undertaken in many contemporary peacebuilding processes can be roughly categorised into four types. First, the initial step in rebuilding sustainable and effective legal systems in war-affected societies is (re)constructing the constitutional frameworks of governance. Although interim constitutions can be developed through negotiation between the representatives of military factions and intervening actors, a new constitution can be durable and stable only when it is carefully designed through a process of inclusive participation. Furthermore, the constitution needs to provide an impartial political climate in which all social groups can pursue their goals, and it should make provision for peaceful means of resolving the conflicts of interests between social groups.

Second, the structural reform of judicial and legal institutions is also pursued. Ensuring the independence of judicial decisions from the influence of political, governmental and military actors is a prerequisite of good judicial performance. In addition, any inconsistencies in the aims, functions, scope of responsibilities and operating principles of different legal institutions that have served to undermine the rule of law need to be addressed.

Third, many reconstruction programmes include projects for strengthening the capacity of judicial institutions. While some programmes focus on training new judges, court staff and lawyers, other programmes pay more attention to introducing new court administration systems and providing new technology (e.g. computer systems for case tracking). The improvement of prison conditions and security is another important issue to be considered.

Last but not least, making the judicial system more available and affordable to all people is another commonly pursued legal system reform. This type of reform is an essential element in the creation of a durable peace in societies in which many people have participated in military combat because people in these societies have rarely had any access to a reliable legal system or methods of resolving or expressing their problems and disputes. Some frequently used methods include public education about their rights to bring legal complaints, provision of alternative dispute resolution (e.g. neighbourhood counsellors, local mediation mechanisms and informal legal enquiry services) and support for legal advocacy NGOs.

Case study: Truth and Reconciliation Commission in South Africa

Pursuing both justice and social reconciliation has constantly been one of the key challenges in most contemporary peacebuilding programmes. While the methods for justice may provoke strong resistance and violent actions, too much amnesty may allow the structural issues that caused armed conflicts to remain. For instance, the truth commissions implemented in Latin American countries, like Uruguay, Argentina and Chile in the 1980s, presented the negative consequences of the efforts for 'generous forgiveness.' In these countries, the provisions of a blanket amnesty to the previous antihumanitarian crimes left the new governments with few ways to present 'new' standards of social justice. Moreover, by limiting the mandates of the commissions to the investigation of missings and killings, a wide range of human rights violations (i.e. rape and torture) were left undiscovered. The decision to prohibit the identification of the perpetrators made the commissions fail to provide proper opportunities for victims' pain and anguish to be acknowledged. As a result, the truth commissions in the 1980s achieved highly limited successes in bringing the former perpetrators into the process of truth revelation/punishment, in recognising the victims' pains and suffering, and in facilitating solid ground for social reconciliation.

A few years after these failures, the South African government initiated the Truth and Reconciliation Commission in May 1995, when the legal framework of the commission was officially endorsed by President Nelson Mandela. The Commission was composed of seventeen commissioners with some 300 staff members; moreover, it had three subcommittees that dealt with three distinct dimensions of social reconciliation. Whilst the Human Rights Violation Committee aimed to receive testimonies from victims, the Reparation and Rehabilitation Committee was in charge of proposing public policies for reparation and social reconciliation. The main task of the Amnesty Committee was receiving and reviewing the amnesty applications.

The leading actors – including Archbishop Desmond Tutu, who structured the Commission – were aware of the failures of the reconciliation initiatives in Latin American countries. Thus, the main objective of the Commission was to develop "a method that would not provoke the bloodbath that many feared, but that would acknowledge the competing historical narratives . . . and facilitate reconciliation" (Rigby 2001: 126). In order to avoid the pitfalls apparent in the preceding mechanisms in Latin America, South Africa applied the following actions.

First, it tried to make the all procedures of the truth commission's activities public and to involve as many people as possible. The government hosted a large number of public debates on the structure, composition and mandates of the truth commission; moreover, it welcomed mass media coverage of the details of the activities. For instance, the commission held a large number of public meetings with local communities, civil organisations and religious associations across the country in 1995 in order to raise public awareness. Approximately 21,000 statements from victims were gathered and were usually heard in public places such as church halls and civic centres (USIP n.d.a.).

Second, regarding the issue of impunity, forgiveness was granted only to the people who acknowledged their past deeds; a collective amnesty was not provided. Former perpetrators had to submit amnesty applications, providing the details on their criminal activities, to the Committee by 10 May 1997. Moreover, in order to avoid 'victor's justice,' such applications were requested both from former oppressors as well as from anti-apartheid fighters. In total, 7,112 applications were received, and many of the applicants were required to physically attend the Commission offices to provide further details. Eventually, amnesty was granted in 849 cases. The names of perpetrators were also included in the final report of the Commission.

Third, the Committee tried to recognise not only individual violence but also institutional and structural violence during apartheid. Consequently, a number of special hearings were held on the "role of business, the media, the health sector, the faith communities, the trade unions, and the judiciary system" (Rigby 2001: 131). The final report of the Committee covered the structural issues, historical background and institutional environment that had nurtured violence and discrimination.

Fourth, the Commission also proposed a number of important actions of reparation. The suggestions include a wide range of issues from material aid such as financial grants to more symbolic, social and structural support, such as the revisions of legal provisions in favour of social minorities. The President's Fund was established in 2003 to provide reparation to the victims of apartheid, but the process of distribution has been very slow.

After the final report was submitted in 1998, various efforts were made to continue the process of social reconciliation. For instance, President Mandela gave an official apology to the victims on behalf of the country while a government body was established to monitor the implementation of the Commission's recommendations (the Institute for Justice and Reconciliation). Despite its significant limitations such as the unimplemented provisions of reparation and the refusal of revolutionary leaders' commitment, the truth commission in South Africa is considered a relatively successful model that shows the significant contribution of public participation.

Conclusion

This chapter has discussed the issues related to justice and reconciliation in the aftermath of violent conflicts. First, it gave an overview of the contribution of justice and reconciliation to peacebuilding in conflict-affected countries. After presenting the definition of the concept of transitional justice, the first part of the chapter revealed the four dimensions that justice should consider: the right to know, the right to reparation, the guarantee of nonrecurrence of human rights abuses and the right to justice. In addition, it presented three dimensions of reconciliation: acknowledgement and contrition from the perpetrators of antihumanitarian acts, and forgiveness from the victims. Moreover, three methods for promoting justice and reconciliation were introduced: truth-telling, trial and prosecution and reparation and compensation. Finally, some of the forms of truth and reconciliation commission were discussed by focusing on their mandates and contributions to peace promotion in war-affected countries.

Despite their usefulness as observed in recent examples, key methods such as truth commissions and international tribunals have presented various limitations. While some attempts failed due to lack of substantial enforcing power (e.g. the truth commissions in Latin America), others were criticised as biased in favour of a certain group of (international or domestic) actors (e.g. international tribunal for the former Yugoslavia). More importantly, the achievements of these methods were considered much less significant than the massive costs to operate these mechanisms. Thus, as discussed in this chapter, many people have argued that these mechanisms are ineffective and inefficient.

Such criticisms make highly valid points. Nevertheless, to be fair, it should also be noted that the process of pursuing social reconciliation and justice is highly complex and painful. A social justice or reconciliation programme cannot be completed through a few years' events. Instead, the transformation of people's atrocities or hatred normally takes several generations and as such requires the commitment of a majority of the social actors. Hence, in this sense it is too ambitious to expect the previously implemented mechanisms in conflict-affected countries to have brought about significant differences within short periods of time. Moreover, from a practical perspective, more proactive community-led initiatives for promoting social transformation should supplement the existing mechanisms. Ultimately, social justice and reconciliation can only be achieved through constructing some form of human community where people can share the same future.

Discussion questions

•   Considering the required time and costs, is an international tribunal a useful form of bringing past war crimes into justice?
•   Can 'forgetting' be a suitable response to the past war crimes?
•   Is justice necessary for reconciliation? If yes, on a continuum of justice, where should that be located?
•   Are there potential alternatives to the conventional punitive trials for reconfirming justice in the war-affected societies?

Notes

1 Amnesia is sometimes employed as a means of letting go of the past. In the initial phases of the post-conflict period, when the complicity of the grassroots membership of both sides in past events is so widespread, agreeing 'to forget the past' is considered a useful method of preventing further social tensions from arising.
2 In many cases, indigenous ways of promoting social reconciliation are employed alongside the traditional methods previously mentioned. In some cases, the use of traditional rituals of reacceptance to readmit perpetrators into communities was an important part of reconciliation (e.g. in Cambodia), while in others religious amnesty played a critical role in the reintegration of former combatants into civil societies (e.g. El Salvador).

Recommended reading

Breen-Smyth, M. (2007) Chapters 2 and 5, in *Truth Recovery and Justice after Conflict: Managing Violent Pasts*. London: Routledge: 6–21, 67–90.
Goldstone, R. (1996) 'Justice as a Tool for Peace-Making: Truth Commissions and International Criminal Tribunals'. *New York University Journal of International Law and Policy* 23: 485–503.Lederach, J. P. (1999) Chapter 6, in *Building Peace: Sustainable Reconciliation in Divided Societies*. Washington, DC: United States Institute of Peace.
Mani, R. (2005) 'Balancing Peace with Justice in the Aftermath of Violent Conflict'. *Development* 48 (3): 25–34.
Rigby, A. (2001) 'Introduction', in *Justice and Reconciliation: After the Violence*. Boulder, CO: Lynne Rienner.Skaar, E., Gloppen, S. and Suhrke, A. (eds.) (2005) *Roads to Reconciliation*. Oxford: Lexington Books.

Online resources

For more details of International Criminal Tribunals and Truth Commissions, please see: International Criminal Tribunal for former Yugoslavia (ICTY)   http://www.icty.org
International Criminal Tribunal for Rwanda (ICTR)   http://www.unictr.org
South African Truth Commission   http://www.justice.gov.za/trc/
Special Court for Sierra Leone   http://www.rscsl.org/

Conclusion

This book has explored a wide range of issues relevant to contemporary peacebuilding efforts by focusing on three specific dimensions. First, it reviewed a number of the core concepts related to peace, violent conflict and peacebuilding. Following this, practical aspects of peacebuilding were examined from both procedural (conflict resolution, post-conflict reconstruction and conflict transformation) and thematic perspectives (security, political, socio-economic reconstructions and justice and reconciliation). In addition to introducing the key features of peacebuilding activities, this volume presented their major achievements and limitations, the barriers prohibiting successful peacebuilding, and practical suggestions proposed to overcome these challenges. Finally, the peacebuilding programmes implemented in Afghanistan, Bosnia-Herzegovina, Cambodia, Colombia, Eastern Slavonia, El Salvador, Kenya, Kosovo, Mozambique, South African and Timor-Leste were examined as case studies. Through these discussions, this book has aimed to provide readers with an opportunity to reflect upon contemporary international peace-related activities with the benefit of a broader understanding of overall peacebuilding processes.

In reflecting on the achievements and limitations of the peacebuilding programmes implemented over the past two decades, a range of efforts to make peacebuilding more effective and sustainable emerged. Although many of these trends were introduced in the previous chapters, the significance of a few new developments was presented only briefly in order to focus on the key features of peacebuilding practice. Hence, as concluding remarks, this chapter revisits the following issues.

Prioritising and setting peacebuilding objectives

It is crucial that the peacebuilding process establishes a vision that can be shared by all or most stakeholders so that they can contribute to the process effectively. This can only be achieved by involving as many stakeholders as possible in the process through an action-planning methodology. Peacebuilding should not be planned away from the locale of that conflict-affected environment. Stakeholders need to perceive and experience that their concerns, priorities and objectives are being consulted, considered, negotiated and incorporated in the reconstruction planning as much as possible. Unfortunately, in too many peacebuilding environments the prioritisation and setting of reconstruction objectives are carried out from a largely utilitarian, external and technical perspective.

There are a number of reasons for this. First, it should be accepted that it is not an easy challenge and it is often impossible to secure the full support of all stakeholders. Invariably, there are parties in a peacebuilding environment that are prepared to act as 'spoilers.' It is necessary to be realistic regarding what can be achieved in ensuring a comprehensive support for the reconstruction agenda. Nevertheless, the handling of this challenge by both international and national actors has been far from exemplary in recent times, which brings us to the second issue. The way this challenge tends to be tackled is often based on a Darwinian approach of the survival of the fittest. In other words, whoever manages to get their voice heard tends to get an upper hand in the building up of this vision. For example, when the international community intervenes and acts as a third party in a peacebuilding environment, the local politicians they work with tend to be those who waged the conflict. In the 'peace-building marketplace,' peace is often 'traded' for political opportunity or economic advantage, or to put it another way, there may be no option but to work with the belligerents of a conflict (Miall, Ramsbotham and Woodhouse 1999) – but this does not mean that this should be the only way ahead.

It is also important to build up a range of methodologies so that the reconstruction agenda is not completely dominated by a few internal actors, and in order for civil society to contribute to the process on an equal basis. All too often the way in which the international community tackles this challenge has a significant negative impact. For example, by rushing to organise the first post-conflict elections before the society and the sociopolitical environment are actually ready for it, those belligerents or politicians involved in the conflict will turn themselves into the legally elected representatives of the people. Not surprisingly, the vision set for reconstruction comes to reflect only the views, opinions and agendas of those involved in waging the conflict.

However, this is on the assumption that the international community approaches this challenge from a totally neutral perspective and it is all up to internal actors, and this is clearly wrong. In the contemporary practice of establishing a vision for peacebuilding, external actors tend to play a central role without leaving much space for the inclusion of such issues as what and how internal actors would envisage for the reconstruction process to take place. Such a view of reconstruction also tries to set quantifiable goals and objectives for all activities, some of which are largely in the sociopolitical and cultural realms of life and not easily quantifiable in numbers and statistics. They are also naturally value based, and therefore those objectives set by the international community would not necessarily reflect what would really be desired by war-affected communities. The internal and external agendas concerning what constitutes that reconstruction vision, how it can be achieved, and what would be the expected outcomes from this process can be completely different. For example, it is often the case that external actors would like to see a sectoral process, or in other words, a compartmentalisation of the process, while internal actors would prefer a process in which inter-linkages between different areas and priorities are well recognised. Internal actors may be more prepared to make sacrifices in short-term gains in order to establish stronger long-term prospects. At the same time, the agenda of external actors tends to dictate to the contrary, since they would often prefer quick, uncomplicated and cheap solutions to long-term involvements with complex structures and mechanisms based on local sociopolitical and cultural frameworks.

Transition from emergency relief to development

One direction in which peacebuilding efforts are moving is reflected in their attempts to address the complex conditions of conflict resolution and post-conflict development in a more comprehensive way. Until the mid-1990s, emergency relief and humanitarian aid tended to be regarded as independent areas. On the one hand, major relief agencies refused to be affected by the agenda of political peacebuilding actors or international development agencies, while, on the other, international peacebuilding organisations did not include emergency relief as a part of their operation plans. Hence, despite the efforts of various actors, there were a large number of emergency relief aid programmes aimed at providing urgent necessities that failed to address issues like institutional fragility, low trust in government, lack of social reintegration and insignificant private investment.

However, after having implemented a number of peacebuilding programmes for several years, international peace-supporting actors recognised that many war-affected communities continue to have various problems that could lead to the resumption of violent conflict. Hence, both relief actors and development agencies reconsidered their mandates, budgets and activities in order to address this problem. Relief and development began to be considered as different parts of a more comprehensive peacebuilding. In 1994, the US Agency for International Development (USAID) established the Office of Transition Initiative, and in 1996 the UK's Department for International Development established a Conflict Policy Unit. These two groups were created in order to explore and develop the links between relief and development. In addition, the United Nations Development Programme (UNDP) created an Emergency Response Division in 1997 and set transformation as an important goal of the unit.

At the same time, new priorities began to be emphasised in major peacebuilding plans. For instance, the transformation from 'food aid' to 'poverty reduction' is one of the key aims in agricultural reconstruction. In recent programmes in Rwanda, Mozambique, Somalia and Afghanistan, the provision of seeds and tools (rather than food) has been adopted as a method of enhancing productivity among farmers and promoting sustainable agricultural rehabilitation. Moreover, the need for a number of new efforts to provide more comprehensive support to seed systems, agricultural systems and broader livelihood systems was recognised (Christoplos, Longley and Slaymaker 2004: 17).

Coordination of peacebuilding programmes

If 'connecting emergency relief with development' is a comprehensive approach in terms of time sequence, 'coordination of peacebuilding programmes' is a type of comprehensive effort regarding actors. Over the past decade, the differences and contradictions between the principles and positions of different peacebuilding organisations hindered effective collaboration. As discussed in Chapter 5, many of the weaknesses in contemporary peacebuilding programmes are reported to be a consequence of the lack of coordination.

Recognising the importance of coordination, intensive interaction, information sharing, respect for norms and mutually agreed rules, the establishment of a coordination body for peacebuilding actors has been suggested in many academic papers and practical reports. As a prominent coordinating actor, then UN Secretary-General Kofi Annan highlighted the importance of aid coordination in 1997 by stressing the need for "coherent, effective, and timely assistance to those in need" (Strand 2005: 89). In particular, the promotion of enhanced civil-military collaboration is considered a key requirement for successful post-conflict reconstruction (de Coning 2006).

Various suggestions have been made in an effort to improve the effectiveness of collaboration by overcoming these challenges (Herrhausen 2007; Lotze, de Carvalho and Kasumba 2008). One example is the issue of access restriction. Proponents argue that limiting the number of participating organisations can enhance unity within the coordinating body (association) by increasing the chances of interaction between the members, increase mutual understanding and assist in developing communication protocols or work routines.

Another example is reputation. High reputation is a practical, useful method for attracting greater funding from external donors and, at a more fundamental level, is considered an important value by many peacebuilding organisations and humanitarian agencies. Hence, coordinating bodies can regulate participating actors' opportunistic behaviour by drawing on and exploiting their concern with achieving and maintaining a good reputation.

A more subtle but fundamental approach concerns organisational culture. Organisational culture refers to "ideas and values . . . that are specific to a given organization and have special relevance to its members" (Rodrigues 2006: 538) and includes various forms such as myth, ritual and symbol that encourage participating actors to make efforts to achieve their common goals. Once coordinating bodies and other member organisations create an organisational culture that transcends ownership, collaboration will be significantly easier.

Mobilising adequate resources

One of the most critical challenges to be overcome for the sustainability of peacebuilding strategies is the mobilisation of adequate resources. The landscape of post-conflict reconstruction experiences around the world shows that there are often two major problems in the realisation of this task. The first is in regard to the type of resources that are given a priority, which tend to be more financial and physical than human and organisational. The second shortcoming relates to the timing and amount of resources provided in the progression from relief to reconstruction.

The scale of the challenge of rebuilding conflict-affected communities requires the development of collaborative structures of governance with the participation of actors from national and local authorities, local NGOs and grassroots-level organisations, the international aid community (donors and NGOs) and the private sector. The absence of any of these actors, particularly local ones, could result in programme failure, long delays in responding to urgent needs, the waste of scarce resources and, most significantly, in renewed conflict. However, the critical question in resource mobilisation concerns what kind of resources should be given priority and who should coordinate the process. The current practice often focuses on those financial resources which are provided from external to internal actors, and invariably the process is led and coordinated by external actors, forcing internal actors to assume a 'support' role in 'helping' the work of the international community.

The transfer of financial resources for reconstruction comes with a package of conditionality that may range from economic and social requirements to political ones. It is in the process of this 'power' transfer that it is often made clear the agendas, aspirations and values of the international community are 'expected,' and 'required,' or sometimes even imposed on the local context. The prioritisation of financial resources creates a multilayered, hierarchical system of decision making in which the quantity of funds to be provided, and to whom, forms the main element of relationships between different agencies. In return, such a structure usually creates its own dynamics of power relations such as those between donors and governments, donors and international NGOs, international and local NGOs and local NGOs and community-based organisations. Instead of such a financial-centric focus in resource mobilisation, the priority should be given to the empowering and enablement of local human resources. Such a perspective can place local agencies in the driving seat of the process, supported by external actors if, as and when needed. The reconstruction strategy adopted by the international community would have to entail more than simply working with local actors, and it would need to ascertain what would be the most empowering means of transferring know-how, experiences and financial resources to local actors.

The challenge of the timing and scope of financial resources is often a critical issue because policy makers in conflict-affected environments frequently assume that external resources will remain consistent throughout the period needed for the reconstruction and development of the war-torn areas. In reality, international experience has shown that donor interest reaches its peak in the aftermath of establishing peace and declines sharply thereafter. This is of course in direct contrast to the needs of war-affected areas. It is often the case that with an increasing media attention during peace negotiations, the international community tends to be much more willing to make generous pledges for reconstruction. To a large extent this generosity may be only for the cameras, and pledges made may be conveniently forgotten or reduced once the war-affected country in question starts to enjoy a certain level of security and stability.

Nontraditional methods of peacebuilding

The development of new methods is also a characteristic of contemporary peacebuilding. Due to the involvement of more diverse actors and the emergence of new technology, both conflict resolution and post-conflict reconstruction are supported by new tools for pursuing their goals. In this section, a few examples related to new technologies, new actors and new strategies are presented to demonstrate the multiple directions of such new development.

In terms of technology, social media such as YouTube, Facebook, Flickr, Twitter and WordPress provide inexpensive, convenient and useful channels for many NGOs and individuals to influence peacebuilding activities. First, these methods have proved a highly useful tool in enabling these actors to publicise issues globally. In recent major civil movements and intrastate conflicts, such as the social mobilisation in North Africa and Middle East (popularly known as the Arab Spring) and the antigovernment demonstrations in Burma, people posted videos, photos and articles reporting the most up-to-date stories through these media. Second, mass media is a useful tool for showing the collective will of the people. By providing easy and convenient ways of expressing their opinions (e.g. clicking 'Like' on a Facebook post), such media allow individuals who are interested in certain issues but are unable to take proactive action to join the movements that they are interested in through such 'micro-actions.'

In terms of actors, interreligious dialogue is another discernible trend. As the number of religion-involved conflicts rapidly increased in the post–Cold War period (e.g. the 9/11 terror attack based on Islamic fundamentalism and the conflicts in the former Yugoslavia fuelled by religious tensions), the efforts of religious actors to create new peace initiatives are also increasing. Representative examples of this new form of peacebuilding initiative are the interfaith dialogue between the Roman Catholic Church and its Anglican counterpart in Northern Ireland, and the meetings between religious leaders in Israel and Palestine. Whereas traditional peacebuilding methods generally focus on substantive and material reconstruction, such religious dialogues attempt to address the psychological and emotional aspects of peacebuilding.

As a strategic method, an open-ended, flexible approach is adopted by many peacebuilding organisations. Traditionally, most major organisations applied a blueprint approach towards peacebuilding programmes that set their goals and fixed implementation schedules for their achievement. By contrast, an open-ended approach starts programmes with long-term visions and a number of initial goals; then more realistic targets and plans are developed and revised according to the progress of the programmes. Although such an approach might initially appear to be directionless and less effective than traditional approaches, it has proved to be a useful tool for achieving goals in the face of a range of issues in postwar societies that prevent peacebuilders from setting predetermined goals (e.g. undeveloped or underdeveloped infrastructure, security instability, a high illiteracy rate, limited experience with democratic practices, people's psychological war trauma and serious corruption).

Final note

Overall, peacebuilding is a highly complex and problematic task, which is likely to face a wide range of sociopolitical, economic and cultural challenges and ethical concerns. It should be remembered that the practice of peacebuilding is likely to be a 'messy' business, and building peace is likely to be the continuation of armed conflict politics, but simply through different means – the Clausewitz in reverse, as pointed out by Miall et al. (1999). Divided communities with their broken societal relationships; low security and instability challenges; destroyed infrastructure and dysfunctional services; nonexistent or badly dissolved governance structures; the absence of any type of bureaucracy to channel the state authority to ordinary citizens; widespread dynamics of war economy and relief dependency; crippled human resources and lost opportunities; a ruined economy – these are just some of the critical areas that peacebuilding would need to respond to in order to open up new opportunities and perspectives for sustainable peace. However, peacebuilding planned and implemented in a technocratic way by envisaging the challenge as different pieces of puzzle in the shape of different programmes and projects would likely fall short in achieving sustainable peace.

Peacebuilding as a process rather than a collation of different programmes would need to place the emphasis on the transformative impact of such programmes, or in other words, peacebuilding would need to be about building societal relationships as part of undertaking post-conflict reconstruction. It needs to address the root causes of the problem with its reformative characteristics, while considering its impact on interwoven societal relationships at both the horizontal and vertical levels. One of the main reasons for the failure of peacebuilding is the ill-defined and ad hoc way in which relationships between different agencies, authorities, institutions and processes at the macro, meso and micro levels. To achieve this, peacebuilding needs to adopt new ways of hearing the voices of ordinary conflict-affected people, but more importantly, peacebuilding needs to be prepared to act upon according to the issues, needs, expectations and aspirations identified by that voice rather than preset agendas of the internal and external elites. In doing this, the three key principles of human security – 'freedom from fear,' 'freedom from want' and 'freedom to live in dignity' – should set the overall guidance for the purpose of peacebuilding.

Useful online resources

Materials on peacebuilding practice

Berghof Handbook of Conflict Transformation (Bergh of Foundation)
http://www.berghof-handbook.net/articles/

Teaching Resources and Simulations (United States Institute of Peace)
http://www.usip.org/category/course-type/teaching-resources

Conflict analysis sources

Conciliation Resources
http://www.c-r.org/

International Alert
http://www.international-alert.org/

International Crisis Group
http://www.crisisgroup.org/

Relief Web
http://reliefweb.int

Databases on peace and conflict

Database of Peace Research Institute Oslo (PRIO)
http://www.prio.org/Data/Database of Stockholm

International Peace Research Institute (SIPRI)
http://www.sipri.org/databases

Peace Accord Matrix (University of Notre Dame)
https://peaceaccords.nd.edu

Uppsala Conflict Data Program
http://www.pcr.uu.se/research/UCDP/

Peacebuilding practitioners' networks

Alliance for Peacebuilding
http://www.allianceforpeacebuilding.org/

Peace and Collaborative Development Network
http://www.internationalpeaceandconflict.org/

Free-access online periodicals

African Journal on Conflict Resolution
http://www.accord.org.za/publications/ajcr

Asian Journal of Peacebuilding
http://tongil.snu.ac.kr/xe/ajp

Berghof Dialogue Series
http://www.berghof-handbook.net/dialogue-series

International Journal of Peace Studies
http://www.gmu.edu/programs/icar/ijps/

Journal of Conflict Transformation and Security
http://cesran.org/jcts

Peace, Conflict and Development
http://www.bradford.ac.uk/ssis/peace-conflict-and-development/

Bibliography

Addison, T. and Brück, T. (eds.) (2009) *Making Peace Work: The Challenges of Social and Economic Reconstruction*. Basingstoke: Palgrave Macmillan.

Alison, M. (2006) *Women and Political Violence: Female Combatants in Ethno-national Conflict*. London: Routledge.

Alkire, S. (2003) *A Conceptual Framework for Human Security*. Working Paper No. 2. Oxford: Centre for Research on Inequality, Human Security and Ethnicity.

Anderlini, S. N. (2007) *Women Building Peace: What They Do, Why It Matters*. Boulder, CO: Lynne Rienner.

Arafat, J. (2000) *Minimum Standards and Essential Needs in a Protracted Refugee Situation: A Review of the UNHCR Programmes in Kakuma, Kenya*. Geneva: Evaluation and Policy Analysis Unit, United Nations High Commissioner for Refugees (UNHCR).

Arnson, C. and Azpuru, D. (2003) 'From Peace to Democratization: Lessons from Central America', in *Contemporary Peacemaking: Conflict, Violence and Peace Processes*, edited by Darby, J. and Mac Ginty, R. Houndmills: Palgrave Macmillan: 197–211.

Aron, R. (1966) *Peace and War: A Theory of International Relations*. New York: Doubleday.

Avruch, K. (1998) *Culture & Conflict Resolution*. Washington, DC: United States Institute of Peace Press.

Axelrod, R. (1990) *Evolution of Co-operation*. Harmondsworth: Penguin.

Ballard, B. (2002) *Reintegration Programmes for Refugees in South-East Asia: Lessons Learned from UNHCR's Experience*. Geneva: UNHCR.

Baranyi, S. and North, L. (1996) *The United Nations in El Salvador: The Promise and Dilemmas of an Integrated Approach to Peace*. CERLAC Occasional Paper. North York, ON: Centre for Research on Latin America and the Caribbean (CERLAC).

Barash, D. P. and Webel, C. P. (2009) *Peace and Conflict Studies* (2nd ed.). Thousand Oaks, CA: Sage: 3–12.

Barnes, K. (2011) 'The Evolution and Implementation of UNSCR 1325', in *Women, Peace and Security: Translating Policy Into Practice*, edited by Olonisakin, F., Barnes, K. and Ikpe, E. London: Routledge: 15–34.

Bayer, R. (2010) 'Peaceful Transitions and Democracy'. *Journal of Peace Research* 47 (5): 535–46.

Bebbington, A. (1999) 'Capital and Capabilities: A Framework for Analyzing Peasant Viability, Rural Livelihoods and Poverty'. *World Development* 27 (12): 2021–44.

Bekoe, D. and Parajon, C. (2007) 'Women's Role in Liberia's Reconstruction'. Washington, DC: United States Institute of Peace. Available at: http://www.usip.org/publications/women-s-role-in-liberia-s-reconstruction (Accessed on 25 May 2015).

Bellamy, A. J., Williams, P. and Griffin, S. (2004) *Understanding Peacekeeping*. Cambridge: Polity Press.

Bellamy, A. J., Williams, P. and Griffin, S. (2010) *Understanding Peacekeeping*, edited by Bellamy, A. and Williams, P. Cambridge: Polity.

Bercovitch, J. (ed.) (2002) *Studies in International Mediation*. Houndmills: Palgrave Macmillan.

Bercovitch, J. and DeRouen, K. (2005) 'Managing Ethnic Civil Wars: Assessing the Determinants of Successful Mediation'. *Civil Wars* 7 (1): 98–116.

Berghof Foundation (2012) *Berghof Glossary on Conflict Transformation: 20 Notions for Theory and Practice*. Berlin: Berghof Foundation.

Boege, V., Brown, A., Clements, K. and Nolan, A. (2008) *Towards Effective and Legitimate Governance: States Emerging From Hybrid Political Orders*. Brisbane: Australian Centre for Peace and Conflict Studies, University of Queensland.

Borzyskowski, I. (2015) 'Peacebuilding Beyond Civil Wars: UN Election Assistance and Election Violence'. A paper presented at the 8th Annual Conference on the Political Economy of International Organizations, Hertie School of Governance, Berlin, 12–14 February.

Boulding, E. (2000) *Cultures of Peace: The Hidden Side of History*. Syracuse, NY: Syracuse University Press.

Bouta, T. (2005) *Gender and Disarmament, Demobilization and Reintegration*. The Hague: Netherlands Institute of International Relations.

Boyce, W., Koros, M. and Hodgson, J. (2002) *Community Based Rehabilitation: A Strategy for Peacebuilding*. Hamilton, ON: Humanities Department, McMaster University. Available at: http://www.ncbi.nlm.nih.gov/pmc/articles/PMC139991/ (Accessed on 17 June 2013).

British House of Commons, International Development Committee (2006) *Conflict and Development: Peacebuilding and Post-conflict Reconstruction: Sixth Report of Session 2005–06*. London: Stationery Office.

Bryden, A. and Hänggi, H. (eds.) (2004) *Reform and Reconstruction of the Security Sector*. Geneva: Geneva Centre for the Democratic Control of Armed Forces (DCAF).

Burton, J. (1990) *Conflicts: Resolution and Prevention*. Houndmills: Macmillan.

Bush, B. and Folger, J. (1994) *The Promise of Mediation: Responding to Conflict Through Empowerment and Recognition*. San Francisco: Jossey-Bass.

Butler, R. (2013) 'Deforestation Rate Falls in Congo Basin Countries'. Available at: http://news.mongabay.com/2013/0722-congo-basin-rainforest.html (Accessed on 9 June 2015).

Buxton, J. (2008) *Reintegration and Long-Term Development: Linkages and Challenges Thematic*. Working Paper No. 5. Bradford: University of Bradford.

Calame, J. and Pasic, A. (2009) *Post-conflict Reconstruction in Mostar: Cart Before the Horse, Divided Cities/Contested States*. Working Paper Series No. 7. Available at: http://www.conflictincities.org/PDFs/WorkingPaper7_26.3.09.pdf (Accessed on 28 September 2015).

Call, C. T. (2003) 'Democratisation, War and State-Building: Constructing the Rule of Law in El Salvador'. *Journal of Latin America Studies* 35: 827–62.

Call, C. T. (2008) 'Knowing Peace When You See It: Setting Standards for Peacebuilding Success'. *Civil Wars* 10 (2): 173–94.

Call, C. T. and Stanley, W. (2003) 'Military and Police Reform After Civil War', in *Contemporary Peacemaking: Conflict, Violence and Peace Processes*, edited by Darby, J. and Mac Ginty, R. Houndmills: Palgrave Macmillan: 212–23.

Cambodian Women's Development Agency (CWDA) (n.d.) 'About Us'. Available at: http://www.cwdagency.org/cpu (Accessed on 2 June 2015).

Caplan, R. (2002) *A New Trusteeship? The International Administration of War-Torn Territories*. Adelphi Paper No. 341. Oxford: Oxford University Press.

Carbonnier, G. (2009) 'Private Sector', in *Post-conflict Peacebuilding: A Lexicon*, edited by Chetail, V. Oxford: Oxford University Press: 245–55.

Carment, D. and Rowlands, D. (1998) 'Three's Company: Evaluating Third-Party Intervention in Intrastate Conflict'. *Journal of Conflict Resolution* 42 (5): 572–99.

Chambers, R. and Conway, G. (1991) *Sustainable Rural Livelihoods: Practical Concepts for the 21st Century*. Discussion Paper No. 296. Brighton: Institute of Development Studies.

Chandler, D. (1999) *Bosnia: Faking Democracy After Dayton*. London: Pluto Press.

Checa Hidalgo, D. (2008) 'Non-violence in Conflict Zones; Peace Brigades International'. *UAEMex* 48: 120–43.

Cheldelin, S., Druckman, D. and Fast, L. (2003) *Conflict: From Analysis to Intervention*. London: Bibbles.

Chesterman, S. (2007) 'Ownership in Theory and in Practice: Transfer of Authority in UN Statebuilding Operations'. *Journal of Intervention and Statebuilding* 1 (1): 3–26.

Chetail, V. (ed.) (2003) *Peacebuilding and Post-conflict Reconstruction: A Practical and Bilingual Lexicon*. Oxford: Oxford University Press.

Chetail, V. (ed.) (2009) *Post-conflict Peacebuilding: A Lexicon*. Oxford: Oxford University Press.

Chikwanha, A. B. (2009) 'Conclusion – Closing the Gap Between Theory and Practice of Criminal Justice in Africa', in *The Theory and Practice of Criminal Justice in Africa, African Security Initiative*. Monograph 161. Pretoria: Institute for Security Studies: 111–16.

Chipkin, I. and Ngqulunga, B. (2008) 'Friends and Family: Social Cohesion in South Africa'. *Journal of Southern African Studies* 34 (1): 61–76.

Chopra, J. (2000) 'The UN's Kingdom of East Timor'. *Survival: Global Politics and Strategy* 42 (3): 27–40.

Christoplos, I., Longley, C. and Slaymaker, T. (2004) *The Changing Roles of Agricultural Rehabilitation: Linking Relief, Development and Support to Rural Livelihoods*. London: Overseas Development Institute.

Clements, K. (1997) Peace Building and Conflict Transformation'. *Peace and Conflict Studies* 4 (1): 3–13.

Clements, K. (2008) *Traditional, Charismatic and Grounded Legitimacy: Study for GTZ*. Brisbane: Australian Centre for Peace and Conflict Studies, University of Queensland.

Cobham, A. (2005) 'Causes of Conflict in Sudan: Testing the Black Book'. *European Journal of Development Research* 17 (3): 462–80.

Colletta, N. J. and Cullen, M. L. (2000) *Violent Conflict and the Transformation of Social Capital: Lessons from Cambodia, Rwanda, Guatemala, and Somalia*. Washington, DC: World Bank.

Collier, P. (1999) 'On the Economic Consequences of Civil War'. *Oxford Economic Paper* 51 (1): 168–83.

Collier, P., Hoeffler, A. and Sambanis, N. (2005) 'The Collier-Hoeffler Model of Civil War Onset and the Case Study Project Research Design', in *Understanding Civil War: Evidence and Analysis*, edited by Collier, P. and Sambanis, N. Washington, DC: World Bank: 1–34.

Commission on Human Security (2003) *Human Security Now: The Report of the Commission on Human Security*. Available at: http://ochaonline.un.org/OchaLinkClick.aspx?link=ocha&docId=1250396 (Accessed on 17 June 2013).

Conflict Prevention Forum (n.d.) *A Toolbox to Respond to Conflicts and Build Peace*. Available at: http://www.creativeassociatesinternational.com/CAIIStaff/Dashboard_GIROAdminCAIIStaff/Dashboard_CAIIAdminDatabase/resources/ghai/toolbox.htm (Accessed on 17 June 2013).

Cooke, B. and Kothari, U. (2001) *Participation: A New Tyranny?* London: Zed Books.

Costi, A. (2006) 'Hybrid Tribunals as a Viable Transitional Justice Mechanism to Combat Impunity in Post-conflict Situations'. *New Zealand Universities Law Review* 22 (2): 213–39.

Crisp, J. (2001) *Mind the Gap! UNHCR Humanitarian Assistance and the Development Process*. Geneva: UNHCR. Available at: http://www.jha.ac/articles/u043.htm (Accessed on 17 June 2013).

Crocker, C. A., Hampson, F. O. and Aall, P. R. (1999) *Herding Cats: Multiparty Mediation in a Complex World*. Washington, DC: United States Institute of Peace Press.

CSIS/AUSA [Center for Strategic and International Studies and the Association of the United States Army] (2002) *Post-Conflict Reconstruction Task Framework*. Available at: http://csis.org/images/stories/pcr/framework.pdf (Accessed on 28 September 2015)

Culbertson, R. and Pouligny, B. (2007) ' "Re-imagining Peace" after Maa Crime: A Dialogical Exchange Between Insider and Outsider Knowledge', in *After Mass Crime: Rebuilding States and Communities*, edited by Pouligny, B., Chesterman, S. and Schnabel, A. Tokyo: United Nations University Press: 271–87.

Curle, A. (1994) 'New Challenges for Citizen Peacemaking'. *Medicine and War* 10 (2): 96–105.

Darby, J. and Mac Ginty, R. (eds.) (2003) *Contemporary Peacemaking: Conflict, Violence and Peace Processes*. Houndmills: Palgrave Macmillan.

de Coning, C. (2006) 'Civil-Military Coordination and UN Peacebuilding Operations'. *African Journal on Conflict Resolution (AJCR)* 5 (2): 89–118.

Dogra, N. (2011) 'The Mixed Metaphor of "Third World Woman": Gendered Representations by International Developments'. *Third World Quarterly* 32 (2): 333–48.

Dollar, D. and Kraay, A. (2002) 'Growth Is Good for the Poor'. *Journal of Economic Growth* 7: 195–225.

Donais, T. (2009) 'Empowerment or Imposition? Dilemmas of Local Ownership in Post-conflict Peacebuilding Processes'. *Peace & Change* 34 (1): 3–26.

Doyle, M. (2005) 'Three Pillars of Liberal Peace'. *American Political Science Review* 99 (3): 463–66.

Doyle, M. W. (1996) 'Strategies of Enhanced Consent', in *Preventing Conflict in the Post-communist World*, edited by Chayes, A. and Chayes, A. H. Washington, DC: Brookings Institution: 483–506.

Easterly, W. (1999) 'Life During Growth'. *Journal of Economic Growth* 4: 239–76.

Edgren, G. (2003) *Donorship, Ownership and Partnership, Issues Arising From Four SIDA Studies of Donor-Recipient Relations*, SIDA Studies in Evaluation 03/03. Stockholm: Infocenter, SIDA.

Elbadawi, I. and Sambanis, N. (2000) 'Why Are There So Many Civil Wars in Africa? Understanding and Preventing Violent Conflict'. *Journal of African Economies* 9 (3): 244–69.

Evans, M. (2005) 'Post-war Reconstruction and Public Administration', in *After the Conflict: Reconstruction and Development in the Aftermath of War*, edited by Barakat, S. London: IB Tauris: 191–212.

Fearon, J. D., Humphreys, M. and Weinstein, J. M. (2009) 'Can Development Aid Contribute to Social Cohesion After Civil War? Evidence From a Field Experiment in Post-conflict Liberia'. *American Economic Review: Papers & Proceedings* 99 (2): 287–91. Available at: http://www.aeaweb.org/articles.php?doi=10.1257/aer.99.2.287 (Accessed on 17 June 2013).

Ferroni, M., Mateo, M. and Payne, M. (2008) *Development Under Conditions of Inequality and Distrust – Social Cohesion in Latin America*. Washington, DC: International Food Policy Research Institute.

FIDA-Kenya (2013) *Traditional Justice Systems in Kenya: A Study of Communities in Coast Province, Kenya*. Available at: http://fidakenya.org/wp-content/uploads/2013/08/Traditional-Justicefinal.pdf (Accessed on 17 June 2013).

Fischer, M. (2006) *Civil Society in Conflict Transformation: Ambivalence, Potentials, and Challenges*. Berlin: Berghof Research Center for Constructive Conflict Management: 11–22.

Fischer, M. and Ropers, N. (2004) 'Introduction', in *Berghof Handbook for Conflict Transformation*, edited by Berghof Foundation. Berlin: Berghof Foundation.

Fisher, R., Ury, W. and Patton, B. (1991) *Getting to Yes: Negotiating an Agreement Without Giving In* (2nd ed.). Sydney: Century Business.

Fisher, R. J. (1997) 'Interactive Conflict Resolution', in *Peacemaking in International Conflict: Methods and Techniques*, edited by Zartman, I. W. and Rasmussen, J. L. Washington, DC: United States Institute of Peace Press: 239–72.

Fisher, R. J. (2001) 'Social-Psychological Processes in Interactive Conflict Analysis and Reconciliation', in *Reconciliation, Justice, and Coexistence: Theory and Practice*, edited by Abu-Nimer, M. Lanham, MD: Lexington Books: 25–45.

Francies, D. (2004) *Culture, Power Asymmetries and Gender in Conflict Transformation*. Berlin: Berghof Foundation.

Fred-Mensah, B. (2004) 'Social Capital Building as Capacity for Postconflict Development: The UNDP in Mozambique and Rwanda'. *Global Governance* 10 (4): 437–57.

Freedman, L. (1998) 'International Security: Changing Targets'. *Foreign Policy* 110: 48–63.

Furnari, E., Oldenhuis, H. and Julian, R. (2015) 'Securing Space for Local Peacebuilding: The Role of International and National Civilian Peacekeepers'. *Peacebuilding*. doi:10.1080/21647259.2015.104 0628Futamura, M., Newman, E. and Tadjbakhsh, S. (2010) *Towards a Human Security Approach to Peacebuilding*. Research Brief No. 2. Tokyo: United Nations University.

Futamura, M. and Notaras, M. (2011) *Local Perspectives on International Peacebuilding*. Research Article Series. Tokyo: United Nations University. Available at: http://unu.edu/publications/articles/local-perspectives-on-international-peacebuilding.html#info (Accessed on 2 June 2015).

Galtung, J. (1964) 'An Editorial'. *Journal of Peace Research* 1: 1–4.

Galtung, J. (1967) 'Peace Research: Science or Politics in Disguise?' *International Spectator* 21 (19): 1573–1603.

Galtung, J. (1969) 'Violence, Peace, and Peace Research'. *Journal of Peace Research* 6 (3): 167–91.

Galtung, J. (1996) *Peace by Peaceful Means: Peace and Conflict, Development and Civilization*. London: Sage.

GAO [US Government Accountability Office] (2007) *Securing, Stabilizing, and Reconstructing Afghanistan: Key Issues for Congressional Oversight* (GAO-07–801SP). Washington, DC: GAO.

Gerstl, A. N. (2015) 'Ownership of International Peacebuilding Programmes by Local Governance Institutions: Case Study of Gulu District in Northern Uganda', in *Local Ownership in International Peacebuilding: Key Theoretical and Practical Issues*, edited by Lee, S. and Özerdem, A. Oxon: Routledge: 156–77.

Gloppen, S. (2005) 'Roads to Reconciliation: A Conceptual Framework', in *Roads to Reconciliation*, edited by Skaar, E., Gloppen, S. and Suhrke, A. Oxford: Lexington Books: 17–54.

Goetschel, L. (2009) 'Conflict Transformation', in *Post-conflict Peacebuilding: A Lexicon*, edited by Chetail, V. Oxford: Oxford University Press: 92–104.

Greene, A. B. (2009) 'Vocational Training in Post-war Sierra Leone and Liberia', in *International Handbook of Education for Changing World of Work*, edited by Maclean, R. and Wilson, D. Amsterdam: Springer Netherlands: 827–34.

Gurr, T. R. (1970) *Why Men Rebel*. Princeton: Princeton University Press.

Haider, H. (2009) *Community-Based Approaches to Peacebuilding in Conflict-Affected and Fragile Contexts*. Issue Paper. Birmingham: International Development Department, University of Birmingham. Available at: http://www.gsdrc.org/docs/open/EIRS8.pdf (Accessed on 17 June 2013).

Hänggi, H. (2004) 'Conceptualising Security Sector Reform and Reconstruction', in *Reform and Reconstruction of the Security Sector*, edited by Bryden, A. and Hänggi, H. Geneva: Geneva Centre for the Democratic Control of Armed Forces (DCAF): 3–13.

Hänggi, H. (2010) 'Establishing Security in Conflict-Affected Societies: How to Reform the Security Sector', in *International State Building and Reconstruction Efforts: Experience Gained and Lessons Learned*, edited by Krause, J. and Mallory, C. K. Opladen: Barbara Budrich: 77–98.

Harrington, C. B. and Merry, S. E. (1988) 'Ideological Production: The Making of Community Mediation'. *Law & Society Review* 22: 709–35.

Harris, D. (2012) *Civil War and Democracy in West Africa: Conflict Resolution, Elections and Justice in Sierra Leone and Liberia*. London: IB Tauris.

Harris, I. (2004) 'Peace Education Theory'. *Journal of Peace Education* 1 (1): 5–20.

Haughton, J. (1998) *The Reconstruction of War-Torn Economies*. Technical Paper. Cambridge: Harvard University Press.

Haynes, J. (2011) *Religion, Politics and International Relations: Selected Essays*. London: Routledge.

Hazan, P. (2009) 'Reconciliation', in *Post-conflict Peacebuilding: A Lexicon*, edited by Chetail, V. Oxford: Oxford University Press: 256–67.

Hazen, J. (2007) 'Can Peacekeepers Be Peacebuilders?' *International Peacekeeping* 14 (3): 323–38. Heathershaw, J. (2008) 'Unpacking the Liberal Peace: The Dividing and Merging of Peacebuilding Discourse'. *Millennium: Journal of International Studies* 36 (3): 597–621.

Heathershaw, J. (2013) 'Towards Better Theories of Peacebuilding: Beyond the Liberal Peace Debate'. *Peacebuilding* 1 (2): 275–82.

Herrhausen, A. (2007) *Coordination in United Nations Peacebuilding – A Theory Guided Approach*. WZB Discussion Paper. Berlin: Wissenschaftszentrum Berlin für Sozialforschung.

Hideaki, S. (2015) 'Local Ownership as a Strategic Guideline for Peacebuilding', in *Local Ownership in International Peacebuilding: Key Theoretical and Practical Issues*, edited by Lee, S. and Özerdem, A. Oxon: Routledge: 156–77, 39–54.

Hofman, M. and Delaunay, S. (2010) *Afghanistan: A Return to Humanitarian Action*. Special Report – Médecins Sans Frontières (11 March). Available at: http://www.doctorswithoutborders.org/publications/article.cfm?id=4311&cat=special-report (Accessed on 17 June 2013).

Höglund, K. and Orjuela, C. (2012) 'Hybrid Peace Governance and Illiberal Peacebuilding in Sri Lanka'. *Global Governance: A Review of Multilateralism and International Organizations* 18 (1): 89–104.

Honwana, A. (1998) 'Sealing the Past, Facing the Future: Trauma Healing in Rural Mozambique'. *Accord* 3: 75–81.

Hulme, D. (2008) *The Story of the Grameen Bank: From Subsidised Microcredit to Market-Based Microfinance*. BWPI Working Paper No. 60. Manchester: Brooks World Poverty Institute.

Huntington, S. (1993) 'The Clash of Civilizations?' *Foreign Affairs* (Summer): 22–49.

Hutchful, E. (2009) *Security Sector Reform Provisions in Peace Agreements*. London: Department for International Development (DFID).

Ikeda, D. (2012) *Human Security and Sustainability: Sharing Reverence for the Dignity of Life*. 2012 Peace Proposal. Available at: http://www.sgi.org/assets/pdf/peaceproposal2012.pdf (Accessed on 17 June 2013).

International Center for Transitional Justice (ICTJ) (2013) 'What Is Transitional Justice?' Available at: http://ictj.org/about/transitional-justice (Accessed on 17 June 2013).

International Committee of the Red Cross (ICRC) (n.d.) 'Philippines: Civilians Suffer Impact of Armed Clashes in Central Mindanao'. Available at: https://www.icrc.org/en/document/philippines-civilians-suffer-impact-armed-clashes-central-mindanao (Accessed on 28 September 2015)

International Commission on Intervention and State Sovereignty (ICISS) (2001) *Responsibility to Protect*. Ottawa, ON: International Development Research Centre.

International Criminal Tribunal for the Former Yugoslavia (ICTY) (1994) *First Annual Report* (UN Doc. A/49/342, 29 August 1994). Available at: http://www.icty.org/x/file/About/Reports%20and%20Publications/AnnualReports/annual_report_1994_en.pdf (Accessed on 28 September 2015).

International Criminal Tribunal for the Former Yugoslavia (ICTY) (2012) 'About ICTY'. Available at: http://www.icty.org/sections/AbouttheICTY (Accessed on 17 June 2013).

International Institute for Democracy and Electoral Assistance (IDEA) (2003) *Reconciliation After Violent Conflict*. Stockholm: International IDEA. Available at: http://www.idea.int/publications/reconciliation/upload/reconciliation_chap09.pdf (Accessed on 17 June 2013).

Jeong, H. (2005) *Peacebuilding in Postconflict Societies: Strategy & Process*. Boulder, CO: Lynne Rienner.

Jeong, H. (2008) 'Approaches to Understanding Conflicts', in *Understanding Conflict and Conflict Analysis*. London: Sage: 3–19.

Jeong, H. (2010) 'Concepts and Practice', in *Conflict Management and Resolution: An Introduction*. London: Routledge: 131–50.

Jones, R. (2005) 'Conflict Poverty Reduction', in *After the Conflict: Reconstruction and Development in the Aftermath of War*, edited by Barakat, S. London: IB Tauris: 101–22.

Joshi, M., Lee, S. Y. and Mac Ginty, R. (2014) 'Just How Liberal Is the Liberal Peace?' *International Peacekeeping* 21 (3): 364–89.

Juhn, T. (1998) *Negotiating Peace in El Salvador: Civil-Military Relations and the Conspiracy to End the War*. Houndmills: Macmillan.

Junne, G. and Verkoren, W. (2005) *Postconflict Development: Meeting New Challenges*. Boulder, CO: Lynne Rienner.

Kaag, M., Berkel, R., Brons, J., Bruijn, M., Dijk, H., Haan, L., . . . Zoomers, A. (2004) 'Ways Forward in Livelihood Research', in *Globalization and Development: Themes and Concepts in Current Research*, edited by Kalb, D., Pansters, W. and Siebers, H. Dordrecht: Kluwer: 49–74. Kaldor, M. (2006) *New & Old Wars*. Cambridge: Polity.

Kaldor, M. and Vashee, B. (1997) *New Wars: Restructuring the Global Military Sector*. London: Pinter Press.

Keith, J. and Gurr, T. R. (1995) 'Tracking Democracy's Third Wave with the Polity III Data'. *Journal of Peace Research* 32: 469–82.

Keohane, R. and Nye, J. (1977) *Power and Interdependence: World Politics in Transition*. Boston: Little, Brown.

Kerkkänen, A. (2009) 'Human Security – A Paradigm for Contemporary Peacebuilding', in *Human Security in Peacebuilding*, edited by Korhonen, S. Kuopio: Crisis Management Center Finland: 9–23.

Körppen, D., Schmelzle, B. and Wils, O. (2008) *A Systemic Approach to Conflict Transformation: Exploring Strengths and Weaknesses*. Berlin: Berghof Research Center for Constructive Conflict Management.

Krause, K. and Jütersonke, O. (2005) 'Peace, Security and Development in Post-conflict Environments'. *Security Dialogue* 36 (4): 447–62.

Krippner, S. and McIntyre, T. (eds.) (2003) *The Psychological Impact of War Trauma on Civilians: An International Perspective*. Westport, CT: Greenwood.

Kumar, C. and Haye, J. (2011) 'Hybrid Peacemaking: Building National "Infrastructures for Peace"'. *Global Governance* 18: 13–20.Lambourne, W. (2004) 'Post-conflict Peacebuilding: Meeting Human Needs for Justice and Reconciliation'. *Peace, Conflict and Development* 4. Available at: http://www. peacestudiesjournal.org.uk/dl/PostConflictPeacebuilding.PDF (Accessed on 17 June 2013).

Langer, A. (2005) 'Horizontal Inequalities and Violent Group Mobilization in Côte d'Ivoire'. *Oxford Development Studies* 33 (1): 25–45.

Langer, A. and Brown, G. (2007) *Cultural Status Inequalities and Group Mobilisation*. CRISE Working Paper No. 41. Oxford: Centre for Research on Inequality, Human Security and Ethnicity (CRISE), University of Oxford.

La Rosa, A.M. and Philippe, X. (2009) 'Transitional Justice', in *Post-conflict Peacebuilding. A Lexicon*, edited by Chetail, V. Oxford: Oxford University Press: 368–79.

Lederach, J.P. (1999) *Building Peace: Sustainable Reconciliation in Divided Societies*. Washington, DC: United States Institute of Peace Press.

Lederach, J.P. (2003) *The Little Book of Conflict Transformation*. Intercourse, PA: Good Books.

Lee, S. (2014) 'Seeking a New Generation of the Critical Scholarship'. *Peacebuilding* 2 (3): 351–57.

Lee, S. and Park, W. (2015) 'Nurturing Local Voice: The UNDP's Local Empowerment Programmes in Cambodia', in *Local Ownership in International Peacebuilding: Key Theoretical and Practical Issues*, edited by Lee, S. and Özerdem, A. Abingdon: Routledge: 135–55.

Lee, S.Y. (2011) 'The Limit of Ethnocentric Perceptions in Civil War Peace Negotiations'. *Conflict Resolution Quarterly* 28 (3): 349–73.

Lee, S.Y. and Mac Ginty, R. (2012) 'Context and Post-conflict Referendums'. *Nationalism and Ethnic Politics* 18 (1): 43–64.

Lee, S.Y. and Özerdem, A. (2015a) 'Exit Strategies', in *Routledge Companion to Humanitarian Action*, edited by Mac Ginty, R. and Peterson, J. Oxon: Routledge: 372–84.

Lee, S.Y. and Özerdem, A. (eds.) (2015b) *Local Ownership in International Peacebuilding*. Oxon: Routledge.

Leslie, H. (2000) 'Conceptualising and Addressing the Mental Health Impacts of Gender Roles in Conflict and Peacemaking'. *Development Bulletin* 53: 65–69.Leslie, H. (2001) 'Healing the Psychological Wounds of Gender-Related Violence in Latin America', in *Gender, Development and Humanitarian Work*, edited by Sweetman, C. London: Oxfam: 50–59.

Leslie, J. (1995) 'Towards Rehabilitation: Building Trust in Afghanistan'. *Disaster Prevention and Management* 4 (1): 27–31.

Lewicki, R.J., Saunders, D.M. and Minton, J.W. (2001) *Essentials of Negotiation*. Boston: McGraw-Hill.

Lewicki, R.J., Weiss, S.E. and Lewin, D. (1992) 'Models of Conflict, Negotiation and Third Party Intervention: A Review and Synthesis'. *Journal of Organizational Behavior* 13: 209–52.

LICADHO (2015) 'Cambodia's Concessions'. Available at: http://www.licadho-cambodia.org/land_concessions/ (Accessed on 28 September 2015).

Liden, K. (2009) 'Building Peace Between Global and Local Politics: The Cosmopolitical Ethics of Liberal Peacebuilding'. *International Peacekeeping* 16 (5): 616–34.

Locula, J.M. (2011) 'Reparation of Victims: Seeking a Bottom-Up Approach to Transitional Justice'. *Peace and Conflict Monitor*. Available at: http://www.monitor.upeace.org/printer.cfm?id_article=792 (Accessed on 25 June 2015).

Lopes, C. and Theisohn, T. (2003) *Ownership, Leadership and Transformation: Can We Do Better for Capacity Building?* London: Earthscan.

Lopez-Pintor, R. (1997) 'Reconciliation Elections: A Post-Cold War Experience', in *Rebuilding Societies After Civil War: Critical Roles for International Assistance*, edited by Krishna, K. Boulder, CO: Lynne Rienner: 43–61.

Lotze, W., de Carvalho, G. B. and Kasumba, Y. (2008) *Peacebuilding Coordination in African Countries: Transitioning From Conflict. Accord* Occasional Paper Series 3 (1). Available at: http://www.accord.org.za/downloads/op/op_2008_1.pdf (Accessed on 17 June 2013).

Lyons, T. (1999) *Voting for Peace: Postconflict Elections in Liberia*. Washington, DC: Brookings Institution Press.

Lyons, T. (2004) 'Transforming the Institutions of War: Post-conflict Elections and the Reconstruction of Failed States', in *When States Fail: Causes and Consequences*, edited by Rothbert, R. I. Princeton, NJ: Princeton University Press: 269–318.

Mac Ginty, R. (2008) 'Indigenous Peace-Making Versus the Liberal Peace'. *Cooperation and Conflict* 43 (2): 139–88.

Mac Ginty, R. (2010) 'Hybrid Peace: The Interaction Between Top-Down and Bottom-Up Peace'. *Security Dialogue* 41 (4): 391–412.

Mac Ginty, R. (2011) *International Peacebuilding and Local Resistance: Hybrid Forms of Peace*. Houndmills: Palgrave Macmillan.

Mackenzie-Smith, A. (2015) 'Complex Challenges Facing Contemporary Local Ownership Programmes: A Case Study of South Sudan', in *Local Ownership in International Peacebuilding: Key Theoretical and Practical Issues*, edited by Lee, S. and Özerdem, A. Oxon: Routledge: 55–73.

Maley, W. (2010) *Afghanistan – Reconstruction Challenges and Dilemmas*. Civil-Military Working Paper 8/2010. Canberra: Australian Civil-Military Centre.

Malone, D. and Nitzschke, H. (2009) 'Economic Agendas in Civil Wars: What We Know, What We Should Know', in *Making Peace Work: The Challenges of Social and Economic Reconstruction*, edited by Addison, T. and Brück, T. Basingstoke: Palgrave Macmillan: 31–50.

Mancini, L. (2005) *Horizontal Inequalities and Communal Violence: Evidence from Indonesian Districts*. CRISE Working Paper No. 22. Oxford: Centre for Research on Inequality, Human Security and Ethnicity (CRISE), University of Oxford.

Maney, G., Ibrahim, I., Higgins, G. and Herzog, H. (2006) 'The Past's Promise: Lessons from Peace Processes in Northern Ireland and the Middle East'. *Journal of Peace Research* 43: 181–200. Marino, P. (2005) *Beyond Economic Benefits: The Contribution of Microfinance to Post-conflict Recovery in Asia and the Pacific*. Available at: http://www.microfinancegateway.org/gm/document-1.9.28735/30876_file_Microfinance_and_co.pdf (Accessed on 3 July 2013).

Martz, E. (2010) *Trauma Rehabilitation After War and Conflict*. New York: Springer.

McIntosh, M. and Hunter, A. (2010) *New Perspectives on Human Security*. Sheffield: Greenleaf.

McLeod, D. and Dávalos, M. (2007) 'Post-conflict Employment and Poverty Reduction'. A paper prepared for the UNDP Bureau of Development Policy. New York: UNDP.

Miall, H. (2004) *Conflict Transformation: A Multi-dimensional Task*. Berlin: Berghof Foundation.

Miall, H., Ramsbotham, O. and Woodhouse, T. (1999) *Contemporary Conflict Resolution*. Cambridge: Polity.

Miller, B. (2005) 'When and How Regions Become Peaceful: Potential Theoretical Pathways to Peace'. *International Studies Review* 7: 232.

Miller, M. A. and Bunnell, T. (2011) *Post-disaster Urban Renewal: Memories of Trauma and Transformation in an Indonesian City*. ARI Working Paper No. 154. Singapore: Asia Research Institute.

Minear, L. and Donini, A. (2005) 'International Troops, Aid Workers and Local Communities: Mapping the Perceptions Gap'. *Humanitarian Exchange* 32: 26–29.

Minow, M. (2000) 'The Hope for Healing: What Can Truth Commissions Do?', in *Truth v. Justice: The Morality of Truth Commissions*, edited by Rotberg, R. and Thompson, D. Princeton, NJ: Princeton University Press: 235–60.

Mirbagheri, S. and Farid, M. (2012) *War and Peace in Islam: A Critique of Islamic/ist Political Discourses*. Basingstoke: Palgrave Macmillan.

Mitchell, C. (2002) 'Beyond Resolution: What Does Conflict Transformation Actually Transform?' *Peace and Conflict Studies* 9 (1): 1–23.

Montville, J. V. (1993) 'The Healing Function in Political Conflict Resolution', in *Conflict Resolution Theory and Practice: Integration and Application*, edited by Sandole, D. and van der Merwe, H. New York: Manchester University Press: 112–27.

Moore, C. W. (1986) *The Mediation Process: Practical Strategies for Resolving Conflict.* San Francisco: Jossey-Bass.

Mullen, J. (2008) 'Rural Poverty', in *The Companion to Development Studies* (2nd ed.), edited by Desai, V. and Potter, R. Oxon: Routledge: 143–46.

Munuve, P. (2013) *Refugees as Peacebuilders: Fact or Myth?* Master's thesis, Coventry University, Coventry.

Murithi, T. (2006) 'African Approaches to Building Peace and Social Solidarity'. *African Journal on Conflict Resolution* 6 (2): 9–34. Available at: http://www.accord.org.za/downloads/ajcr/ajcr_2006_2.pdf (Accessed on 17 June 2013).

Myrttinen, H., Naujoks, J. and El-Bushra, J. (2014) *Re-thinking Gender in Peacebuilding*, London: International Alert. Available at: http://www.international-alert.org/sites/default/files/Gender_RethinkingGenderPeacebuilding_EN_2014.pdf (Accessed on 25 May 2015).

Negroponte, D. V. (2005) *Conflict Resolution at the End of the Cold War: The Case of El Salvador, 1989–1994.* Ph.D. thesis, Georgetown University, Washington, DC.

Newbrander, D. (2012) 'Liberal Peace: A Dyad of Democracy and Economic Interdependence, Grounded in Agent Desires'. *Monitor* (Fall): 34–48.

Newman, E., Paris, R. and Richmond, O. (eds.) (2009) *New Perspectives on Liberal Peacebuilding.* Tokyo: United Nations University Press.

Newsom, J. (2002) 'Bougainville Microfinance: Rebuilding Rural Communities After the Crisis'. *Development Bulletin* 57. Canberra: ANU Development Studies Network: 85–88.

Notter, J. and Diamond, L. (1996) *Building Peace and Transforming Conflict: Multi-track Diplomacy in Practice.* Occasional Paper No. 7. Washington, DC: Institute for Multi-track Diplomacy.

Obi, C. (ed.) (2007) *Perspectives on Côte d'Ivoire: Between Political Breakdown and Postconflict Peace.* Discussion Paper No. 39. Uppsala: Nordic Africa Institute.

Öjendal, J. and Lilja, M. (2009) *Beyond Democracy in Cambodia: Political Reconstruction in a Post-conflict Society.* Copenhagen: NIAS Press.

Olonisakin, F., Barnes, K. and Ikpe, E. (eds.) (2011) *Women, Peace and Security: Translating Policy Into Practice.* London: Routledge.

Oxfam (2014) *Conflict Transformation: Transforming Cultures of Violence to Overcome Injustice and Poverty.* Oxfam Humanitarian Policy Note (February). Available at: https://www.oxfam.org/sites/www.oxfam.org/files/hpn-conflict-transformation-240214-en.pdf (Accessed on 26 May 2015).

Özerdem, A. (2008) *Post-war Recovery: Disarmament, Demobilization and Reintegration.* New York: IB Tauris.

Palmer, D. S. (2006) *U.S. Relations with Latin America During the Clinton Years.* Gainesville: University Press of Florida.

Parajon, D. (2007) 'Women's Role in Liberia's Reconstruction'. Available at: http://www.usip.org/publications/women-s-role-in-liberia-s-reconstruction (Accessed on 6 May 2015).

Paris, R. (2001) 'Human Security: Paradigm Shift or Hot Air?' *International Security* 26 (2): 87–102.

Paris, R. (2004) *At War's End: Building Peace After Civil Conflicts.* Cambridge: Cambridge University Press.

Paris, R. (2010) 'Saving Liberal Peacebuilding'. *Review of International Studies* 36 (2): 337–65.

Peake, G., Gormley-Heenan, C. and Fitzduff, M. (2004) *From Warlords to Peacelords: Local Leadership Capacity in Peace Processes.* Londonderry: International Conflict Research (INCORE), University of Ulster.

Porter, E. (2007) *Peacebuilding: Women in International Perspective.* London: Routledge.

Purdeková, A. (2011) *Rwanda's Ingando Camps: Liminality and the Reproduction of Power.* Working Paper Series No. 80. Oxford: Refugee Studies Centre, University of Oxford.

Ramcharan, B. G. (2009) 'Peace Process', in *Post-conflict Peacebuilding: A Lexicon*, edited by Chetail, V. Oxford: Oxford University Press: 228–44.

Ramsbotham, O., Woodhouse, T. and Miall, H. (2005) *Contemporary Conflict Resolution* (2nd ed.). Cambridge: Polity.

Ramsbotham, O., Woodhouse, T. and Miall, H. (2011) *Contemporary Conflict Resolution* (3rd ed.). Cambridge: Polity.

Ratner, S. (1997) *The New UN Peacekeeping: Building Peace in Lands of Conflict After the Cold War*. London: Macmillan.

Reardon, B.A. (1988) *Comprehensive Peace Education*. New York: Teachers College Press.

Reich, H. (2006) *'Local Ownership' in Conflict Transformation Projects: Partnership, Participation or Patronage?* Berghof Occasional Paper No. 27. Berlin: Berghof Research Center for Constructive Conflict Management.

Reydams, L. (2005) 'The ICTR Ten Years On: Back to the Nuremberg Paradigm?' *Journal of International Crime Justice* 3 (4): 977–88.

Richmond, O. (2005) *The Transformation of Peace*. Basingstoke: Palgrave Macmillan.

Richmond, O. (2006) 'The Problem of Peace: Understanding the "Liberal Peace" '. *Conflict, Security and Development* 6 (3): 291–314.Richmond, O. (2007) *The Transformation of Peace*. Houndmills: Palgrave.

Richmond, O. (2015) 'The Dilemmas of a Hybrid Peace: Negative or Positive?' *Cooperation and Conflict* 50 (1): 50–68.

Richmond, O. and Franks, J. (2011) *Liberal Peace Transitions: Between Statebuilding and Peacebuilding*. Edinburgh: Edinburgh University Press.

Richmond, O. and Mac Ginty, R. (2014) 'Where Now for the Critique of the Liberal Peace?' *Cooperation and Conflict* 50 (2): 171–89.

Richmond, O. and Mitchell, A. (2011) *Hybrid Forms of Peace: From Everyday Agency to Post-liberalism*. Houndmills: Palgrave Macmillan.

Rigby, A. (2001) *Justice and Reconciliation: After the Violence*. Boulder, CO: Lynne Rienner.

Roberts, D. (2011) *Liberal Peacebuilding and Global Governance: Beyond the Metropolis*. London: Routledge.

Rodrigues, S. B. (2006) 'The Political Dynamics of Organizational Culture in an Institutionalized Environment'. *Organization Studies* 27 (4): 537–57.

Ropers, N. (2008) 'Systemic Conflict Transformation: Reflections on the Conflict and Peace Process in Sri Lanka', in *A Systemic Approach to Conflict Transformation: Exploring Strengths and Limitations*, edited by Körppen, D., Schmelzle, B. and Wils, O. Berlin: Berghof Research Center for Constructive Conflict Management: 11–41.

Rosenberg-Friedman, L. (2003) 'Religious Women Fighters in Israel's War of Independence: A New Gender Perception, or a Passing Episode?' *Journal of Jewish Women's Studies & Gender Issues* 6: 119–47.

Ross, M. H. (2007) *Cultural Contestation in Ethnic Conflict*. Cambridge: Cambridge University Press.

Rothstein, R. L. (2007) 'The Timing of Negotiations: Duelling Metaphors'. *Civil Wars* 9 (3): 262–81.

Rupesinghe, K. (1998) *Civil Wars, Civil Peace*. London: Pluto.

Russett, B. (1993) *Grasping the Democratic Peace: Principles for a Post–Cold War World*. Princeton, NJ: Princeton University Press.

Russett, B. and O'Neal, J. R. (2001) *Triangulating Peace: Democracy, Interdependence, and International Organizations*. New York: W.W. Norton.

SAFE (1996) *Annual Report 1996*. Dublin: SAFE.

Sandy, L. and Perkins, R. (2008) *The Nature of Peace and Its Implications for Peace Education*. Oslo: University of Oslo. Available at: http://www.uio.no/studier/emner/jus/jus/ENGSEMJ/v08/undervisningsmateriale/IL%20&%20HR/Topic%202%20-%20Reading.pdf (Accessed on 3 January 2013).

Sassòli, M. (2009) 'Reparation', in *Post-conflict Peacebuilding: A Lexicon*, edited by Chetail, V. Oxford: Oxford University Press: 279–90.

Schmelzle, B. and Fischer, M. (eds.) (2009) *Peacebuilding at a Crossroads? Dilemmas and Paths for Another Generation*. Berghof Dialogue Series No. 7. Berlin: Berghof Foundation.

Schnabel, A. and Tabyshalieva, A. (eds.) (2012) *Defying Victimhood: Women and Post-conflict Peacebuilding*. Tokyo: United Nations University Press.

Sedra, M. (2013) 'Security Sector Reform', in *Routledge Handbook on Peacebuilding*, edited by Mac Ginty, R. London: Routledge: 211–24.

Sen, A. (1981) *Poverty and Famines: An Essay on Entitlements and Deprivation*. Oxford: Oxford University Press.

Sen, A. (2003) *The Human Security Report*. New York: UN Commission on Human Security.

Servaes, S. and Birtsch, N. (2008) *Engaging With Victims and Perpetrators in Transitional Justice and Peace Building Processes*. Paper presentation. Bern: Working Group on Development and Peace and KOFF.

Sherriff, A. and Barnes, K. (2008) *Enhancing the EU Response to Woman and Armed Conflict*. ECDPM Discussion Paper No. 84. Maastricht: European Centre for Development Policy Management (ECDPM).

Shinoda, H. (2008) *The Difficulty and Importance of Local Ownership and Capacity Development in Peacebuilding*. Hiroshima: Institute for Peace Science, Hiroshima University.

Shinoda, H. (2015) 'Local Ownership as a Strategic Guideline for Peacebuilding', in *Local Ownership in International Peacebuilding*, edited by Lee, S. Y. and Özerdem, A. Oxon: Routledge: 19–38.

Sisk, T. and Reynolds, A. (eds.) (1998) *Elections and Conflict Management in Africa*. Washington, DC: United States Institute for Peace.

Sjoberg, L. (2010) 'Women Fighters and the "Beautiful Soul" Narrative'. *International Review of the Red Cross* 92 (877): 53–68.

Smith, D. (2004) *Trends and Causes of Armed Conflict*. Berlin: Berghof Foundation.

Smith, J.D.D. (1994) 'Mediator Impartiality: Banishing the Chimera'. *Journal of Peace Research* 31 (4): 445–450.

Sommers, M. (2002) *Children, Education and War: Reaching Education for All (EFA) Objectives in Countries Affected by Conflict*. Washington, DC: World Bank.

Standish, K. and Kertyzia, H. (2015) 'Looking for Peace in the National Curriculum of England'. *Journal of Peace and Justice Studies* (forthcoming).

Starkey, B., Boyer, M.A. and Wilkenfeld, J. (1999) *Negotiating a Complex World: An Introduction to International Negotiation*. Lanham, MD: Rowman & Littlefield.

Strand, A. (2005) 'Aid Coordination: Easy to Agree on Difficult to Organise', in *After the Conflict: Reconstruction and Development in the Aftermath of War*, edited by Barakat, S. London: IB Tauris: 87–100.

Synott, J. (2005) 'Peace Education as an Educational Paradigm: Review of a Changing Field Using an Old Measure'. *Journal of Peace Education* 2 (1): 3–16.

Truth and Reconciliation Commission of South Africa (2000) *From Rhetoric to Responsibility: Making Reparations to the Survivors of Past Political Violence in South Africa*. TRC Final Report. Available at: http://www.csvr.org.za/wits/papers/papr2r2.htm (Accessed on 17 June 2013).

Tschirgi, N. (2013) 'Securitization and Peacebuilding', in *Routledge Handbook on Peacebuilding*, edited by Mac Ginty, R. London: Routledge: 197–210.

United Nations (UN) (2004) *A more secure world: Our shared responsibility*. New York: United Nations. Available at: http://www.un.org/en/peacebuilding/pdf/historical/hlp_more_secure_world.pdf (Accessed on 28 September 2015).

United Nations (UN) (2004) *Secretary-General's Report on the Rule of Law and Transitional Justice in Conflict and Post-Conflict States* (UN Doc. S/2004/616). Available at: http://www.unhcr.org/4506bc494.html (Accessed on 17 June 2013).

United Nations (UN) (2009) *United Nations Policy for Post-conflict Employment Creation, Income Generation and Reintegration*. Geneva: UNDP/ILO. Available at: http://www.ilo.org/wcmsp5/groups/public/@ed_emp/@emp_ent/@ifp_crisis/documents/publication/wcms_117576.pdf (Accessed on 17 June 2013).

United Nations (UN) (2010) *Reconstructing Public Administration After Conflict: Challenges, Practices and Lessons Learned.* New York: United Nations.UNDP Disaster Management Team (1994) *Humanitarian Principles and Operational Dilemmas in War Zones.* New York: UNDP.

UNESCO-UNEVOC (2007) *Education for Livelihoods and Civic Participation in Post-conflict Countries: Conceptualizing a Holistic Approach to TVET Planning and Programming.* UNESCO-UNEVOC Discussion Paper Series No. 3. Bonn: UNESCO-UNEVOC International Centre.

United Nations Development Programme (UNDP) (1994) *Human Development Report.* New York: Oxford University Press. Available at: http://hdr.undp.org/en/media/hdr_1994_en_contents.pdf (Accessed on 17 June 2013).

United Nations Development Programme (UNDP) (2001) *Peace-Building from the Ground-Up: A Case Study of UNDP's CARERE Programme in Cambodia 1991–2000.* Phnom Penh: UNDP/ Cambodia.

United Nations Development Programme (UNDP) (2003) *United Nations Development Programme: Human Development Report 2002.* New York: UNDP.

United Nations Development Programme (UNDP) (2008) *Post-conflict Economic Recovery: Enabling Local Ingenuity.* New York: Bureau for Crisis Prevention and Recovery, UNDP.

United Nations General Assembly (UNGA) (2000) *Report of the Panel on United Nations Peacekeeping (the Brahimi Report)* (UN Doc. A/55/305–S/2000/809) Available at: http://www.un.org/en/ga/search/view_doc.asp?symbol=A/55/305 (Accessed on 22 October 2015).

United Nations General Assembly (UNGA) (2000) *Support by the United Nations System of the Efforts of Governments to Promote and Consolidate New or Restored Democracies* (UN Doc. A/55/489). Available at: http://www.un.org/documents/ga/docs/55/a55489.pdf (Accessed on 2 June 2015).

United Nations General Assembly (UNGA) (2007) *Support by the United Nations System of the Efforts of Governments to Promote and Consolidate New or Restored Democracies* (UN Doc. A/55/489, 2000).

United Nations Security Council (UNSC) (1995) *Supplement to an Agenda for Peace* (UN Doc. A/50/60-S/1995/1). Available at: http://www.un.org/documents/ga/docs/50/plenary/a50-60.htm (Accessed on 22 October 2015).

United Nations Security Council (UNSC) (2000) *Women as Active Agents in Peace and Security – UN Security Council Resolution 1325* (UN Doc. S/RES/1325). Available at: http://daccess-dds-ny.un.org/doc/UNDOC/GEN/N00/720/18/PDF/N0072018.pdf?OpenElement (Accessed on 6 May 2015).

United Nations Security Council (UNSC) (2004) *The Rule of Law and Transitional Justice in Conflict and Post-conflict Societies: Report of the Secretary-General* (UN Doc. S/2004/616). Available at: http://www.unrol.org/files/2004%20report.pdf (Accessed on 27 May 2015).

United Nations Security Council (UNSC) (2008) *Security Council Resolution 1820 – Adopted by the Security Council at its 5916th Meeting, on 19 June 2008* (UN Doc. S/RES/1820). Available at: http://www.securitycouncilreport.org/atf/cf/%7B65BFCF9B-6D27–4E9C-8CD3-CF6E4FF96FF9%7D/CAC%20S%20RES%201820.pdf (Accessed on 2 June 2015).

United Nations Security Council (UNSC) (2009) *Security Council Resolution 1888 – Adopted by the Security Council at its 6195th Meeting, on 30 September 2009* (UN Doc. S/RES/1888). Available at: http://www.unelections.org/files/SC_Resolution1888(2009)_30September2009.pdf (Accessed on 2 June 2015).

United Nations Security Council (UNSC) (2013a) *UN Security Council Resolution 2106* (UN Doc. S/RES/2106). Available at: http://peacemaker.un.org/sites/peacemaker.un.org/files/SC_ResolutionWomen_SRES2106(2013)(english).pdf (Accessed on 6 May 2015).

United Nations Security Council (UNSC) (2013b) *Report of the Secretary-General on Women and Peace and Security* (UN Doc. S/2013/525). New York: United Nations.

United Nations Secretary General (UNSG) (1992) *An Agenda for Peace: Preventive Diplomacy, Peacemaking and Peace-keeping* (UN Doc. A/47/277 – S/24111, 17 June). New York: United Nations.

United Nations Secretary General (UNSG) (1996) *Agenda for Democratization* (UN Doc. A/51/761) Available at: http://www.un.org/fr/events/democracyday/pdf/An_agenda_for_democratization.pdf (Accessed on 22 October 2015).

United Nations Secretary General (UNSG) (2004) *A More Secured World: Our Shared Responsibility* (UN Doc. A/59/565) Available at: http://www.un.org/en/peacebuilding/pdf/historical/hlp_more_secure_world.pdf (Accessed on 22 October 2015).

United Nations Secretary-General (UNSG) (1993) *Report on the Work of the Organisation From the Forty-Seventh to the Forty-Eighth Session of the General Assembly*. New York: United Nations.

United Nations Secretary-General (UNSG) (2001) *Yearbook of the United Nations 1998*. New York: United Nations.

United Nations Secretary-General (UNSG) (2002) *United Nations System Support for Capacity Building: Report of the Secretary-General* (UN Doc. E/2002/58, 14 May). New York: United Nations.

United Nations Secretary-General (UNSG) (2005) *In Larger Freedom: Towards Development, Security and Human Rights for All* (UN Doc. A/59/2005, 21 March). Available at: http://www.un.org/en/ga/search/view_doc.asp?symbol=A/59/2005 (Accessed on 6 May 2015).

United Nations Secretary-General (UNSG) (2006) *Importance of National Ownership, Building Effective Public Institutions: Opening First Session of Peacebuilding Commission* (UN Doc. SG/SM/10533 PBC/2, 23 June). New York: United Nations.

United Nations Secretary-General (UNSG) (2009) *Report of the Secretary-General on Peacebuilding in the Immediate Aftermath of Conflict* (UN Doc. A/63/881-S/2009/304). Available at: http://www.un.org/en/peacebuilding/pbso/pdf/s2009304.pdf (Accessed on 2 June 2015).

United Nations Secretary-General (UNSG) (2011) *Preventive Diplomacy: Delivering Results* (UN Doc. S/2011/552, 26 August). New York: United Nations.

United States Institute of Peace (USIP) (2009) *Guiding Principles for Stabilization and Reconstruction*. USIP and U.S. Army Peacekeeping and Stability Operations Institute. Washington, DC: United States Institute of Peace Press.

United States Institute of Peace (USIP) (2011) *Social Reconstruction and Human Security*. Available at: http://www.usip.org/education-training/courses/enhancing-social-well-being-fragile-states (Accessed on 17 June 2013).

United States Institute of Peace (USIP) (n.d.a.) 'Market Economy Sustainability'. Available at: http://www.usip.org/guiding-principles-stabilization-and-reconstruction-the-web-version/9-sustainable-economy/market-eco (Accessed on 2 June 2015).

United States Institute of Peace (USIP) (n.d.b.) 'Social Reconstruction'. Available at: http://www.usip.org/guiding-principles-stabilization-and-reconstruction-the-web-version/10-social-well-being/social-reco (Accessed on 28 September 2015)

UN Peacebuilding Support Office and UN Development Program (2010) *E-discussion on Economic Revitalization and Peacebuilding*. New York: United Nations. Available at: http://www.un.org/en/peacebuilding/pdf/doc_wgll/e_consultation_summary.pdf (Accessed on 17 June 2013).

Uppsala Conflict Data Program (2009) *Peace Agreements in Armed Conflicts 1989–2006*. Available at: http://www.pcr.uu.se/research/UCDP/graphs/charts_and_graphs.htm (Accessed on 17 June 2013).

van Zyl, P. (2005) 'Promoting Transitional Justice in Post-Conflict Societies', in *Security Governance in Post-Conflict Peacebuilding*, edited by Bryden, A. and Hanggi, H. Geneva: Geneva Centre for the Democratic Control of Armed Forces (DCAF): 209–32.

Vaux, T. (2001) *The Selfish Altruist: Relief Work in Famine and War*. London: Earthscan.

Väyrynen, R. (1991) *New Directions in Conflict Theory: Conflict Resolution and Conflict Transformation*. London: Sage.

Wallensteen, P. (2007) *Understanding Conflict Resolution*. London: Sage.

Walter, B. F. (2002) *Committing to Peace: The Successful Settlement of Civil Wars*. Princeton, NJ: Princeton University Press.

Watkins, M. and Rosegrant, S. (2002) *Breakthrough International Negotiation*. Hoboken, NJ: Wiley.

Weissbrodt, D. (2005) *Truth and Reconciliation Commissions*. Human Rights Resources Center. Available at: http://www.hrusa.org/workshops/humphrey/workshop/PublicForum/Truth%20and%20Reconciliation.pdf (Accessed on 17 June 2013).

Welchman, L. and Hossain, S. (eds.) (2005) *'Honour' Crimes, Paradigms, and Violence Against Women*. London: Zed Books.

Wilén, N. (2009) 'Capacity-Building or Capacity-Taking? Legitimizing Concepts in Peace and Development Operations'. *International Peacekeeping* 16 (3): 337–51.

Williams, P. and Scharf, M. (2002) *Peace With Justice?: War Crimes and Accountability in the Former Yugoslavia*. Lanham, MD: Rowman & Littlefield.

Wils, O. and Unger, B. (2006) *Systemic Conflict Transformation: Guiding Principles for Practitioners and Policy Makers Working on Conflict*. Berlin: Berghof Research Center.

World Bank (1998) *Post-Conflict Reconstruction: The Role of the World Bank*. Washington, DC: World Bank.

World Bank (2015) 'State and Peacebuilding Fund'. http://www.worldbank.org/en/news/feature/2015/02/02/state-peace-building-fund-spf-our-niche-where-work (Accessed on 2 June 2015).

Wulf, H. and Debiel, T. (2009) *Conflict Early Warning and Response Mechanisms: Tools for Enhancing the Effectiveness of Regional Organisations?* Crisis States Working Papers Series No. 2. London: Destin Development Studies Institute.

Yarn, D. (ed.) (1999) *Dictionary of Conflict Resolution*. San Francisco: Jossey-Bass.

Young, N. (ed.) (2010) *The Oxford International Encyclopedia of Peace*. Oxford: Oxford University Press: 407–8.

Zartman, I. W. (2003) 'The Timing of Peace Initiatives: Hurting Stalemates and Ripe Moments', in *Contemporary Peacemaking: Conflict, Violence and Peace Processes*, edited by Darby, J. and Mac Ginty, R. Houndmills: Palgrave Macmillan: 19–29.

Zetter, R. (2005) 'Land, Housing, and the Reconstruction of the Built Environment', in *After the Conflict: Reconstruction and Development in the Aftermath of War*, edited by Barakat, S. London: IB Tauris: 155–72.

Index

Note: Page numbers with *f* indicate figures, those with *t* indicate tables, and those with *b* indicate boxes.

Lightning Source UK Ltd.
Milton Keynes UK
UKHW030613110220
358514UK00012B/98